How to Read
Superhero
Comics and Why

Geoff Klock

continuum
NEW YORK • LONDON

2002

The Continuum International Publishing Group Inc
370 Lexington Avenue, New York, NY 10017

The Continuum International Publishing Group Ltd
The Tower Building, 11 York Road, London SE1 7NX

www.continuumbooks.com

Library of Congress Cataloging-in-Publication Data

Klock, Geoff.
    How to read superhero comics and why / Geoff Klock.
        p.   cm.
    Includes bibliographical references and index.
    ISBN 0-8264-1418-4 (hbd)—ISBN 0-8264-1419-2 (pbk)
    1. Comic books, strips, etc.—United States—History and criticism.
    I. Title.
    PN6725 .K59 2002
    741.5'0973—dc21

                                        2002005803

ISBN: 0-8264-1418-4 (hb)
           0-8264-1419-2 (pb)

[A] sacred history indeed, but still a more sacred ideal, a transcendent version or representation, under intenser and more expressive light and shade, of human life and its familiar or exceptional incidents, birth, death, marriage, youth, age, tears, joy, rest, sleep, waking—a mirror, towards which men might turn away their eyes from vanity and dullness, and see themselves therein as angels, with their daily meat and drink, even, become a kind of sacred transaction—a complementary strain or burden, applied to our every-day existence, whereby the stray snatches of music in it re-set themselves, and fall into the scheme of some higher and more consistent harmony. A place adumbrated itself in his thoughts, wherein those sacred personalities, which are at once the reflex and the pattern of our nobler phases of life, housed themselves; and this region in his intellectual scheme all subsequent experience did but tend still further to realize and define. Some ideal, hieratic persons he would always need to occupy it and keep a warmth there. And he could hardly understand those who felt no such need at all, finding themselves quite happy without such heavenly companionship, and sacred double life, beside them.

—Walter Pater, "The Child in the House"

THE GENERAL: Oh, my God. Why?

JAKITA WAGNER: Because it's what we do. We gather information on the hidden wonders of the world.

ELIJAH SNOW: Mystery archeologists. There's a hundred years of fantastic events that the Planetary intends to excavate.

JAKITA WAGNER: We're mapping the secret history of the twentieth century.

—Warren Ellis, *Planetary*

A number of talented improvisers have attempted to enlarge the role [of the cowboy], giving us, for instance, the scholar-cowboy: "All I eat is beans cooked over a mesquite fire, but I also speak Chaucer." The role is legitimized by the cachet of scholarship, and we are made more comfortable in it. It is not necessary that we speak Chaucer; it is enough that we are told that Chaucer and mesquite fires may safely coexist.

—Donald Barthelme, *Culture, Etc.*

Special thanks to Professor Ernest Gilman, Professor Robert Gurland, Professor Perry Meisel, David Barker, Professor Rosa Eberly, Professor Diane Davis, Scott Blackwood, Will Brooker, Jason Smith, Ximena Gallardo, Brad Winderbaum, Topical Steve, Jill Duffy, Tadzio Koelb, Mike Holohan, Sara Reiss, Brenda and Barry Reiss, Professor Bill Bridges, Emily Golden, all the scholars at the Warren Ellis Forum (LP2001AD, James Moar, Aman Chaudhary, etc.), and my parents, Don and Diane Klock, without whom this would not have been possible.

Contents

Introduction

S uperhero comic books do strange and wonderful things when exposed to literary and psychoanalytic theory. No kidding. For years I read poetry and poetic theory in school, and I read superhero comics for fun. After a while I started having a hard time separating the two activities. This book is what I learned from that juxtaposition. If you read poetry, poetics, or literary criticism, you will be surprised to find how superhero comic books fall in line, in an interesting way, with what you have been reading; you may also pick up a few new tricks to take back to poetry along the way. If you read superhero comic books, you will find a new way of looking at them, which will stay with you long after you sell this book for more comics. If you don't know literary criticism or superhero comics, then you have made an efficient choice in picking up the volume in your hands; if you come to find either subject half as engaging as I do, your money will be well spent. The following introduction is designed to put us all on the same page with a general sketch of the argument presented in this book, some info on superhero comics and their relation to the unconscious, a rejection of structural mythology as a guiding principle in the study of popular culture, an explanation of why this study does not fall under the heading of "cultural studies," a short introduction to the method used here (with some handy definitions), and a coda on canon formation, with an explanation of how the works discussed were selected.

To start: in setting out a definition of the superhero in *Superheroes: A Modern Mythology,* Richard Reynolds cites "Lost Parents" as the first of seven features of the superhero narrative. He writes that it is "a key preoccupation. . . . Superman is separated from his natural parents, and so his extraordinary powers are not represented in a straightforward parent-to-child relationship. Few superheroes enjoy uncomplicated relationships with parents who are regularly present in the narrative."[1] I would like to begin this study with a personal spin on Reynolds's state-

---

[1] Richard Reynolds, *Superheroes: A Modern Mythology* (Jackson: University Press of Mississippi, 1992), 12.

ment, inspired by the literary theory of Harold Bloom: "Few superhero narratives enjoy uncomplicated relationships with prior parent-narratives, which are (all too) regularly present in the narrative." And from there, the superhero comics get really interesting.

A General Sketch of the Argument Presented

Superhero comic books are traditionally thought to have at least two distinct periods, at least two major waves of creativity: the golden age and the silver age. The distinction between the two periods is as blurry as the distinction between any two movements in the history of literature or art. For purposes of this argument, however, only a reductive sketch will be presented here, as the works looked at in this study draw upon this simplified conception. The golden age was the birth of the superhero proper out of the pulp novel characters of the early 1930s and was primarily associated with the DC Comics Group. Superman (1938), Batman (1939), Green Lantern (1940), and Wonder Woman (1941) are the most famous creations of this period. In the early 1960s, Marvel Comics launched a completely new line of heroes, the primary figures of the silver age: the Fantastic Four (1961), Spider-Man (1962), the Incredible Hulk (1962), the X-Men (1963), the Avengers (1963), Iron Man (1963), and Daredevil (1964). As has been discussed elsewhere,[2] this second wave of superheroes was as different from the first as the first wave was from the pulps. Warren Ellis, referring to the (very simplified) above distinction as the first and second movement, suggests the birth of a third movement "somewhere between Frank Miller on *Daredevil* [May 1979–February 1983] and Alan Moore on *Marvelman* [March 1982–August 1984]"[3] and claims that as of 1997 the comic book world stood at the close of the third movement. He then hints at the coming fourth movement.

The modest goal of the present book is to present a different paradigm for recognizing the "third movement" of superhero comic books

---

[2] See Greg McCue, *Dark Knights: The New Comics in Context* (London: Pluto Press, 1988), 35–53. This is also an excellent place to begin for those seeking a more detailed and subtle discussion of the paradigm shift that resulted in the golden age becoming the silver.

[3] Warren Ellis, *From the Desk of Warren Ellis,* vol. 1 (Urbana, IL: Avatar, 2000), 11.

and to avoid at all costs the temptation to refer to this movement as "postmodern," "deconstructionist," or something equally tedious.[4] Chapter 0 looks at *Crisis on Infinite Earths*: while *Crisis* stands outside the arc of strong work that makes up the body of this study, it sets in motion much that follows, and is thus marginalized in the chapter layout. Chapter 1 covers what Ellis refers to as the third movement, the revolutionary works of Frank Miller and Alan Moore in the 1980s, the end of the silver age. Like Samuel Beckett as the last modernist, or Cormac McCarthy's *Border Trilogy* as the extrapolation of the American cowboy myth to its natural terminus, *Batman: The Dark Knight Returns* (1986) and *Watchmen* (1986) represent the culmination of the silver age, and a powerful response to the waning of the imaginative wave launched a quarter of a century earlier. These works are the birth of self-consciousness in the superhero narrative, what I call—taking a cue from Harold Bloom—the revisionary superhero narrative. Here, the building density of tradition becomes anxiety, the superhero narrative becomes literature. If, as Alfred North Whitehead said, "[t]he safest general characterization of the European philosophical tradition is that it consists of a series of footnotes to Plato,"[5] then the contemporary superhero narrative might be viewed as consisting of a series of footnotes to Miller and Moore. Chapter 2 focuses on *Marvels* (1994), *Astro City* (1995), and *Kingdom Come* (1996), which attempt to grapple with their role as inheritors of those texts, as possible candidates for the beginning of the next phase of the superhero narrative, but find themselves too hampered by the influence, and burden, of *The Dark Knight Returns* and *Watchmen*. *Kingdom Come* is successful in building a bridge between the tradition of the past and the innovations of the future, but a deep current of nostalgia remains. As the culmination of this nostalgic vain, Alan Moore launches an entire

---

[4] The back cover of *Squadron Supreme* reads "Before *Watchmen*, before *Marvels*, before *Kingdom Come*—there was *Squadron Supreme*, a deconstructionist parable of the superhero paradigm in a real world setting. Published before such stories became commonplace, it set the standard for post-modernist superhero fiction, and influenced a generation of creators." Mark Gruenwald et al., *Squadron Supreme* (New York: Marvel Comics, 1997, second printing, back cover). Even the normally unhoodwinkable Alan Moore has referred to postmodern heroes, and a new superhero comic book, *The Monarchy*, has been using the term in the diegetic narrative.

[5] Quoted from Introduction to Plato, in *From Plato to Nietzsche*, 2nd ed., ed. Forrest E. Baird and Walter Kaufmann (Upper Saddle River, NJ: Prentice Hall, 1997), 5.

company—America's Best Comics—writing all five titles himself in a grand "retro" examination of every aspect of superhero literature. Chapter 3 examines the impact of Moore's work, which closes the book on the silver age (and the golden, for that matter), bequeathing it a kind of afterlife where it can live forever. Grant Morrison and Warren Ellis are the first to explore the future, as discussed in Chapter 4. Morrison and Ellis discover a bombastic rhetoric with which to deal with these texts and the influence they transmit. Their work connects the silver age to the next phase of superheroes that is fully realized at Wildstorm, the subject of chapter 5. The revisionary superhero narrative culminates in *Planetary*, Ellis's "superhero as literary critic." *Planetary* retroactively structures tradition in such a way as to present the successors to the silver age in *Stormwatch* and its continuation in *The Authority, Wildcats,* and *Planetary.* A brief epilogue will begin thinking about the landscape changed by these powerful titles and the first genuine break from the Silver Age with a look at *Marvel Boy*, Grant Morrison and Frank Quitely's *New X-Men*, and Peter Milligan and Mike Allred's *X-Force.* 'A Frequently Asked Question' will sketch a line of thought in M. Night Shyamalan's *Unbreakable*, which gives the revisionary superhero narrative a representation on film. In the annotated bibliography readers will be given a sense of some important work that, for various reasons, was not covered in this study.

Superhero Comic Books and Their Relation to the Unconscious

Superhero comic books and psychoanalysis have a close relationship that should be kept in mind in any explication of the genre. Stated in more detail below, superhero comic books have a peculiar relation with their own continuity (the literal narrative elements of a character's story) and tradition (the more general conventions of the superhero genre, so tight and narrow as to come close to another level of continuity). Continuity is especially paradoxical for long-running characters. On some level, events make up a character's history (e.g., Batman began fighting crime in an era when he could refer to World War I as the "Great War") but also could not logically occur when a reader considers that character's history as a whole (e.g., Batman never seems to age, although he has come in contact with more contemporary situations). It is this storytelling background that accounts for what Umberto Eco calls, in probably the most insightful comment on the subject, the "oneiric climate" of the superhero story, "where what has happened before and what has happened after appear extremely hazy. The narrator picks up the strand of the event again and again, as if he had forgotten to say something and wanted to add details to what has already been said."[6] A superhero narrative read in the context of its continuity is akin to Woody Allen's mythological beast with the head of a lion and the body of a lion, but not the same lion.

The superhero comic book was practically launched with the death of Sigmund Freud; Dr. William Moulton Marston, a psychologist (and inventor of the lie detector), created Wonder Woman only two years later. While it would be irresponsible to read too much into these auspicious beginnings, it must be noted that superhero comic books have a rather high level of interaction with psychoanalysis and psychoanalytic criticism, as commentators as far apart as Dr. Fredric Wertham and Richard Reynolds (with his oedipal analyses, derived from Joseph Campbell's theory that all mythologies are essentially the same) would agree. The reason, put simply, is this: any given superhero narrative stands in relation to its conflicted, chaotic tradition, and continuity as the ego stands in relation to the unconscious. Carl Jung's words on the latter subject capture precisely the ambivalent relationship of a superhero story to its continuity and tradition:

> From this discredited and rejected region comes the new afflux of energy, the renewal of life. But what is this discredited and rejected source of vitality? It consists of all those psychic contents that were repressed because of their incompatibility with conscious [read: contemporary narrative] values—everything hateful, immoral, wrong, unsuitable, useless, etc., which means everything that at one time or another appeared so to the individual concerned. The danger now is that when these things reappear in a new and wonderful guise, they may make such an impact on him that he will forget or repudiate all his former values. What he once despised now becomes the supreme prin-

---

[6] Umberto Eco, *The Role of the Reader: Explorations in the Semiotics of Texts* (Bloomington: Indiana University Press, 1979), 114.

ciple, and what was once truth now becomes error. This reversal of values is similar to the devastation of a country by floods.[7]

Given this homogeneity, it is no wonder that Harold Bloom's poetics (based so heavily on Freud) and the writings of Lacanian psychoanalytic theorist Slavoj Žižek, as well as their quite considerable influences (Jung, Emerson, Nietzsche, the Bible, etc.), should reveal so much about the workings of this strange genre of literature.

Popular Culture: Carl Jung, Joseph Campbell, and Claude Lévi-Strauss

One work stands out in particular in a discussion of superhero comic books and psychoanalysis, and the reason for its omission in this study deserves attention. Sam Kieth's *The Maxx* (1994) stands as one of the stranger spins on the superhero motif in recent memory. The Maxx is a superhero (complete with a mask and purple spandex) who is homeless and lives in a box. While his city is plagued by a serial rapist (Mr. Gone), he becomes entangled with a cynical feminist social worker named Julie Winters. To complicate matters, the Maxx also flashes between two worlds, the city and Pangea (or "the Outback"), a kind of mythical primitive Australia, where the Maxx is the protector of the Leopard Queen (Julie Winters as a bad paperback cover, as noted by the characters themselves). What is interesting is that in the course of the story it becomes increasingly clear to the characters that the complicated fantasy world they inhabit and their interpersonal relationships are lifted almost directly from the metaphors of Jungian psychology and some passages from Claude Lévi-Strauss. When Julie Winters was a child, she found a wounded rabbit and tried to nurse it back to health. It became increasingly sick in a box under her bed until her mother took it away with the usual platitudes about "going to a better place now." Late that night, Julie witnessed her mother killing the wounded rabbit with a shovel, but she never spoke of the incident. She escaped into a pretend world, the Outback, where she was queen. When she was raped as a college stu-

---

[7] C. G. Jung, *Psychological Types,* trans. H. G. Baynes (Princeton, NJ: Princeton University Press, 1990), 266.

dent, she escaped into a world of tough posturing and cynical control of other people's lives. A homeless man she hit with her car became tangled up in her world, at once a man, a superhero, and a rabbit (a fact that explains his excessively large feet and hunched appearance). Kieth takes from Jung and Lévi-Strauss a combination of a "soul-image" (anima/animus) and a spirit animal. Jung writes:

> The soul-image is a specific image among those produced in the unconscious. Just as the persona, or outer attitude, is represented in dreams by images of definite persons who possess the outstanding qualities of the persona in especially marked form, so in a man the soul, i.e. anima, or inner attitude, is represented in the unconscious by definite persons with the corresponding qualities. Such an image is called a "soul-image." Sometimes these images are of quite unknown or mythological figures. . . . [W]ith women the animus is personified as a man. . . . In all cases where there is an identity with the persona, and the soul accordingly is unconscious, the soul-image is transferred to a real person. . . .
>
> . . . The projection of the soul-image offers a release from preoccupation with one's inner process so long as the behavior of the object is in harmony with the soul-image. The subject is then in a position to live out his persona and develop it further. The object, however, will scarcely be able to meet the demands of the soul-image indefinitely. . . .
>
> . . . For an idealistic woman, a depraved man is often the bearer of the soul-image; hence the "savior fantasy" so frequent in such cases.[8]

Lévi-Strauss writes that the rabbit's split nose and upper lip have a connection in many mythologies to incipient twinhood (the creature was nearly divided in two), and that many mythologies, such as the Bible, offer twins of vastly different natures:

---

[8] Ibid., 470–72. Quoted from the definitions section, all internal references have been removed (e.g., in the original quotation, *unconscious* is italicized and linked to its definition elsewhere in the section).

This explains why, in this mythology, the hare as a god has an ambiguous character which has worried commentators and anthropologists: Sometimes he is a very wise deity who is in charge of putting the universe in order, and sometimes he is a ridiculous clown who goes from mishap to mishap. And this also is best understood if we explain the choice of the hare by the Algonkian Indians as an individual who is between the two conditions of (*a*) a single deity beneficent to mankind and (*b*) twins, one of whom is good and the other bad. Being not yet entirely divided in two, being not yet twins, the two opposite characteristics can remain merged in one and the same person.[9]

These elements, combined with the feminism of Camille Paglia and some Daliesque imagery, form the basis of *The Maxx*. This kind of analysis, however, amounts to little more than extensive footnoting. The whole argument might be summarized as "See C. G. Jung's *Psychological Types,* pp. 470–472, and Claude Lévi-Strauss's *Myth and Meaning,* p. 33." Unless previously unexposed to Jung and Lévi-Strauss, the reader is given nothing new.

In the same vein, superheroes will not be discussed here in light of the Jung–Lévi-Strauss–Campbell triad. While readers might expect such an exegesis, this study will not conclude that Batman, Superman, and Wonder Woman are the thousand-and-first, -second and -third faces of Campbell's monomythical "Hero with a Thousand Faces." "Why is mythology everywhere the same, beneath its varieties of costume?"[10] was not selected as an epigraph to this work. Nowhere here will it be claimed that the superhero is best understood in terms of

> *separation–initiation–return*: which might be named the nuclear unit of the monomyth.
> *A hero ventures forth from the world of common day into a region of supernatural wonder: fabulous forces are there encountered and a decisive victory is won: the hero comes back from this mysterious adventure with the power to bestow boons on his fellow man.*[11]

---

9 Claude Lévi-Strauss, *Myth and Meaning* (New York: Schocken Books, 1978), 33.

10 Joseph Campbell, *The Hero with a Thousand Faces* (Princeton, NJ: Princeton University Press, 1949), 4.

11 Ibid., 30 (Campbell's emphasis).

Superheroes are not a valuable source of study because they are a "modern mythology," (Reynolds), which like all mythologies are

> controlled and intended statements of certain spiritual principles, which have remained constant throughout the course of human history as the form and nervous structure of the human physique itself. Briefly formulated, the universal doctrine teaches that all the visible structures of the world—all things and beings—are the effects of a ubiquitous power out of which they rise, which supports and fills them during the period of their manifestation, and back into which they must ultimately dissolve.[12]

This initial sketch of unused theory would not be complete without mentioning that superheroes will not be read as Jungian archetypes or expressions thereof. The following quote from Jung expresses what will not be done here, and its final line hints at the reason.

> I call the image primordial when it possesses an archaic character. I speak of its archaic character when the image is in striking accord with familiar mythological motifs. It then expresses material primarily derived from the collective unconscious. . . .
>
> The primordial image, elsewhere also termed archetype, is always collective, i.e., it is at least common to entire peoples or epochs. In all probability the most important mythological motifs are common to all times and races; I have, in fact, been able to demonstrate a whole series of motifs from Greek mythology in the dreams and fantasies of pure-bred Negroes suffering from mental disorders.[13]

The superhero comic book is not interesting because it

> derives its convincing power from the unconscious archetype, which, as such, is eternally valid and true. But this truth is so universal and so symbolic that it must first be assimilated to the recognized and recognizable knowledge of the time before it can become a practical truth of any value for life.[14]

---

[12] Ibid., 257.
[13] Jung, 443.
[14] Ibid., 381.

These kinds of observations in regard to popular culture have become tedious, and it should be the place of future criticism to provide something more than structural mythology and systems like it. These approaches fall under the heading of maieutics (a word derived from the Greek *maicutikos,* "midwifery"): they are designed to make us recognize something previously latent in our mind rather than tell us something we did not know before. This book will use several critical models in its description of how certain specific superhero texts function in relation to their influences—what Matthew J. Pustz calls "comics literacy"[15]—in order to situate the next generation of superheroes. Focusing on a dialectic of continuity and discontinuity rather than continuity pushed to the level of archetype, this book will demonstrate how the superhero text, despite its obvious poetic debt, *becomes new.* A few insightful comments from Campbell and Jung will help make this argument, but we will not help make theirs.

The Place of Cultural Studies

Academic approaches to superhero comic books take three major forms: structural mythology (discussed above), cultural history (*Comic Book Nation*; *Dark Knights: New Comics in Context*), and cultural studies (*Black Superheroes, Milestone Comics, and Their Fans*; *Comic Book Culture*). This book will attempt something more in the vein of literary criticism, what Oscar Wilde called "the only civilized form of autobiography":

> That is what the highest criticism really is, the record of one's own soul. It is more fascinating than history, as it is concerned simply with oneself. It is more delightful than philosophy, as its subject is concrete and not abstract, real and not vague. It is the only civilized form of autobiography, as it deals not with the events, but with the thoughts of one's life; not with life's physical accidents of deed or circumstance, but with the spiritual moods and imaginative passions of the mind.[16]

---

[15] Matthew J. Pustz, *Comic Book Culture* (Jackson: University Press of Mississippi, 1999), 110–156.

[16] Oscar Wilde, *The Artist as Critic,* ed. Richard Ellmann (Chicago: University of Chicago Press, 1968), 365.

This rather different approach to popular culture, as the passage above suggests, is less concerned with much that cultural studies, for example, finds fascinating: sociology, demographics, economics, interviews, reader response, and media reaction. Harold Bloom has this to say about source study (something one might expect from an approach that regards the anxiety of influence):

> All criticisms that call themselves primary vacillate between tautology—in which the poem is and means itself—and reduction—in which the poem means something that is not itself a poem. Antithetical criticism must begin by denying both tautology and reduction, a denial best delivered by the assertion that the meaning of a poem can only be a poem, but *another poem—a poem not itself.* And not a poem chosen with total arbitrariness, but any central poem by an indubitable precursor, even if the ephebe *never read* that poem. Source study is wholly irrelevant here; we are dealing with primal words, but antithetical meanings, and an ephebe's best misinterpretations may well be of poems he has never read.[17]

While I would not slander cultural studies in any way—both literary criticism and cultural studies have blind spots, and each sees something the other does not—I would defend my own position with yet another aphorism from Bloom:

> Beware the rhetorical or ironic impersonalist, whether traditionalist or deconstructionist, whose cool tone is a reaction-formation defense of a private quest for power. The self-dramatizing pragmatist, whatever his defenses, is more authentically representative of the perpetual otherness of poetry.[18]

A Statement on Criticism and Intentionality

Because this study draws heavily on Harold Bloom's anxiety of influence poetics, and because an approach to popular culture that is primarily

---

[17] Harold Bloom, *The Anxiety of Influence* (Oxford: Oxford University Press, 1973), 70 (Bloom's emphasis).
[18] Harold Bloom, *Agon* (Oxford: Oxford University Press, 1982), 41.

literary criticism might cause consternation for those anticipating the more usual cultural studies approach, a few passages from *The Anxiety of Influence, A Map of Misreading,* and *Agon* might help to situate the reading presented here. The word *trope* is used throughout this book in its dictionary form, though it might be unfamiliar to some. Derived from the Greek *tropos,* "turn" (*heliotrope,* for example, means to turn toward the sun), trope refers to any sign with a meaning beyond its literal interpretation (i.e., one that turns from literal meaning). I chose the word *sign* carefully here because *trope* is a broad term that includes every kind of metaphor, and is not limited to words. This is especially important in a study dealing with a medium composed of words and pictures. I will argue, for example, that Warren Ellis's Four Voyagers (*Planetary* 6) are a trope of Marvel's Fantastic Four, which is to say that while the Four Voyagers are characters in themselves, they are also an interpretation/ metaphor of characters that have come before.

Influence, misreading, and *misprision* are the most important terms and the ones used in a sense beyond their dictionary meanings.

> "Influence" is a metaphor, one that implicates a matrix of relationships—imagistic, temporal, spiritual, psychological—all of them ultimately defensive in their nature. What matters most . . . is that the anxiety of influence *comes out of* a complex act of strong misreading, a creative interpretation that I call "poetic misprision." What writers may experience as anxiety, and what their works are compelled to manifest, are the *consequence* of poetic misprision rather than the *cause* of it. The strong misreading comes first; there must be a profound act of reading that is a kind of falling in love with a literary work. That reading is likely to be idiosyncratic, and it is almost certain to be ambivalent, though the ambivalence may be veiled. Without Keats's reading of Shakespeare, Milton and Wordsworth, we could not have Keats's odes and sonnets and his two *Hyperions.*[19]

Influence, then, is a critical fiction, and misreading and misprision are acts of interpretation that create new texts. This act of interpretation is not a special act preformed on a given reading, but a quality inherent in

---

[19] Bloom, *Anxiety,* xxiii (Bloom's emphasis)

the act of reading itself. Misprision is something that every strong reader does, and the critical exegesis of this act of reading is never objective. It too is caught up in the matrix it describes:

> Reading . . . is a belated and all-but-impossible act, and if strong is always a misreading. . . . Criticism may not always be an act of judging, but it is always an act of deciding, and what it tries to decide is meaning. . . .
> . . . Influence, as I conceive it, means that there are *no* texts, but only relationships *between* texts. These relationships depend on a critical act, a misreading or misprision, that one poet performs upon another, and that does not differ in kind from the necessary critical acts preformed by every strong reader upon every text he encounters. The influence-relation governs reading as it governs writing, and reading is therefore a miswriting just as writing is a misreading. As literary history lengthens, all poetry necessarily becomes verse-criticism, just as all criticism becomes prose-poetry.
> The strong reader, whose readings will matter to others as well as to himself, is thus placed in the dilemmas of the revisionist, who wishes to find his own original relation to truth.[20]

> To read actively is to make a fiction as well as to receive one, and the kind of active reading we call "criticism" or the attempt to decide meaning, or perhaps to see whether meaning *can* be decided, always has a very large fictive element in it. . . . "Reading" is a heuristic process, a path-breaking into inventiveness.[21]

This book will demonstrate that superhero comic books are an especially good place to witness the structure of misprision, because as a serial narrative that has been running for more than sixty years, reinterpretation becomes part of its survival code. Bloom would suggest that novels, poems, and plays, often viewed as closed structures, are best seen in a

---

[20] Harold Bloom, *A Map of Misreading* (Oxford: Oxford University Press, 1975), 3–4 (Bloom's emphasis).
[21] Bloom, *Agon,* 238 (Bloom's emphasis).

continuous line with the history of their literature, a paradigm Batman fans have known for years.

The objection might be made that a reliance on Bloom causes this book to elevate the superhero comic book writer to the untouchable status of the cinema auteur. This would not be entirely incorrect in regard to the perspective of the work, but it must be distinguished from a person actually believing Warren Ellis to be beyond mortal ken. Viewing reading as a heuristic process, the assumption that the comic book storyteller is the guiding force behind a work will yield some powerful results. In Bloom's words, "[E]ach of us carries about a Shakespeare or a Tolstoy or a Freud who is our fiction. . . . That author is perhaps our myth, but the experience of literature partly depends upon that myth."[22] Elsewhere Bloom writes, "[W]hether the theory is correct or not may be irrelevant to its usefulness for practical criticism."[23] The fact that intentionality itself is an enabling fiction used by the critic to present an imaginative vision cannot be emphasized enough. *Baywatch* may be regarded as trash put together by those with no intentions beyond ogling girls, but the truth of this observation does not invalidate its (possible) reception in Brazil as a brilliant satire of American consumer culture. While this latter perspective may elevate the *Baywatch* creators to a level they do not deserve, such is the price of the perspective. As Kenneth Burke writes, drawing on the etymological link between theory and sight, "[A] way of seeing is always a way of not seeing."[24]

With this in mind, it must be noted that, like film, comic books as a medium are characterized by a high degree of collaboration. The statement that the meaning of a comic book is strongly shaped by forces such as the comic book industry (editors, market analysis) and comic book fandom (e.g., fan fiction) is by no means incorrect, but this study takes the position that these are highly accidental extratextual materials organized by a visionary storyteller, alongside genre and narrative elements. While this single-author perspective has been appropriate in the history of literature, comic books present the reader with a storyteller that is most often multiple.

---

[22] Harold Bloom, *The Book of J* (New York: Vintage, 1990), 19.

[23] Bloom, *Map,* 10.

[24] Kenneth Burke, *Permanence and Change,* 3rd ed. (Berkeley: University of California Press, 1984), 49.

To separate the comic book writer from the comic book artist in a discussion of the medium is to miss the dimension of exchange inherent in comic book production. The writer may provide for the artist a description of a story element, in which case, comment on the art or design should really be aimed at the writer. Alternatively, an artist might justify a design on the basis of a small background narrative explaining what occurred in the imaginary narrative that precedes any work of fiction. This "background information" might factor into the story at some point, and in that case comments on the writing should now be directed at the artist. Some comic books go so far in acknowledging the give-and-take between writers and artists that both the writer and the artist are simply credited as "storytellers," a move that more adequately portrays the roles involved. These entities we are confronted with are hybrid beings, and when this book speaks, for the sake of simplicity, of Warren Ellis's visionary handling of *Planetary,* it should not be forgotten that it is just as much artist John Cassaday and colorist Laura Depuy's visionary handling. It is just as much John Cassaday's *Planetary* and Laura Depuy's *Planetary* as Warren Ellis's *Planetary.* (It is even, to some degree, Wildstorm's *Planetary.*) Writing about individuals qua artist or writer is, however, unavoidable, and this hybrid collaborative creator should be kept in mind throughout.

If this book does draw attention to the "writer" more than the "artist," then, this is because of a bias that connects the narrative with the writer and because more often than not this book analyzes the more abstract "story," only occasionally providing detailed commentary on specific images. The legal difficulty of obtaining images for reproduction in this book only compounds the problem, and it should be insisted that this work in no way intends to value writers over artists as the creative force behind the comic books discussed.

And so . . .

Like Perry Meisel's *The Cowboy and the Dandy,*[25] this work is an attempt to provide an alternative to Bloom's elitism:

> Canon-formation is not an arbitrary process, and is not, for more than a generation or two, socially or politically deter-

---

[25] Perry Meisel, *The Cowboy and the Dandy* (New York: Oxford University Press, 1999).

mined, even by the most intense of literary politics. Poets survive because of inherent strength; this strength is manifested through their influence upon other strong poets. . . . Poems stay alive when they engender live poems, even through resistance, resentment, misinterpretation; and poems become immortal when their descendants in turn engender vital poems. Out of the strong comes forth strength, even if not sweetness, and when strength has imposed itself long enough, then we learn to call it tradition whether we like it or not.[26]

There is a lot of truth in this statement, but Bloom would see the superhero comic book in a losing competition with the poems of Wallace Stevens. Presented here is a superhero mini-canon where *Batman: The Dark Knight Returns* and *Watchmen* are the strongest work in the tradition (and some certainly do not like it, as we will see), engendering vital stories in their genre. A discussion on the relative merits of Wallace Stevens and Grant Morrison will take us nowhere. As Raymond Chandler writes, "Within its frame of reference, which is the only way it should be judged, a classic is a piece of writing which exhausts the possibilities of its form and can hardly be surpassed,"[27] and I am inclined to agree with him.

This book, then, will be highly selective within its own frame of reference, and many works in the superhero genre will be absent from this discussion, including many superhero comics recently labeled revisionary, or revisionist. In the wake of *The Dark Knight Returns* and *Watchmen,* the phrase *revisionary superhero narrative* has been used by the comic book reading community to denote any superhero story that attempts a reworking of given characters or concepts. It occurs in this book, not in the sense of a revisionary history, but in the sense of Bloom's strong poetic revision through misprision: it is the wish of the revisionist to find an original relation to truth. What should be emphasized in the use of the word *revisionary* here is not "revise" but "visionary." In the latter sense, it is not a value-neutral term. John Byrne's reworking of Superman and Wonder Woman, Mark Waid on *The Kingdom,* Todd McFarlane's *Spawn,* Mark Gruenwald's *Squadron Supreme,* Rick Veitch's *One* (textual

---

[26] Bloom, *Map,* 200.

[27] Raymond Chandler, *Trouble Is My Business* (New York: Random House, 1939), x.

priority here is not a matter of simply being early), and even Neil Gaiman's *Sandman* (whose work, though strong, leaves behind the superhero genre completely) are not truly revisionary and are not covered here. Any history of the superhero story would be grossly incomplete without them, but this is not a history. This study, which nowhere claims to be exhaustive, presents an argument only through those superhero comic books that are both strong and representative.

To be more reader friendly, this book argues for the future of the superhero narrative across those works readily available to consumers at local comic book stores, bookstores, or Internet vendors in the form of trade paperbacks. TPBs (as they are called) collect comic book plot arcs, mini-series, and even whole series into easily available bookshelf editions. The overlap between those interested in literary theory and superhero comic books is not large, and in-depth sections on *Miracleman, Animal Man, Doom Patrol,* and *Flex Mentallo* would only alienate all but the most dedicated fans, as it would mean hours searching across back-issue bins and Internet auctions for those works one issue at a time, only to follow an argument just as easily presented across reprinted work. The reader should have no difficulty obtaining any work discussed in chapters 0 through 5, though the argument is accessible to anyone who has read only a few of the materials discussed.

Also absent from this study are those works that are part of the superhero genre because the superhero genre offered the only mainstream outlet for comic book creators. As Brian Michael Bendis writes in *Fortune and Glory:*

> See, in the world of comics, if you don't do superheroes, you're alternative. In comics, if it don't have a cape, or claws, or, like, really giant, perfectly spherical, chronic back-pain-inducing breasts involved in it it's alternative. The closest analogy I can think of is the difference between mainstream and independent film. . . . What I mostly write and draw is crime fiction. If you don't normally read comics and you're asking yourself: what's so alternative about crime fiction? Go to the top of the page and start reading again.[28]

---

[28] Brian Michael Bendis, *Fortune and Glory: A True Hollywood Comic Book Story* (Oni Press, 2000), #1.

Frank Miller entered the industry with the intention to concentrate on crime comics but found superheroes to be the only game in town. Because of this, Miller's work on the superhero title *Daredevil,* while being tremendous in its own right, did not factor into this book as highly as might be assumed at first glance. In a work on crime comics, Miller's *Daredevil* would be the first post-Wertham chapter (his *Sin City* might be the last), but here is little more than a lead-in to the realism (and revisionary realism) of his *Batman: The Dark Knight Returns.* This state of nearly-but-not-quite-out-of-the-genre should in no way reflect on the quality of works that are really a compromise formation, like Miller's *Daredevil,* Bendis's *Powers,* and Alan Moore's *Swamp Thing.* These are works that, while powerful and important, are only part of the superhero genre for marketing reasons: for the purposes of this book, they can hardly be considered superhero narratives at all.[29]

---

[29] These compromise formations account for the lasting power of a genre many would like to see abolished to make way for a more varied market. The superhero narrative has proved itself able to accommodate a wide range of stories under its banner, grouping together such disparate titles as Frank Miller's *Elektra: Assassin* and Marvel's *Infinity Gauntlet.*

Melancholy and the Infinite Earths

Will Brooker, in an unpublished essay on *Flex Mentallo,* gives a precise account of *Crisis on Infinite Earths* for those unfamiliar with the work. He writes:

The Crisis on Infinite Earths was a twelve-part maxiseries run by DC Comics in 1985. Its principle aim was to clean up the mess of narrative parallel universes which DC's writers had established over the past forty-five years, in order to start afresh with a single, easy-to-follow continuity. It achieved this aim by combining all of the possible earths into one, and killing off all the characters who didn't fit. The stories which had occurred "pre-Crisis" were therefore made unofficial, outside continuity, and would never be referred to again.[30]

In practice the Crisis did make DC's narrative universe more accessible to new readers. However, it also served the purpose of wiping out almost five decades of superhero history, and rewriting its main characters according to the more "serious," "adult" ethos of the mid-1980s. . . . Post-Crisis, the embarrassing moments of the 1950s and 1960s could simply be wiped out of history. There was to be no Rainbow Batman, for instance, no Bat-Mite, no Ace the Bat-Hound, no Batman in Ancient Rome, no Robin shouting "Come on, big boy!" to a pink alien.[31]

The word *crisis* derives from the Greek *krisis,* "judgment," and as Brooker makes clear, *Crisis on Infinite Earths* (1985) is interesting in its (editorial)

---

[30] Will Brooker, "Hero of the Beach: Flex Mentallo at the End of the Worlds," unpublished.
[31] Ibid.

judgment on DC's superhero comic book universe. *Crisis,* by Marv Wolfman and George Pérez, begins with the idea that the universe was meant to be one whole and unified structure, but was unnaturally splintered into a multiverse. This multiverse was an architecture of parallel worlds that house various interpretations and alternate histories of established characters: a Superman married to Lois Lane, a Batman whose parents were never killed, a world where the superheroes of World War II fight Adolf Hitler eternally, an evil mirror image of the Justice League of America (the Crime Syndicate—Superman, Batman, Wonder Woman, the Flash, and Green Lantern—become the villainous Ultra-Man, Owl-Man, Superwoman, Johnny Quick, and Power Ring). *Crisis* reveals that this situation of alternate histories is not natural but the result of a disaster that occurred eons ago. The planet Oa lies at the center of the universe, as a perfectly evolved scientific utopia; it is here that one man dares to use a powerful machine to look into the only realm of knowledge forbidden by tradition, the origins of the universe. His hubris results in a chain reaction that sends shock waves back in time, creating a situation in which the universe not only becomes a shattered and unstable multiverse, but always has been. The metaphor of this biblically styled story is unavoidable: by looking into origins, existence is splintered into a variety of mutually exclusive interpretations that have no center. The current state of the DC universe—all of the continuity problems and confusions and paradoxes, Umberto Eco's oneiric climate—is the retroactive result of looking too closely for a guiding and originating principle.

Two creatures are spun out of this catastrophe, powered by the energy released: the benevolent Monitor (raised on the moon of Oa) and the evil Anti-Monitor (raised on the moon's antimatter counterpart). Representatives for the forces of Order and Chaos, their birthplaces on matter and antimatter counterparts of a satellite of Oa, they are born literally slightly off-center. The Anti-Monitor gains power over his eternal foe, the Monitor, by destroying whole universes (remember, this is a multiverse). In the main battle between the Anti-Monitor and the Monitor's recruited superheroes, the universe is reborn the way it was meant to be: as a single unified whole. The Anti-Monitor did not simply eliminate whole universes (such as the world of the Crime Syndicate) but made it so that they never existed in the first place. *Crisis on Infinite Earths* was not designed to simply change the DC universe but to retroactively restructure it around a new organizing principle, specifically, the "adult ethos" Brooker mentions above, the very significant demographic shift that made the target audience of the comic book companies eighteen to twenty-four-year-old college-educated males. Comic books were now expected to tell stories for adults using the building blocks of children's literature. Characters made obsolete by *Crisis* were engulfed by white energy that looked a lot like the blank page taking over, and Superman's origin, for example, was retold by John Byrne putting Superman in the position of meeting his old enemies for the first time again. Krypton was redesigned, and the Legion of Super Pets (superpowered animals added as comic relief to *Superman* in the 1950s) were nowhere to be seen. They had not been killed; they simply never existed in the first place.

This was not the finest writing in the history of superhero comics. It was in many ways merely a marketing gimmick, forcing readers to buy all twelve issues to understand the changes being imposed on all their favorite characters and the universe they inhabited, and to make the DC universe simpler to comprehend for new readers and readers who preferred the more manageable continuity of Marvel. *Crisis on Infinite Earths,* however, started the new interpretation of superheroes. Retroactive changes, reimaginings, reinterpretations, revisiting origins, and revisions became major storytelling tools, tools that, rather than overturning the difficulties of continuity, fit in nicely with Eco's "oneiric quality." The irony of *Crisis* was that its methodology, in simplifying continuity, was used to make superhero comic books all the more complex, convoluted, and rich: any attempt at simplifying continuity into something streamlined, clear, and direct—from *Batman: Year One* and *Daredevil: The Man Without Fear* to Marvel Comic's *Ultimate X-Men* and *Ultimate Spider-Man*—only results in another layer of continuity. To a large degree, the changes imposed by *Crisis* did not stick, and the DC universe was left even more chaotic than before.

The last Superman story before the *Crisis* revamp and John Byrne's *Man of Steel* was Alan Moore's *Superman: Whatever Happened to the Man of Tomorrow?* One of the most beloved Superman stories of all time, it begins with a poem:

This is an IMAGINARY STORY
(which may never happen, but then again may)

about a perfect man who came from the sky and did only good.
It tells of his twilight, when the great battles were over and great
     miracles long since performed;
of how his enemies conspired against him and of that final war
     in the snowblind wastes beneath the Northern Lights;
[....]
This is an IMAGINARY STORY . . .
Aren't they all?[32]

Imaginary stories were those "what ifs" that were not supposed to affect established continuity but ended up creating an alternate continuity of their own and were about to be wiped out by *Crisis*. Here, Moore recognizes the absurdity of delineating between "real" fictional stories and "imaginary" ones, and his statement is a defense against the changes he knows are coming to *Superman. Whatever Happened to the Man of Tomorrow?* delights in every aspect of Superman's chaotic continuity, however absurd, that is about to be erased, and even manages to feature a moment with Krypto the Superdog, doomed not to make it out of *Crisis,* that is one of the few genuinely poignant *Superman* moments. In the story, all of Superman's enemies attack at once, and he must retreat into his Fortress of Solitude and protect his loved ones against a threat that—for the first time in his life—he believes he cannot stop. It turns out to be a malevolent Mxyzptlk behind it all: Superman kills him and, because he has broken his vow never to take a life, retires. His powers removed forever, he lives happily ever after with Lois Lane and lets the world believe Superman is dead. Moore's "last Superman story," while nostalgic about the rich (if sometimes ridiculous) continuity about to be wiped out, achieves a premature melancholy.

In the years after *Crisis,* DC would set up an "Elseworlds" banner that would feature alternative takes on established heroes—Batman as a vampire, Batman in the nineteenth century, Superman initially crashing to Earth in the Soviet Union. Unlike the imaginary stories of previous decades no attempt was made to give these "worlds" a metaphysical framework. There are no "parallel timelines" or an alternate Earth orbiting directly opposite ours, or Earth's antimatter counterpart. By

---

[32] Alan Moore, Kurt Swan, et al., *Superman: Whatever Happened to the Man of Tomorrow?* (New York: DC Comics, 1997).

2000, the industry would tolerate exactly the situation lamented as lost in *Whatever Happened to the Man of Tomorrow?*: Grant Morrison and Frank Quitely's stand-alone graphic novel *JLA: Earth-2*. *Earth-2* is the story of the Crime Syndicate of Amerika mysteriously alive and kicking and not under the "Elseworlds" banner, even though they were visibly killed off in *Crisis on Infinite Earths*. It is this continuity in ambiguity that is a unifying feature of the pre-Wildstorm works given attention in this book.

The multiverse is reduced to a universe at the end of *Crisis*. But the earlier ambiguity will make itself felt in the revisionary superhero narrative, which exists (in part) to come to terms with it. This ambiguity will expand until the multiverse is reinstalled as a concept in several forms: Mark Waid's *The Kingdom* (1999) introduces to the DC universe the concept of hypertime:

> Hypertime. The vast, interconnected web of parallel timelines which comprise all reality. . . . an unpredictable multi-verse, an infinite realm of parallel worlds where reality as you know it has taken different twists and turns. . . . Events of importance often cause divergent "tributaries" to branch off the main timestream. . . . On occasion those tributaries return—sometimes feeding back into the central timeline, other times overlapping it briefly before charting an entirely new course.[33]

Alan Moore created a similar concept for Image Comics in his *1963* (1993), which, in debt to the story by Jorge Luis Borges of the same name, he calls the Aleph: "a point from which all other points are visible . . . windows to other universes."[34] In his work on Awesome Comics'

---

[33] Mark Waid et al., *The Kingdom* (New York: DC Comics, 1998), 226–227. Note the phrase *twists and turns,* derived from the first line of Robert Fagles's translation of Homer's *Odyssey*. What is interesting is that the word Fagles is trying to communicate (a word that has given many of Homer's translators difficulty) is the Greek *polytropon,* or "many ways." *Tropos* (the dictionary form of *tropon*) is the ancient Greek source of the English word *trope,* or metaphor. Waid's conception recognizes, on some level, what Warren Ellis' Snowflake instinctively knows: the conception of the multiverse is a vision of "polytropes," or various metaphors, misreadings, and misprisions, of superhero continuity. Homer, *The Odyssey,* trans. Robert Fagles (New York: Penguin, 1996).
[34] Alan Moore et al., *1963* (Fullerton, CA: Image Comics, 1993), #6.

Supreme, he introduced a similar space for *Supreme* continuity, called "the Supremacy."[35] Waid's description of hypertime is accompanied by visuals of DC universe continuity wiped out by *Crisis on Infinite Earths*; Moore's Aleph contains visuals of independently owned comic books—including Frank Miller's *Sin City,* Dave Sim's *Cerebus,* and Scott McCloud's *Understanding Comics*—suggesting a multiverse that includes links to more than just one company's comic book universe. Grant Morrison's *Marvel Boy* (2000) introduces Macrospace into the Marvel universe: "Splintered across the endless, infinite worlds of the superspectrum: the immense rainbow of realities, where everything you ever imagined is just as real as everything else and all at once."[36] Morrison's description is accompanied by visuals of several universes, including one that alludes to Wildstorm's *Authority* and *Planetary.*

In an objective superhero history of the DC universe, Waid's concept of "hypertime" brings the DC universe to full multiplicity of storytelling, encompassing every DC universe yarn in a metaphysical framework of intersecting timelines. In this study of the revisionary superhero narrative, the Snowflake from Warren Ellis's *Planetary* is the cathexis of these narrative trends and a link to them all. Waid's hypertime, Moore's Aleph, and Morrison's Macrospace are statements about continuity and possibility in the superhero story, but Warren Ellis's *Planetary* (1998) presents us with a version that brings with it an imaginative and persuasive force that assures, despite chronology, its priority in the tradition of the superhero narrative.

Crisis would fail miserably as an attempt at simplification, giving the world a DC universe that made even less sense than before. What would change in the next fifteen years (in the works that are discussed in chapters 1 through 5) is the perspective that saw unwieldy chaos as a bad thing. Like many aspects of superhero comic books, what appears to a newcomer or outside observer as a drawback or flaw turns out to be, upon closer inspection, one of the genre's unique strengths. The path that gets the superhero story from the reduction of chaotic continuity in a single fictional universe through the burden of continuity and tradition to *Planetary*'s Snowflake is the focus of this book.

---

[35] Alan Moore et al., *Supreme* (Fullerton, CA: Maximum Press, 1996), vol. 3, #41.

[36] Grant Morrison, J. G. Jones, et al., *Marvel Boy* (New York: Marvel Comics, 2000), #5.

1

The Bat and the Watchmen

INTRODUCING THE REVISIONARY
SUPERHERO NARRATIVE

A succession of men had sat in that chair. I became
aware of that thought suddenly, vividly, as though
each had left a little of himself between the four walls
of these ornate bulkheads; as if a sort of composite
soul, the soul of command, had whispered suddenly
to mine of long days at sea, and of anxious moments.

—Joseph Conrad, *The Shadow Line*

Frank Miller's *Batman: The Dark Knight Returns* (1986) and Alan Moore's *Watchmen* (1986) are the first instances of a kind of literature I am going to identify as the revisionary superhero narrative: a superhero text that, in Harold Bloom's words, is a "strong misreading" of its poetic tradition, a comic book whose "meaning" is found in its relationship with another comic book. Although strong work existed in comics before this point—in the works of Will Eisner and Jack Kirby, for example—it is with these titles that, to quote critic Perry Meisel, referring to the blues tradition after swing, "a tradition now [exists] sufficiently dense with precedent to cause the kinds of self-consciousness and anxiety with which we [as students of literature] are familiar."[37] I will trace the development of this new kind of comic book—this new kind of literature—from its inauguration in 1986 to its present-day form, marking its changes, shifts, and misprisions, noting its differences and similarities to other forms of literature, but primarily

---

[37] Perry Meisel, *The Cowboy and the Dandy* (New York: Oxford University Press, 1999), 55–56.

trying to approach superhero comic books on their own terms rather than as analogous to existing poetics. Rather than present an introduction for those who do not read comic books regularly or discuss how the revisionary superhero narrative functions entirely in the abstract, then begin an analysis of the specifics, I will dive right into a reading of *Batman: The Dark Knight Returns* and *Watchmen,* including side discussions into the shorter *Batman: Year One* and *Batman: The Killing Joke.* They are interesting texts in themselves as well as paradigmatic of this genre, and comments for the nonspecialist (in academia or comic books) will be incorporated throughout. Together, they mark a first phase of development, the transition of the superhero from fantasy to literature. As Bloom writes:

> With marvelous significance for any theory of fantasy which is not content [as this work is not] with mere formalism or structuralism, Freud hypothesized that as infants we begin by living in fantasy. But when fantasy ceases to bring actual satisfaction then infantile hallucinations end, and the reality-principle begins to enter, together with a lengthening of attention-span, judgment, and the first sense of memory.[38]

The Dark Knight Returns and *Watchmen* are a judgment, and the superhero narrative's first sense of memory, its transition to the "reality principle."

I

Frank Miller: *Batman: The Dark Knight Returns* and *Batman: Year One*

In his introduction to *Batman: The Dark Knight Returns,* Alan Moore gives the reader the first hint toward understanding the relation that this work has with the complex tradition in which it participates. He writes:

> [Miller] has taken a character whose every trivial and incidental detail is graven in stone on the hearts and minds of comic fans

---

[38] Bloom, *Agon,* 203.

that make up his audience and managed to dramatically redefine that character without contradicting one jot of the character's mythology. Yes, Batman is still Bruce Wayne, Alfred is still his butler and Commissioner Gordon is still the chief of police, albeit just barely. There is still a young sidekick named Robin, along with a batmobile, a batcave and a utility belt. The Joker, Two-Face and the Catwoman are still in evidence amongst the roster of villains. Everything is exactly the same, except for the fact that it's all totally different.[39]

Batman: The Dark Knight Returns is the first work in the history of super-hero comics that attempts a synthesis of forty-five years of preceding Batman history in one place. Prose summaries giving a sense of how the Dark Knight has been portrayed over the decades have already been written.[40] To avoid redundancy, let me cite one example of Batman's contradictory portrayal as emblematic. The adventures of a superhero are published serially, and thus continuity is established from episode to episode, as in television. Unlike television, however, the serial adventures of individual superheroes have been running for decades, and as fictional characters these heroes do not age. Batman, for example, has remained a perennially young twenty-nine-year-old since his appearance in 1939, even though the environment in which he fights has changed month by month to remain contemporary. While certain writers and artists have had long runs with a single character, each superhero has had a number of different writers and artists over its run, crossing decades in American history. Since no single creator is essential to the continuation of any given character across the run of a series, many successful superhero titles are still in publication. Comic books are open-ended and can never be definitively completed, as even canceled titles might be revived and augmented by new creators.

This creates a number of interesting paradoxes that the revisionary superhero narrative will deal with uniquely, as we will see. The reader is given to understand, for example, that the Batman fighting crime in 1939 saying, "Well, Robin, he was a pilot during the war"; the cheery,

[39] Alan Moore, "Introduction," *The Dark Knight Returns* (New York: DC Comics, 1986).

[40] See Les Daniels, *Batman: The Complete History* (San Francisco: Chronicle Books, 1999).

goofy, campy 1960s Batman reciting the proverbial "Good job, old chum" (the basis for the Adam West *Batman* television show); and the solitary, grim, nearly psychotic, nocturnal 1980s Batman who watches Ronald Reagan on television are one and the same continuous character. Frank Miller's *Dark Knight Returns* is a radical move in the history of the superhero narrative because it is the first work that tries to compose a story that makes sense of its history, rather than mechanically adding another story to the Batman folklore. It must participate in the tradition in order to be recognized as a Batman story, but it consciously organizes that tradition in such a way as to comment on forty-five years of Batman comic books. This serves to complicate the assumptions and structure of that tradition. This is why, as Alan Moore notes, every aspect of the Batman that every reader knows so well finds expression here. This reworking organizes the Batman canon's contradictory parts into a coherent whole.

The Dark Knight Returns is one of the most important works in the tradition of superhero narratives because it is the first strong misreading of comic book history, specifically the history of Batman. Miller's work, and some of the work of those around him, can be located near Harold Bloom's concept of revisionary literature, which Bloom describes as "a re-aiming or a looking-over-again, leading to a re-esteeming or a re-estimating. . . . [T]he revisionist strives to *see* again, so as to *esteem* and *estimate* differently, so as to *aim* 'correctively.'"[41] Bloom's theory of revisionism is useful in understanding the way recent superhero narratives function, but the important moments will be where superhero comic books differ, rather than line up, with theories of poetry and other literature. An analysis of *The Dark Knight Returns* will serve as a good introduction to, and paradigm for, the way in which recent superhero narratives function, as it was one of the first, and still one of the strongest, superhero misprisions. One difference from Bloom's understanding of poetry may already be asserted. Miller is not writing a poem within the determination of strong poetic influence, but writing a character whose aspects are literally formed by his predecessors' works: he cannot come to the character fresh, because everything his predecessors on *Batman* wrote, on some level, did happen to the character he is writing. Batman, like many superheroes, wears his tradition on his

---

[41] Bloom, *Map,* 4 (Bloom's emphasis).

sleeve. The writer of an established superhero finds not only anxiety in past reading (which determines present writing), but in the very *bricolage* of the character's previous narrative. Poetic influence, which Bloom primarily identifies in stylistic terms, often emerges in superhero comic books as elements of the ostensible diegetic narrative, as this study will demonstrate. Miller's task differs from, say, strong poetry in America, because his misreading of Batman is an organization of a host of contradictory weak readings of a single, overdetermined character rather than an overcoming of previous strong effort within a poetic tradition; his effort in organizing them is to converge those weak readings into his own strong vision.

The first aspect of Miller's reorganization is an intense level of realism, the hallmark of his gritty, hard-boiled work on Marvel's *Daredevil* in the early 1980s (more influenced by the novels of Raymond Chandler and Dashiell Hammett than by fantasy/science fiction).[42] This trend reaches its culmination in *The Dark Knight Returns,* in which the Batmobile is sensibly reconceived as a Bat-Tank, and Arkham Asylum, usually portrayed as some kind of medieval dungeon, becomes an actual hospital for the mentally disturbed, complete with doctors and nurses. Miller forces the world of Batman to make sense. On a broad scale, this means introducing realistic time into comic books in a way never done before. First, Batman is aged, a move unheard of in a genre where characters persist for decades untouched by the passage of time. *The Dark Knight Returns* is set in Batman's "future," where he has been in retirement for ten years and is now in his mid-fifties. Gotham City, which in the history of comics has been a kind of abstract fictional stand-in for any urban setting, is given a temporal and spatial specificity very much in line with the New York City of the mid-1980s: the Twin Towers are a clear part of the city's skyline, and Ronald Reagan is president of the United States. So, while the reader is intended to understand *The Dark Knight Returns* as taking place in Batman's "future," it is a future

---

[42] Frank Miller, interview in *Writers on Comics Scriptwriting,* ed. Mark Salisbury (London: Titan Books, 1999), 187. I find it useful to separate the superhero narrative from fantasy/science fiction. The former is most often set in a mythical past with a distinct cosmology, whereas the latter is set in the future and often uses science in a completely different manner. The lines are, of course, blurred but some useful distinctions can be made.

relative to his age. The setting is in fact the contemporaneous 1980s. Miller accomplishes this level of realism—taking time seriously— without breaking from the superhero tradition of always setting the story in contemporary urban America. Aging Batman is the only way to accomplish this and still make narrative sense.

Miller also finds ways to synthesize Batman's confused and contradictory history on a smaller scale. Batman appears throughout *The Dark Knight Returns* in a number of different uniforms, with various Bat-Shield chest emblems reflecting forty-five years of costume design. In one amusing example, readers are finally given an explanation for one of the more confusing aspects of the garb, the eye-catching yellow Bat-Shield on a uniform meant to blend in with shadows. When Batman takes a rifle shot to the chest, which any reader assumes would kill him instantly, it reveals metal shielding. Batman says, "Why do you think I wear a target on my chest—can't armor my head,"[43] and with that one line a thirty-year mystery dissolves as every reader runs mentally through previous stories, understanding that plate as having always been there. This example of Miller's realism is paradigmatic of his revisionary strategy, and is more clearly illustrated by the way he incorporates violence into his narrative.

Miller has often stated that the only thing contemporary comics have learned from *The Dark Knight Returns* is the extreme level of violence it presents.[44] His own work is not so much violent as it is more graphic and more realistic about the violence that has always inhabited superhero narratives. With *The Dark Knight Returns,* the reader is forced to confront what has been going on for years between the panels. Miller's realism operates as a kind of commentary on a genre that has treated its inherent violence with kid gloves. Take, for example, the fact that Batman has in the course of his history gotten into many fights in which he is outnumbered and his opponents are armed with guns. Using only a Batarang and his fists, Batman manages to defeat them all without breaking a sweat. Miller never treats his hero so gently—*his* Batman is almost al-

---

[43] Frank Miller, Klaus Janson, and Lynn Varley, *Batman: The Dark Knight Returns* (New York: DC Comics, 1986), 51.

[44] Miller, "Batman and the Twilight of the Idols: An Interview with Frank Miller," in *The Many Lives of the Batman,* ed. Roberta E. Pearson and William Uricchio (New York: Routledge Press, 1991), 45.

ways wounded, sometimes badly, and the Batarang is reconceived as a kind of bat-shaped throwing star that disarms by slicing into the forearm, rather than its former, sillier portrayal as a boomerang that disarms criminals by knocking weapons out of their hands. The strength of Miller's portrayal leaves readers with the impression that all of Batman's fights must have been of this kind, but that they have been reading a watered-down version of the way things "really happened." It is important to note that powerful reading in superhero narratives often functions in this way: making all other readings appear to have "fallen away" from the strongest version that is retroactively constituted as always already true.

In Eco's oneiric climate, strong work comes to define truth, as narrative continuity is fuzzy at best. Miller's revisionary realism (connected to Freud's reality principle and sense of memory, as quoted above in the passage from Bloom) is only another version of what comic books often accomplish in the narrative, a literal revising of the facts of a comic book character's history on the basis of recent interpretation. Take, for example, the design of Superman's home planet, Krypton. The rendering of a "futuristic" world looks very different today than the rendering done in 1938. Today, however, Krypton is portrayed anew and is expected to be understood by readers as the true rendition of how Krypton *has always* looked. Miller's writing is very conscious of this process and actively strives to participate in comic book tradition, invoking various recognizable aspects in such a way as to recast readers' understanding of what they have seen before. Harold Bloom's remarks on Milton are amusingly relevant. Substituting Miller for Milton, the reader may conceive that—within its field of signifiers—*The Dark Knight Returns* has "the true priority of *interpretation,* the powerful reading that insists on its own uniqueness and its own accuracy. Troping on his forerunners' tropes, [Miller] compels us to read as he reads, and to accept his stance and vision as our origin, his time as true time."[45]

Miller's work internalizes not only fictional determination but also intertextual/historical influence. Early in *The Dark Knight Returns,* Bruce Wayne finds the film *The Mark of Zorro* on television,[46] and the reader is given to understand that this was the movie from which Bruce Wayne

---

[45] Bloom, *Map,* 132 (Bloom's emphasis).
[46] Miller et al., *Batman: The Dark Knight Returns,* 22.

and his parents were returning when his parents were killed. Batman creator Bob Kane has admitted that *The Mark of Zorro* (1920) was an influence in the creation of his superhero.[47] Miller makes the trail of influence in Bruce Wayne's creation of the Batman persona within the fictional history parallel the influence on Kane's portrayal of the character. This is only the first example of how *The Dark Knight Returns* engages and synthesizes not only the fictional tradition of its main character but also the very real history that has surrounded the comic book as a medium.

One key historical intertext for Miller's work is Dr. Fredric Wertham's notorious book, *Seduction of the Innocent*. Published in 1954, the 397-page opus condemned the comic book industry for degrading American values, and for spreading social and moral perversion. His words on superhero comic books still echo in the genre today:

> What is the social meaning of these supermen, superwomen, superlovers, superboys, supergirls, super-ducks, super-mice, super-magicians, super-safe crackers? How did Nietzsche get into the nursery? . . . Superheroes undermine respect for the law and hardworking decent citizens.[48]

He had this illuminating passage specifically devoted to Batman:

> Only someone ignorant of the fundamentals of psychology and the psychopathology of sex can fail to realize a subtle atmosphere of homoeroticism which pervades the adventures of the mature "Batman" and his young friend "Robin." . . . Robin is a handsome ephebic boy, usually shown in his uniform with bare legs. . . . He often stands with his legs spread, the genital region discreetly evident.[49]

Bruce Wayne and Dick Grayson's life in Wayne Manor is described as "the wish dream of two homosexuals living together." The shine on this observation was only made to sparkle more brightly in light of the Adam West *Batman* show that graced the airwaves in the 1960s. Since that

---

[47] McCue, *Dark Knights,* 22.

[48] Fredric Wertham, *Seduction of the Innocent* (New York: Rinehart and Company, 1954), 15.

[49] Ibid., 191. McCue cites these same passages in *Dark Knights.*

time, these terms have colored the impression of Batman for the non—comic book reading public and has forced on the defensive those fans reading the more "serious" Denny O'Neal/Neal Adams Batman of the 1970s, readers who viewed this perspective as insulting, but had no terms in which to reply.[50]

Miller responds to the instincts of mainstream fandom and "refutes" these passé charges without denying Wertham his observation that homoeroticism plays a role in the superhero story. He synthesizes both perspectives, both aspects of the comic book tradition, while remaining inside the framework of the Batman folklore. His conciliatory (and revisionary) move is to cast a girl in the role of the new Robin. The original Robin, Dick Grayson, makes no appearance in *The Dark Knight Returns*: Bruce cryptically informs Commissioner Gordon that they have not spoken for seven years. The second Robin, Jason Todd (whose uniform is seen in a glass case at the center of the Batcave) died, and because Batman feels responsible for Todd's death, he retired ten years ago. Carrie Kelly, the new Robin, is picked up in the course of *The Dark Knight Returns,* and through her gender provides interesting commentary on the role of her young male predecessors.

Several scenes are particularly germane to this discussion. The first occurs after Carrie Kelly is initially brought to the Batcave with an almost mortally wounded Batman. She has saved his life (albeit barely) and tagged along in the Batmobile with conscious plans of becoming the next Robin (she has already crafted a uniform by hand). A young girl waiting with anxiety to discover if her hero will live, she is placed in the role of a concerned wife or lover. Two small panels at the bottom right of the right-hand page show a large hand being placed on her shoulder as she turns her head: the page turn reveals a full-page spread (the comic book equivalent of "music swells"), which is not a reunion kiss, suggested by the lead-in drama, but a completely nonsexual embrace, almost a parody of the lover's embrace.[51] In another scene, Robin nearly falls to her doom but is rescued by Batman. Safe from death but still hovering over the water, she straddles Batman's crotch and clutches to him tightly. Here, the female Robin is cast in the role of the damsel in

---

[50] See Will Brooker, *Batman Unmasked* (New York: Continuum, 2000), 101–170, for an extremely sensitive and cogent discussion of homophobia, Wertham, and *Batman.*
[51] See Miller et al., *Batman: The Dark Knight Returns,* 91–92.

distress (cf. Superman's characteristic swoop downward to catch the recurrently falling Lois Lane), but again the result, which, like the earlier embrace, could be read as sexual (and in the damsel in distress role would be), simply defies the reader to interpret it in this manner.[52] It is difficult to find sexual tension in Batman's "Good soldier. Good Soldier."[53] In both these scenes, the setup hints at the possibility of a sexual reading, then frustrates the fulfillment of this desire. Rather than provide more sexual tension (as a similar situation might in early Hollywood films, which often coded sexual moments in such a way as to be suggestive while avoiding the censors), the dissonance between the erotic frame with which the reader is provided and the ostensible content short-circuits the sexual reading altogether. Those who are familiar with Wertham's book or its echoes—ubiquitous in popular culture parodies of Batman—will be on the lookout for these kinds of homoerotic signifiers, and discover Miller toying with them. Casting Robin as a girl places the sexual relation of Batman and Robin in a more socially acceptable light, as if the sexuality can and thus will be brought out into the open, then still denies that the sexuality is there. The reader is invited to conclude that it never was, that age is the obvious barrier to this reading of the Batman–Robin relationship, not homosexuality. The one moment that does suggest sexuality in Robin comes when she sees the corpses left behind by the Joker. Batman narrates, "A tiny hand tightens its grip on my arm. . . . A girl of thirteen breathes in sharply, suddenly, her innocence lost,"[54] but this must be read in the context of Batman's relationship to the Joker, and the Joker's relation to sexuality within the narrative.

Having evaded Wertham's claims for Batman and Robin, Miller is not so naive as to insist that homoeroticism is entirely absent from the Batman narrative, and in fact provides for it a consequential role in *The Dark Knight Returns*. The final joke on Wertham is Miller's ability to avoid homoeroticism in the Batman–Robin relationship while at the same time raising the question, transferring it to the antagonistic relationship between Batman and the Joker. Miller caters to instincts that Batman and Robin's relationship is not a thinly disguised homoerotic fantasy, but

---

[52] Ibid., 138.

[53] Ibid.

[54] Ibid., 140 (Miller's ellipsis).

also gives Wertham his due by not invoking a reactionary position (as C. S. Lewis did in regard to Shakespeare's sonnets), that the homoerotic has no place at all.

The Joker's role in *The Dark Knight Returns* brings homoerotisism out into the open for one of the first times in mainstream superhero comic books. Like Batman, the Joker has been the subject of various disparate portrayals in the Batman titles and has gone through an equal amount of instability regarding his history and character. A disturbed murderer in the 1940s and early 1950s, he becomes silly rather than evil after the crackdown on violence in comics in 1954 (led by Wertham's book), then slowly returns to his earlier viciousness as comics begin to recover. Miller's Joker has the personality of an aging, degenerate rock star, as murderous as he is effete. *The Dark Knight Returns* portrays the Joker in a role that synthesizes these dual and opposing persona. The dialogue between hero and villain unearths Wertham's general charges of homo-eroticism in Batman, and the shift from Batman/Robin to Batman/Joker makes the claim significantly more interesting and complex. The effect is not, as some have claimed, simply a homophobic attempt to align homosexuality with evil, but rather provides a subterranean connection between two characters who seem, on the surface, to be diametrically opposed.

Sketching out a specific level of connection between antagonists in this work, however, cannot be appreciated without at least mentioning the more general part Batman's villains play in the series. Every major member of the villain's gallery operates as a kind of reflection of some aspect of Batman's personality or role so that an understanding of one of the villains always sheds light on Batman himself. Some examples, expanding Reynolds's observations on the Penguin and Two-Face,[55] will make this clear. Two-Face is always given at least some part in every major Batman story because of his parallel relation to Batman: a success-ful upper-class socialite, the district attorney of Gotham City had half his face scarred by acid thrown when he was prosecuting the mob. This trauma resulted in a split personality and an obsession with duality and the number 2. Bruce Wayne, upon seeing his parents murdered, suffered a similar personality split: the creation of the Batman alter ego. The Penguin reflects the dark side of Bruce Wayne's millionaire capitalist

---

[55] Reynolds, *Mythology*, 68.

playboy routine. Mr. Freeze points out the dark side of Bruce Wayne's utter lack of emotion as Batman. The shape-shifter, Clayface, suggests the anti–essential nature of the Batman/Bruce Wayne relationship, both of which are seen as persona (Batman to scare criminals, Wayne to cover up Batman under the role of a disaffected rich fop). Poison Ivy uses criminal activity (and Batman's vigilante status is, of course, illegal) for a good cause, ecology. The Scarecrow, whose entire existence is devoted to fear, recalls that the intention of the Batman persona is the edge provided by terror. The Mad Hatter's mind control reflects the extremities of Batman's methods of coercion. The Riddler parodies Batman's role as the great detective. Man-Bat provides another example of a Jekyll-and-Hyde transformation that, like Batman, only emerges at night. The Ventriloquist questions, in terms of split personality, who is the puppet and who is the puppeteer. Even a ludicrously silly villain like the Calendar Man, who commits theme crimes once a month, reflects Batman's monthly publishing schedule. Miller actually conceives of Ronald Reagan, who wants Batman brought down, in terms of his reflective relation to the Dark Knight: a spokesman for the president informs the news that "[i]ts noisy, all right. That big cape and pointy ears—it's great show biz. And you know the president knows his show biz."[56] The political similarities between the two is a major theme of *The Dark Knight Returns*. Miller is very aware of this function of Batman's villains and draws the reader's attention to it early. Confronting Batman face to face (as it were), Two-Face asks him what he sees: "I see a reflection, Harvey. A reflection."[57] Under this schema, any understanding of the Joker—violent, insane, or sexually deviant—will reflect an aspect of Batman.

The Joker is clearly in some kind of dormant state at Arkham Asylum, watching television in a common room without his trademark smile—until he hears news reports of Batman's return to the streets. As the smile slowly grows, his only reaction is to say, "Darling"[58] (by which the Joker will refer to Batman throughout *The Dark Knight Returns*). Claiming rehabilitation, he appears on a kind of David Letterman show (along with Dr. Ruth Westheimer). Dr. Wolper, the Joker's psychotherapist, claims, "My patient is a victim of Batman's psychosis," and that

---

[56] Miller et al., *Batman: The Dark Knight Returns,* 66.

[57] Ibid., 55.

[58] Ibid., 41.

the nature of this psychosis is "sexual repression, of course."[59] "We must not restrain ourselves," says the Joker, as he begins his killing spree by kissing the sex therapist, poisoning her.[60] In a later apostrophe to Batman, remarking to himself that he no longer keeps track of how many people he has killed, the Joker coyly notes, "But you do. And I love you for it."[61] Were this sexuality only found in the Joker it would suggest a simple connection between sex ("deviant" sexuality) and evil, but Batman's dealings reveal a complex dynamic at work. Earlier in the narrative, Batman and Two-Face crash through a window together: Batman narrates: "We tumble like lovers,"[62] and the Joker's intriguing combination of feminine and masculine signifiers—the delicate application of makeup, a "tough guy" build, speech affectations, aggressive physical violence—must be seen in light of the fact that the issue devoted to him opens with Batman dressed as a woman.[63] Descending on his most hated villain, the reader is privy to this piece of Batman's interior monologue, ostensibly about finally killing the Joker but suggestive of something else:

> Can you see it, Joker? Feels to me . . . like it's written all over my face. I've lain awake nights . . . planning it . . . picturing it . . . endless nights . . . considering every possible method . . . treasuring each imaginary moment . . . from the beginning, I knew . . . that there's nothing wrong with you . . . that I can't fix . . . with my hands. . . .[64]

The final battle between the two occurs in the Joker's most often-used site, the carnival. A skirmish in the House of Mirrors suggests that the two are dark reflections of each other, and the Joker's death, the consummation of the Batman–Joker relationship referred to in the passage above, occurs, appropriately, in the Tunnel of Love. All this serves to address Wertham's earlier claims about the subtext of superhero literature; in addressing nearly fifty years of comic book history, in trying to make sense of a chaotic tradition, Miller cannot avoid it. He is able to

---

[59] Ibid., 126.

[60] Ibid., 127

[61] Ibid., 140.

[62] Ibid., 54.

[63] Ibid., 106.

[64] Ibid., 142 (Miller's ellipses).

write a Batman without the camp and silliness of the Adam West series (the Dick Sprang years of the comic book) but while still understanding the character as operating over a background informed by a homoerotic subtext. By moving the focus from Robin to the Joker, he swerves from understanding this subtext as specifically linked to superhero narratives (through the sidekick, an archetypal role in superhero stories), suggesting, rather, that it operates in all antagonistic narratives: a relatively pedestrian illustration of the widely accepted Freudian thesis on the link between sexuality and violence (regardless of sexual preference). Miller brings together hero and villain, and hints at the collapse between them. This thesis is reinforced by the observation that moments before his death, the Joker's word bubbles take on the color and shape used to distinguish Batman's speech.

(Looking ahead fifteen years, and to the end of this book, the stage is set for the future of the superhero narrative at Wildstorm, and the reader should catch the stirrings of one of its key aspects here. The golden age at DC was characterized by elements of the fantastic and magical: Wonder Woman was created by a goddess, and Captain Marvel was given his powers by the wizard Shazam. The silver age at Marvel was marked by powers derived from an unflagging faith in all things scientific and radioactive: the powers of the Fantastic Four derived from Cosmic Rays, and Spider-Man gained his abilities from the bite of a radioactive spider. The Wildstorm universe of *The Authority, Planetary,* and *Wildcats,* by contrast, is characterized by a difficulty in distinguishing heroes from villains. This stems largely from the initial atmosphere of the early Wildstorm titles in which the sources of the superpowers (themselves a boon) doubled as the shadowy villain of the story, often a secret government military installation or massive corporation in search of private power. Extrapolated from obvious real-life parallels, this ambivalent relation to government and big business, which provides both towering benefits and sinister motivation, created an ambivalent breed of heroes. The heroes of the Wildstorm universe were left in a moral vacuum their golden and silver age counterparts never had to face. The WildC.A.T.s would find the war they fought had been over for centuries and their cause not as morally pure as they had believed, and Stormwatch would discover their leader an utterly insane madman on a quest for power. Even the upbeat *Gen-13* cannot exist in the Wildstorm universe without the shadowy counterpart of Warren Ellis's *DV8*. A key seed has been set in *Batman:*

The Dark Knight Returns that will reach fruition in *The Authority*—the synthesis of *Stormwatch* and *WildC.A.T.s* and the subject of chapters 4 and 5.)

The collapse between antagonists, however, only points to a larger, more dangerous, pattern of collapse between Batman and his more shadowy reflective antagonist: the political. *The Dark Knight Returns* is also known for overtly engaging political issues, but this observation misses the point that Miller makes in bringing political realities to Batman: comic books have always had a political dimension, usually supporting whatever hegemonic discourse (most often conservative) the decade at hand had to offer. (It is interesting to note in this context that the father of all superhero stories—*Action Comics* 1 (1938) the first appearance of Superman—involved Superman stopping fifth columnists trying to get America "embroiled" in the war in Europe.)[65] Like the issues of homo-eroticism and violence, Miller wants to foreground a submerged aspect of comic book tradition. He chooses, along with cold war Reagan-era politics, a more structural aspect of superhero politics: its fascistic tendencies.

Three aspects of superhero comic books are at work here. First, superheroes, and Batman especially, always rely on physical violence and intimidation to fight crime. Batman himself is not unwilling to be physically brutal to acquire information, for example, and often relies on the threat or implied threat of violence to keep criminals in line. Second, it is often the case that the superhero is a kind of criminal—a vigilante. In these two respects, many masked crime fighters differ from the Ku Klux Klan only in that they are usually afforded socially acceptable status on a large scale.[66] As masked men who take the law into their own hands the superhero comes dangerously close to some of the great evils in American history. Third, superheroes most often occupy a reactionary role, traditionally emerging only to meet a threat to the status quo. Large-scale social changes are a supervillain signature, manifesting when one wishes to take over the world or, alternatively, to destroy all human life, allowing nature to grow without humanity's ecological poisoning, for example. However well intentioned, these kinds of moves almost

---

[65] *Action Comics* (New York: DC Comics, 1938), #1.

[66] This description is perhaps more accurate for DC than the Marvel universe: Captain America and the Avengers are not vigilantes, whereas Spider-Man and the X-Men do not enjoy social acceptance.

always mark someone whom the superhero must stop, even in the case of a fellow superhero. Miller takes into account each of these aspects of the comic book tradition, especially the first two (Alan Moore's *Watchmen,* discussed below, focuses on the third). Where in most superhero stories these issues are usually accepted as assumptions, *The Dark Knight Returns* foregrounds their role as determiners of the text, and complicates them.

Violence in Miller's work has already been discussed in the context of his revisionary realism, but it should be kept in mind when understanding Batman's status as a vigilante, also highlighted in *The Dark Knight Returns.* The work is interspersed with debates about the level of danger this kind of activity entails, and the degree to which Batman himself is a hero or villain. In the context of Batman's overdetermination by his multivectored history, and Miller's organization of that history, the question of Batman's signification is raised in a television debate. An anti-Batman spokesperson debates publicly with Lana Lang, once a love interest for Clark Kent, and thus debating the more idealistic view of superheroes:

> LANA: One almost expects to see the Bat-Signal striking the side of one of Gotham's Twin Towers. Yes, he gave us quite a night. . . .
>
> MORRIE: Sure kept the hospitals busy.
>
> LANA: Yes, Morrie, but I think it is a mistake to think of this in purely political terms. Rather, I regard it as a symbolic resurgence of the common man's will to resist. A rebirth of the American fighting spirit.
>
> MORRIE: Ease up, Lana. The only thing he signifies is an aberrant psychotic force, morally bankrupt, politically hazardous, reactionary, paranoid. . . . [67]

The difficulty is, of course, that Batman has at times signified all of these things. Here, Miller allows Batman's interpretations to engage in dialectic rather than choosing a single perspective. Once again, Miller complicates a key assumption of the Batman tradition: his vigilante, and thus illegal, status. Unlike the comic books that came before, the reader cannot wholeheartedly agree with Batman's methods, but is instead invited to question his extremity.

---

[67] Miller et al., *Batman: The Dark Knight Returns,* 41.

Batman's disregard for civil rights arises only three pages after the debate quoted above. Questioning a suspect who Batman has already left in a neck brace and crutches, the following Clint Eastwoodesque exchange takes place:

> BATMAN: You're going to tell me everything you know, sooner or later. If it's later—I won't mind.
>
> MAN: No!—Stay back—I got rights.—[*Batman throws him through a closed window onto a fire escape*]
>
> BATMAN: You've got rights. Lots of rights. Sometimes I count them just to make myself feel crazy. But right now you've got a piece of glass shoved into a major artery in your arm. Right now you're bleeding to death. Right now I'm the only one in the world who can get youto a hospital in time. . . .[68]

Batman's obsession with control and order, his disregard for civil rights, and his use of violence to force others, though often criminals, into submission to his will point to comic book's (sometimes alluring) flirtation with fascism. Illegal, physically violent coercion plays a role in all superhero stories; it is practically a genre convention. Miller questions its role, highlighting an aspect of those narratives in which every reader has, perhaps unwillingly, participated.

The implied threat of large-scale fascistic control must necessarily underlie superhero stories because of a fundamental power differential. In *Leviathan,* Thomas Hobbes writes that the reason men can bond together in equality to create a civilization is that all men are basically equal: where one excels in physical strength, another may excel in mental ability. The power differences among men are never so great that a few might not band together to stop one.[69] In the world of superhero comics, this is simply not the case. It is conceivable that the seven core members of DC's flagship superhero team, the Justice League of America (which includes Batman, Superman, Wonder Woman, and the Green Lantern), could reduce the world to rubble in a matter of days. So even in regard to "do-gooders," the threat of paternalism cum fascism is always present. Other superhero works, like *Squadron Supreme* and *Kingdom Come,* deal with this aspect of superhero tradition more specifically.

---

[68] Ibid., 44–45.

[69] Thomas Hobbes, "Leviathan" in *From Plato to Nietzsche,* ed. Forrest E. Baird and Walter Kaufmann (Upper Saddle River: Prentice Hall, 1997) 471–512.

In *The Dark Knight Returns,* it remains more of an implied threat, but clearly factors into the notable absence of other superheroes in such a global narrative.

Miller's adumbrated explanation of where all the superheroes have gone suggests the reactionary politics of McCarthy era America, when those who refused to come before the committee investigating communism were blacklisted. More specifically, it recalls Wertham's report, Wertham's report, which called the entire comic book industry into question and caused the cancellation of more than a few titles. Superman's fragmentary internal monologue gives only the briefest hints of what happened in Miller's fictional world, but clearly the understanding of Batman's role must be understood in this context:

> The rest of us learned to cope. The rest of us recognized the danger—of the endless envy of those not blessed. Diana [Wonder Woman] went back to her people. Hal [Jordan: The Green Lantern] went to the stars.[70]

> They'll kill us if they can, Bruce. Every year they grow smaller. Every year they hate us more. We must not remind them that giants walk the earth.[71]

> You were the one they used against us, Bruce. The one who played it rough. When the noise started from the parents' groups and the sub-committee called us in for questioning—you were the one who laughed . . . that scary laugh of yours . . . "[S]ure we're criminals," you said. "[W]e've always been criminals. We have to be criminals."[72]

> I gave them my obedience and my invisibility. They gave me a license and let us live. No, I don't like it. But I get to save lives—and the media stays quiet. But now the storm is growing again. They'll hunt us down again—because of you.[73]

After *Seduction of the Innocent,* the criminal and subversive aspects of comic books were played down but not eradicated. Batman, perhaps the

---

[70] Ibid., 120.
[71] Ibid., 129–130.
[72] Ibid., 135 (Miller's ellipses).
[73] Ibid., 139.

most rebellious of the superheroes, is calling attention to himself again and ignoring the rules, just as Miller's work ignores the Wertham report and the "Comics Code Authority" (the comic book industry's reaction to Wertham, similar to the Production Code Administration which was designed to protect "values and decency" in Hollywood in the 1930s and 1940s).[74] Miller's work consistently flaunts the principles of the code, and is thus the point at which comic books become more interesting for adult readers. Miller puts himself in the position of Batman: Batman's indictment of Superman and the subservience he now stands for is Miller's indictment of the comic book industry for crumbling under the weight of the charges in *Seduction of the Innocent.*

Miller places this difficult structural observation in the context of Reagan-era politics, and once again raises dual aspects of the Batman folklore: Batman's position is that of both a rebel and a dispenser of a new hegemonic discourse. The one must necessarily imply the other because superheroes are in a position of fighting for a world in which they will no longer have a place, in which they will no longer be needed. A successful rebel is a new hegemony, and the sheer power many superheroes wield threatens that success. Because comic book superheroes are produced serially and always take place in contemporary America, it is possible (if not necessary) for characters to be rebels forever. They can continue to fight threats in each issue but still never approach the total eradication of crime. Miller raises the fact that, at least theoretically, each superhero is fighting for an overall change in society, even if in each individual issue the hero is usually reactionary in maintaining the status quo. The rebel/hegemony split once again nods to Wertham's observation that "superheroes undermine respect for the law and hardworking decent citizens" and the historical observation that comic book politics have consistently aligned themselves with dominant social trends. Superman, father of all superheroes—and thus in metonymy for all standard superhero narratives—enters into this discussion as the spokesperson for the latter. Batman speaks to him in apostrophe: "You've always known just what to say. 'Yes' . . . to anyone with a badge—or a flag."[75] In Miller's conception, Superman is a stooge and soldier for an enfee-

---

[74] See Amy Kiste Nyberg, "Seal of Approval: The Origins and History of the Comics Code" (Ph.D. diss., University of Wisconsin-Madison, 1994).

[75] Miller et al., *Batman: The Dark Knight Returns,* 190 (my ellipsis).

bled Ronald Reagan who wants to see Batman stopped because his empowerment—and empowerment of others by example—threatens the social control Reagan has in place. Reagan says:

> I like to think I learned everything I know about running this country on my ranch. I know it's corny but I like to think it. And well, it's all well and good, on a ranch I mean, for the horses to be all different colors and sizes, long as they stay inside the fence. It's even okay to have a crazy bronco now and then, does the hands good to break him in. But if that bronco up and kicks the fence out and gets the other horses crazy, well it's bad for business.[76]

The climax of *The Dark Knight Returns* is the final face-off between Batman and Superman. The rebel threatening a new hegemony against the keepers of the old hegemony and the status quo represent the facing-off of the dialectical aspects of comic book tradition. Both of these aspects have been inherent in the superhero comic tradition, of which Miller has been trying to make sense, attempting a synthesis. Here, the two positions literally battle for control, and the implications of the ending are clear in this context. Batman is clearly the winner before collapsing of a heart attack; but his death is only a ruse, and he lives underground. No longer the visible threat he once was, he allows Superman to ignore him as he prepares students to go above and continue the fight. "The American fighting spirit" (as Lana Lang puts it) appears to have been crushed under the heel of reactionary politics, but it is not dead, only dreaming.[77] The rebellious incarnation of the superhero can never be entirely vanquished, but it will always lurk beneath and haunt the genre, no matter how it may try to conform to external standards.

In this respect, *The Dark Knight Returns* can be read as a kind of fable for comic book tradition, warning against the fascistic impulses inherent in superheroes, in which both the reader and Batman come to a realization of the role that this must play in the superhero narrative. *The Dark Knight Returns* once again responds to contradictory aspects of Batman's

---

[76] Ibid., 84.

[77] Cf. the end of Chuck Palahniuk's *Fight Club,* a work that also engages the problem of the rebel's institution of a new hegemony.

fictional history or tradition: at times, Batman has been written with the understanding that he is low profile, that at least part of his power comes from his status in Gotham City as a kind of urban legend that the criminal underworld fears is real. Batman comes out only at night and might be some inhuman demon or vampire. At other times, particularly in the sunny 1950s and 1960s, but also randomly throughout his career, this has been forgotten, and the reader has seen Batman walking the streets in the daytime, shaking hands with the mayor and Commissioner Gordon, marching in parades, even touring college campuses with Robin. Miller acknowledges both mutually exclusive portrayals, presenting Batman's return as Batman-out-in-the-open-with-a-vengeance—a kind of "return of the repressed" 1960s Batman—then reestablishing his urban legend status at the end of the narrative.

When Miller's Batman emerges from retirement, the immediate issue in question is his visibility. The Bat-Tank in particular lacks a certain level of subtlety. Oliver Queen, known to those with knowledge of the DC universe as the Green Arrow, makes the key statement for understanding the Batman's roll in the political in this work:

> You've always had it wrong, Bruce . . . giving them such a big target. Sure, you play it mysterious—but it's a loud kind of mysterious, man. Especially lately. You've got to learn how to make those sons of bitches work for you. Look—it's been five years since I blew out of prison—and you know I've kept busy—And they've been covering for me, just like they covered up my escape. Sure, they'd love to frost me . . . long as they can do it without admitting I exist. But you, Bruce—man, they *have* to kill you.[78]

Batman's use of conspicuous force parallels the Reagan-era cold war politics: both Batman and Reagan are "fighting crime" in a conspicuous display of power (the Bat-Tank, Reagan's missile,[79] and "real-life" Reagan's Star Wars missile defense shield) to impress the population they want to control. In Miller's realism, where the subtlety of Batman-

---

[78] Miller et al., *Batman: The Dark Knight Returns*, 185–186 (Miller's ellipses).
[79] Ibid., 164.

as-urban-legend is much more believable, any conspicuous display of power will be used for, or by, the government (e.g., Superman's involvement as a tool of the White House) to drum up fear or to gain support for the government (to fight the Russians in Miller's fictional Corto Maltese subplot; or, on the local level, the anti-Batman stance, used to get support for a new and unpopular police chief). In the course of *The Dark Knight Returns*, Batman becomes the worst sort of reactionary fascist terrorizing people into his control with cheap theatrics.

Batman's former status as an urban legend kept him outside of this kind of political struggle (outside being co-opted by the White House or being used in a "Big Brother will save you from the Batman" campaign). In the urban legend position, a warrant for Batman's arrest would have been laughable to a disbelieving public, as if the police department were trying to rid Gotham City of the bogeyman. In the end, Bruce Wayne realizes that the Batman persona is being manipulated and publicly destroys it. An early, proposed ending for *The Dark Knight Returns*[80] placed Batman on a throne, in a cave surrounded by disciples waiting to return, but the finished version makes better sense in the context. Bruce Wayne becomes a teacher, on the floor of the cave, kneeling in plain clothes and speaking to students—some of whom are actually standing above him. The narration tells us he has learned that the world is "plagued by worse than thieves and murderers,"[81] presumably the methods used in fighting them. Miller's text reinstalls Batman as a rebel, as subversive, but with a greater understanding of the power structures involved. Like Shakespeare, Miller's innovation within his tradition is to allow reflection to result in character development.

Batman's understanding of himself must also be seen in terms of Miller's understanding of tradition. The final page of *The Dark Knight Returns* is a vision of Batman overcoming his previous interpretations. On the narrative level, this occurs as the destruction of the Batman persona because of the "interpretations" of the media and the government. On the level of trope, it means the placement of Miller's Batman for the Batman of other writers (e.g., Bob Kane and Dick Sprang). As Bloom says of Childe Roland, "There is only Roland himself to serve both as hero and villain. . . . The Childe stands in judgment against

---

[80] Ibid., appendix.
[81] Ibid., 199.

his own antithetical quest and, however lovingly, against his antithetical precursors as well. . . . [He] is an interpretation of his precursors' quest."[82] Batman's metatextual act of knowledge is of himself and his tradition, of his razing of preceding visions of the Batman: "Here, in the endless cave, *far past the burnt remains of a crimefighter whose time has passed* . . . it begins here—an army—to bring sense to a world plagued by worse than thieves and murderers."[83] Miller's is the Batman who, in his strength, burns his predecessors "whose time has past" (the Batman of 1939; the Batman of 1968; his own Batman persona within *The Dark Knight Returns,* literally burned in the destruction of Wayne Manor), but who also understands that the Batcave, and the Batman comic book, is "endless," that is, serially published. However strong a reading Miller might perform, "it begins here" rather than ends. Batman will continue to be published in the hands of other writers.

The feeling of finality in the last moment of *The Dark Knight Returns* is juxtaposed with a statement of beginning. Just after calling for a lamp to illuminate the darkness of the cave—a new fire, a new Batman past the burnt remains of the old—he informs his students that "we haven't got all night," but thinks to himself, "That's not true . . . we have years—as many as we need."[84] The last we hear of Batman's pedagogy is Miller's imparting of the fecundity of the Batman mythos to future writers, "First we get a steady supply of water. There's a spring right beneath."[85] Miller's powerful misprision of comic book history ends with a troping of superhero narratives as an "endless cave" with a "spring" of contradictory but rich tradition to be drawn upon "right beneath." *The Dark Knight Returns* becomes the *fons et origo* (the fountain-head and the origin) of the revisionary superhero narrative. Miller himself has gone into Batman's fictional history and selected elements for use in his work, taking many elements a lesser writer would have simply ignored, and made them his own. The reader can understand that in his last act of knowledge on the final page, Miller's Batman, to quote Bloom again on Childe Roland:

---

[82] Bloom, *Map,* 117.
[83] Miller et al., *Batman: The Dark Knight Returns,* 199 (my emphasis, Miller's ellipsis).
[84] Ibid. (Miller's ellipsis).
[85] Ibid.

negates the larger part of the poem, a negation that strengthens rather than weakens the poem, because there [he] suffers a unique act of knowledge, an act that clarifies both his personal past and tradition, though at the expense of both presence and present. By "presence" I mean both [his] self-presence [the willing destruction of both the Bruce Wayne and Batman personas past and present], and also the virtual existence of any opposing force in the poem other than [his] internalization of the precursors.[86]

This is what Miller's work is about. Batman's (and Miller's) struggle is not to control any villain but to master preceding visions of himself and his tradition. When the new chief of police confronts Commissioner Gordon as to why he supported a vigilante during his tenure, Gordon's words express an understanding of the interpretive process:

I'm sure you've heard old fossils like me talk about Pearl Harbor, Yindel. Fact is we mostly lie about it. We make it sound like we all leaped to our feet and went after the Axis on the spot. Hell, we were scared. Rumors were flying, we thought the Japanese had taken California. We didn't even have an army. So there we were, lying in bed pulling the sheets over our heads—and there was Roosevelt on the radio, strong and sure, taking fear [read: anxiety] and turning it into a fighting spirit [cf. Lana Lang's description of Batman as the return of the American fighting spirit]. Almost overnight we had our army. We won the war. . . . A few years back . . . a lot of people with a lot of evidence said that Roosevelt knew Pearl Harbor was going to be attacked— and that he let it happen. . . . I couldn't stop thinking how horrible that would be, and how Pearl was what got us off our duffs in time to stop the Axis. But a lot of innocent men died. But we won the war. It bounced back and forth in my head until I realized I couldn't judge it. It was too big, *He* was too big.[87]

---

[86] Bloom, *Map,* 116.
[87] Miller et al., *Batman: The Dark Knight Returns,* 96 (my ellipses).

"I don't see what this has to do with a vigilante," Yindel says. "Maybe you will," is the reply. The relation to Batman is obvious, but in terms of Miller's text, it serves as a statement on the power of the single interpretive (revisionary) stance. There is no stable point from which to pass judgment, no standard other than the strength of the vision—the strength of the personality, be it Batman or Miller. This passage is quoted at length, because it is paradigmatic of a move many revisionist superhero narratives will make, from *Watchmen* to *The Authority,* and a subject to which this book will return.

The role of fascism, the role of forced control in *The Dark Knight Returns,* is clearly reflexive. Batman's imposition of control over the chaotic streets of Gotham City cannot be seen as distinct from Miller's imposition of control over Batman's chaotic narrative tradition and intertexts.[88] In his battle with Superman, Batman narrates:

> You sold us out, Clark. You gave them the power that should have been ours. Just like your parents taught you to. My parents

---

[88] This having been said, it would be simply ignorant to deny that *Batman: The Dark Knight Returns* is a conservative text in the Reagan-era style. It assumes that psychiatric care and civil liberties allow more crime than they prevent, and portrays those trying to curb fascism as Nazis themselves, effectively avoiding debate. Such an inversion of political realities allows comics, and Miller especially, to claim to be attacking what, in practice, they support. Though I believe I offer a persuasive argument for the metaphorical weight of Commissioner Gordon's Pearl Harbor anecdote and Batman's imposition of order on the streets of Gotham City, this should supplement, rather than replace, the knowledge that President Franklin Roosevelt's actions and Batman's formation of an underground "army" (Miller's term) represent the obverse of any democratic process. To quote Whit Stillman's film *Barcelona,* one probably shouldn't forget

> —the message or meaning that's right there on the surface completely open and obvious. They never talk about that. What do you call what's *above* the subtext?
> —The text?
> —OK, that's right, but they never talk about that.

(*Barcelona,* dir. Whit Stillman, perf. Taylor Nichols and Christopher Eigeman. Castle Rock Entertainment, 1994) Edgar Allan Poe's short story *The Black Cat* should also be remembered in this context. Like the anti-abolitionist's short story about the hanging of a black cat from a tree limb, stories exceed intentions. Thanks to Tadzio Koelb for insisting on this note and piercing the author's 'fanboy' prejudices.

taught me a different lesson, lying on the street, shaking in deep shock—dying for no reason at all—they showed me that the world only makes sense when you force it to.[89]

Miller's take on the history of the Dark Knight, and on the contradictory tradition of superhero narratives, is that it will only make sense when you force it to. In a psychomachia, the retired "Batman" taunts the aging Wayne, "You are nothing, a hollow shell, a rusty trap that cannot hold me—smoldering, I burn you."[90] Miller holds the chaos of signifiers that is Batman and ultimately shows his character in the cave "far past the burnt remains of a crimefighter whose time has passed." Miller organizes the contradictory signifying field that surrounds the subject of Batman—which includes figures like Wertham and issues as far apart in the American political sphere as fascism and homosexuality—and forms them into a coherent story that is itself a commentary on the history that has come before, as well as on the tradition of the genre. To (mis)quote Bloom on Milton again: "[Miller's] design is wholly definite, and its effect is to reverse literary tradition. . . . The precursors return in [Miller], but only at his will, and they return to be corrected."[91] Every convention that allows superhero narratives to function, and every intertext, is exposed to the reader with a clarity that at once cleans up comic book history and also complicates it. The superhero narratives of any worth that follow *The Dark Knight Returns* can no longer ignore these determiners on the genre, but must confront both comic book tradition and Miller's influential handling of it: the superhero narrative will forever be under the shadow of the bat.

Before moving on from Miller's Batman, it is important to take a short look at Miller's smaller work *Batman: Year One* (1987), written only a year after *The Dark Knight Returns*. It is a key example of another revisionary strategy complementary to, but not contained in, his earlier work. Central to understanding the revisionary superhero narrative is the re-imagining of origins. Having created the ultimate story of Batman's final phase as a crimefighter, Miller steps back to reconceive Bruce Wayne's

---

[89] Miller et al., *Batman: The Dark Knight Returns,* 192.
[90] Ibid., 25.
[91] Bloom, *Map,* 142.

first year in Gotham City, his creation of the Batman persona, and commissioner Gordon's first year as police lieutenant. The same strategy of revisionary realism is employed, and like *The Dark Knight Returns,* it becomes definitive on the strength of its reading. The interesting thing to note—particularly for its recurrences in other "Year One" projects (e.g., *Daredevil: The Man Without Fear, Superman for All Seasons, JLA: Year One, X-Men: Children of the Atom*)—is the way Miller deals with chronology. Miller revises himself here, severing the unity he has created in *The Dark Knight Returns* by setting the story of Batman's first year in the same period of his aging Batman's final story, a Gotham very clearly meant to be a New York in the mid-1980s. Miller maintains the convention that superhero narratives are set in contemporary America, as he did in *The Dark Knight Returns,* but makes it impossible for a reader to reconcile his two Batman stories. While both must be "true" on the strength of their reading, Batman simply cannot be both twenty-five and fifty-five years old in the 1980s. Miller's "endless cave" can never be closed, finished, or unified due to its serial nature.

True to the methodology of comic book literature, Miller undoes himself before any successor can usurp his position. Bloom writes:

> The strong poet survives because he lives the discontinuity of an "undoing" and an "isolating" repetition, but he would cease to be a poet unless he kept living that continuity of "recollecting forwards," of breaking forth into a freshening that yet repeats his precursors' achievements.[92]

Batman: Year One ends with Batman being summoned for the first time by a newly promoted Commissioner Gordon to stop the Joker's attempted poisoning of the Gotham City reservoir. Longtime readers will recognize this as one of Batman's earliest adventures. Batman's obsessive imposition of order finds a dark mirror in the Joker's obsession with chaos and entropy. The Joker kills because death is the most entropic state. Batman's refusal to kill is one of the defining traits of his character. In *The Dark Knight Returns,* the Joker must die for Miller to achieve his ordered vision. *Year One,* which severs that imposition of order with its temporal paradox, appropriately ends with the Joker's

---

[92] Bloom, *Anxiety,* 83.

reappearance, a character emblematic of the contradictory nature of superhero continuity. To strain a metaphor, it is as if the water in the Tunnel of Love where Miller's Joker died carries him back down the "spring right beneath" the Batcave and releases him at the Gotham City reservoir for one of his first encounters with Batman.[93]

There is also an underlying "joke" in the Joker's reappearance: it is in fact a retelling of one of his first appearances, and is only a reappearance in terms of Miller's work on Batman. The joke, of course, revolves around one of the basic maxims in comic books: no matter how dead a villain seems to be (drowned with no body, blown up, etc.), he or she always returns. After portraying one of the most believable "final" death scenes in the history of comics, which even the most jaded reader would have understood as the true death of the Joker (albeit in a story that takes place in Batman's "future"), Miller "resurrects" him by ending his story of Batman's first year in Gotham with the coming of the Joker: the reinstallation of the contradictory confused history that exposes Miller's organization as only an arbitrary—though powerful and persuasive—synthesis.

Alan Moore: *Batman: The Killing Joke* and *Watchmen*

Just as we closed our discussion of Miller's Batman with the reappearance of the Joker as the emblem of destabilized continuity, I would like to introduce Alan Moore through his examination of the Joker in *Batman: The Killing Joke* (1988). This smaller work provides a foothold into *Watchmen (1987),* an earlier opus that introduced the revisionary superhero narrative. On the surface, *The Killing Joke* investigates the connection between Batman and his archrival according to the schema presented above, in which all of Batman's villains are reflections of himself. Both Batman and the Joker are creations of a random and tragic "one bad day."[94] Batman spends his life forging meaning from the ran-

---

[93] Reminiscent of the fountain in Milton's *Lycidas*; to quote the Scarecrow, ">sigh< That's right—Drive it into the ground. . . . You people don't know when to leave a good metaphor alone, do you?" Alan Brennert et al., "The Brave and the Bold #197," in *The Greatest Batman Stories Ever Told,* ed. Mike Gold (New York: DC Comics, 1988), 327.

[94] Alan Moore, Brian Bolland, and John Higgins, *Batman: The Killing Joke* (New York: DC Comics, 1988), 38.

dom tragedy, whereas the Joker reflects the absurdity of "life, and all its random injustice."[95] The Joker questions which of these reactions is more sane. Images of mirrors, distorting and otherwise, abound. The Joker fails to make Commissioner Gordon crack from "one bad day," and thus fails to prove that the world is only a step away from his madness.

But *The Killing Joke,* as I hope to show, is more significantly about its own construction, the construction of the revisionary superhero narrative, the organization of its own determination. While *The Dark Knight Returns* shows order from the perspective of Batman, *The Killing Joke* shows both the terror and the peculiar joyfulness of living within a fictional world burdened by an insanity of signification, and the anxiety caused by contradictory influence and overdetermination. It takes its place in the initial phase of the revisionary superhero narrative in that it exposes the construction of its own narrative, and superhero narratives in general, through several key reflexive moments and metaphors.

The image with which the story opens (and to which it fades) is that of the concentric rings created by raindrops in a shallow puddle. Miller has already cast forty-five years of fictional superhero history as a spring of water to be drawn upon, and connected the Joker with the element (Michel Foucault remarks in *Madness and Civilization* that "water and madness have long been linked in the dreams of European man.").[96] Bloom writes: "The anxiety of influence is an anxiety in expectation of *being flooded.*"[97] Jung's writings on the unconscious have already been cited in regards to comic book continuity and tradition, and it is important to recall that his dominant metaphor is one of water. I think it can be suggested that Moore picks up on this imagery placing as bookends—and using at two key points within the story—this depiction of rhizomic creation, arbitrarily centered reverberation upon a field of signification that itself has no center. The randomly falling raindrops that create lesser or greater waves upon the puddle's surface stand for individual superhero stories and their effect on the field of storytelling.

The superhero narrative is certainly nonlinear and cannot be said to occur in any particular order over time. Miller has already written Bat-

---

[95] Ibid., 28.

[96] Michel Foucault, *Madness and Civilization,* trans. Richard Howard (New York: Random House, 1965), 12.

[97] Bloom, *Anxiety,* 57 (Bloom's emphasis).

man's future before his past, and set his past in a decade irreconcilable with previous fictional history. Indeed, Miller's *Year One,* set in the 1980s, was followed by *Batman: The Long Halloween* (1998), intended as a kind of "Year Two" but which, barring several anachronisms, seems clearly set in the 1940s. Here again is Eco's oneiric climate. These stories, which all play a role in the creation of Batman, must be seen as rhizomicly structured. Shallow but broad, the puddle emphasizes the tradition or field of signification from which *The Killing Joke* emerges. As the last image, it points to where any Batman work will end up—just another drop in the pond, another arbitrary center of organization that will reverberate into the character's fictional history to greater or lesser effect.[98] The central moment of the text's reflexivity is the Joker's imprisonment of Gordon, his misprision of the superhero narrative into the revisionary realm of Miller and Moore: "God, how boring! The man's [the superhero narrative is] a complete turnip. Take him away and put him in his cage. Perhaps he'll get a little livelier once he's had a chance to think his situation over . . . to reflect upon life, and all its random injustice."[99] At the moment of the ellipsis (Moore's), the Joker places his trademark cane into a puddle of water—like the earlier and later images filled with random reverberating drops—and creates at its center the largest mark with the largest set of concentric waves. *The Killing Joke,* a reflection "upon life and all its random injustice," centered on the Joker, joins the superhero narrative as a large and significant, but arbitrary, drop among others. It enters into this saturation of signifiers (first panel)[100] and will be joined by those in the future (final panel).[101] Comic book history, and any individual character, *is* this rhizomic pattern of intersecting circular waves upon this shallow surface.

So it is no accident that in Moore's version of the Joker's origin, the Joker first glimpses his new reflection in a puddle filled with circular

---

[98] "The life of a man," writes Ralph Waldo Emerson, "is a self-evolving circle, which, from a ring imperceptibly small, rushes on all sides outwards to new and larger circles, and that without end. The extent to which this generation of circles, wheel without wheel, will go, depends on the force or truth of the individual soul." (Ralph Waldo Emerson, "Circles," in *The Portable Emerson,* ed. Carl Bode (New York: Penguin, 1981), 230.

[99] Moore et al., *The Killing Joke,* 28 (Moore's ellipsis).

[100] Ibid., 1.

[101] Ibid., 46.

ripples. Moore's Joker is a washed up comedian who gets mixed up with criminals robbing a chemical plant. He dresses as the Red Hood (to conceal his identity) but must flee when Batman arrives. He swims the polluted channel, but the chemicals have transformed his face, burning his skin white and his hair green. The moment that he becomes insane is clearly marked as the moment he sees his new reflection in the puddle. Jacques Lacan, psychoanalytic theorist, describes the formation of human identity in terms of what he calls the mirror stage.

> The mirror stage describes the formation of the ego via the process of identification; the ego is the result of identifying with one's own specular image. . . . The baby sees its own image as a whole, and the synthesis of this image produces a sense of contrast with the uncoordination of the body, which is experienced as a fragmented body; this contrast is first felt by the infant as a rivalry with its own image, because the wholeness of the image threatens the subject with fragmentation. . . . In order to resolve this aggressive tension, the subject identifies with the image; this primary identification with the counterpart is what forms the ego.[102]

Moore's Joker, then, is reborn (and there are clear images of an unholy baptism in the Joker's emergence from a poisoned body of water), his new identity in part created by the identification of his new face with the image in the water. It is significant in terms of the superhero narrative that the Joker finds this image in a pool that stands for the multiplicity of comic book continuity. Lacan's mirror phase describes how every healthy human being is created as a subject; the Joker's insanity is the result of identifying, not with an image of wholeness and unity (as described above), but with a fragmented background pelted by raindrops. In short, Moore's Joker is insane because his mirror reflects not only his image but also overdetermination and influence. Every ego must identify with what is external, but the Joker is faced with a surplus he cannot hope to control. (The mirrors broken in the Joker's fight with

---

[102] Dylan Evans, *An Introductory Dictionary of Lacanian Psychoanalysis* (New York: Routledge, 1996), 115. Cross-references not noted.

Batman in the Hall of Mirrors must take on added significance in this context.)[103]

It is for this reason that images of organization and disorganization can be found throughout the text. Understanding the Joker as a force of signifying chaos, of disorganization, the fake Joker at Arkham[104] may be quickly spotted by an alert reader, tipped off by his organizing a deck of cards, placing the suits together. The two Joker cards can be seen off to one side—at an angle, not constituting a fifth pile. As in *The Dark Knight Returns,* organization can only be achieved with the Joker(s) out of the way. Miller casts Batman as the great organizer; Moore defines the Joker as a breaker of textual organizers (and texts themselves), explicitly when his Joker assaults Batgirl, whose alter ego, Barbara Gordon, is a librarian, an organizer of texts. After shooting Barbara in the spine and sending her crashing down upon the coffee table, the Joker quips:

> It's a psychological complaint, common amongst ex-librarians. You see, she thinks she's a coffee table edition. Mind you I can't say much for the volume's condition. I mean, there's a hole in the jacket and the spine appears to be damaged. Frankly, she won't be walking off the shelves in that state of repair. In fact, the idea of her walking anywhere seems increasingly remote. But then that's always a problem with softbacks. God, these literary discussions are dry.[105]

---

[103] While this book will not spend time with Grant Morrison's *Animal Man,* the recurrence of the raindrop trope in issue #14 should be noted. Morrison's *Animal Man* also engages issues of convoluted continuity and the continuity excised by *Crisis on Infinite Earths.* Grant Morrison appears in *Animal Man* as himself (and in the final issue meets Animal Man) and thinks about how he will next direct the story. Looking at his image in the water bombarded by raindrops, he describes the image: "Interference patterns of concentric circles like bomb impact diagrams. Like telepathic powers in comics. Like the cup and ring marks on megalithic stones. Like patterns on a holographic plate. The symbol of David Bohm's Implicate Order theory. A vision of a vast, interconnected universe where every part contains the whole. Where the universe is a mirror reflecting itself. . . . I need an idea." Grant Morrison, *Animal Man* (New York: DC Comics, 1989), #14 (my ellipsis). Just as in *The Killing Joke,* the drops represent a surplus of meaning, a mirror of identity, and a vast interconnected universe.

[104] Moore et al., *The Killing Joke,* 3.

[105] Ibid., 14.

This points the reader to a key difference between the two authors: Miller's organization and control of comic book history in his narrative involves metaphors of violence and fascism; Moore's metaphors of organization, as the reader will see through further example, are more often textual and literary.

As the example above suggests, the Joker's dialogue is a great reservoir of reflexivity in *The Killing Joke*. His statement that the amusement park is "garish, ugly, and derelicts have used it for a toilet"[106] might not at first glance appear to be about the throw-away medium which is his home. His comment that "[t]he rides are dilapidated to the point of being lethal, and could easily maim or kill innocent little children,"[107] might not immediately remind one that this pulp art form was actually accused of harming little children in Fredric Wertham's *Seduction of the Innocent* (discussed above). But when the reader sees that almost all of the Joker's dialogue is reflexive in this manner, the larger pattern becomes more convincing. Even the owner's worry that the price of the carnival (which, as the quotes above demonstrate, doubles as the site of the comic book) may be too steep, can be interpreted as pointing to the high sticker price of *The Killing Joke*: as a prestige format book free of advertisements, it costs three to four times the price of an average issue. The Joker's larger speeches especially reflect his awareness of the convoluted rhizomic history in which he participates. When Commissioner Gordon's memory of his horrific capture begins to return as he is led through the abandoned carnival (already established as a trope for the superhero narrative), the Joker says:

> Remember? Ohh, I wouldn't do that! Remembering's dangerous. The past is such a worrying, anxious place. "The past tense," I suppose you'd call it. Ha ha ha. Memory's so treacherous. One moment you're lost in a carnival of delights, with poignant aromas, the flashing neon of puberty, all that sentimental candy-floss . . . the next, it leads you somewhere you don't want to go . . . somewhere dark and cold, filled with the damp, ambiguous shapes of things you'd hoped were forgotten.[108]

---

[106] Ibid., 6.

[107] Ibid.

[108] Ibid., 21 (Moore's ellipses).

The "damp" quality is clearly connected to the raindrop images, to the oversaturation of an anxiety-ridden fictional history ("the past tense") just now becoming sufficiently dense to support the revisionary superhero narrative. What could be more ambiguous than the return of childhood heroes—"carnival of delights . . . flashing neon of puberty, all that sentimental candy-floss"—in a context like *The Dark Knight Returns, The Killing Joke,* or *Watchmen?* Did these childhood heroes not lead readers into questionable politics, madness, and violence, somewhere they didn't want to go? The Joker's recommendation for dealing with overdetermination is the madness of unchained signification: "So when you find yourself locked onto an unpleasant train of thought, heading for places in your past where the screaming is unbearable, remember there's always madness."[109] The Joker suggests that no superhero narrative can possibly carry the weight of its tradition: "Most repulsive of all, are its frail and useless notions of order. . . . If too much weight is placed upon them, they snap."[110] This is a worry that is very visible in *Watchmen,* as we will see.

The most significant moment in the Joker's antimeditation on the superhero narrative is addressed to Batman in a trope used in *The Dark Knight Returns,* the Hall of Mirrors. Reflecting that personal tragedy must have had something to do with the existence of the Batman persona, the Joker says, "Something like that happened to me, you know. I . . . I'm not exactly sure what it was. Sometimes I remember it one way, sometimes another. . . . If I'm going to have a past, I prefer it to be multiple choice! Ha ha ha!"[111] Considering the role of fictional history drawn upon in *The Dark Knight Returns* by Miller to create his Batman and the Joker, it cannot be denied that their pasts certainly are "multiple choice," their history often told one way, then another. *The Killing Joke* includes a retelling of the Joker's origin that appeared in *Detective Comics* #168 (1951),[112] but Moore's fleshed out and slightly different version will come to replace the earlier version on the strength of its revisionary reading. At the moment the Joker muses on his convoluted past, Moore

---

[109] Ibid.
[110] Ibid., 33 (my ellipsis).
[111] Ibid., 39 (Moore's ellipses).
[112] See Sheldon Moldoff and George Roussos, "Detective Comics #168," in *The Greatest Joker Stories Ever Told,* ed. Mike Gold (New York: DC Comics, 1988).

offers the reader another selection in the "multiple choice" question of Batman's continuity. Where Miller works to synthesize the various answers into a coherent whole, Moore allows Batman's continuity to stand separate and unresolved at several key moments, exposing cracks in the sanity of organization, questioning the story's ability to stand without "snapping," under its own weight.

Artist Brian Bolland, rather than follow Miller's unified artistic style in *The Dark Knight Returns,* allows Batman's dialectic history to stand in suspension, inserting at several key points work by other artists from the golden and silver ages in a kind of pastiche. The first occurs in the Batcave, where the reader is given a glimpse of what appears to be a kind of "family photo" of Batman, Robin, Alfred, and Commissioner Gordon, standing alongside several characters from the 1950s who have been literally written out of continuity and treated as if they never existed: Batwoman and the first Bat-Girl (who existed as love interests for several years in order to deny charges of Batman and Robin's homosexuality), the Bat-Mite (a ridiculous magical imp, almost emblematic of the camp and silliness of the Batman of the 1960s), and even Ace the Bat-Hound.[113] The most important thing to note about the "photo" is that it is a piece of art from Batman artist Sheldon Moldoff's tenure on the title inserted into *The Killing Joke* as a photo in the Batcave; looking closely, Batman creator Bob Kane's signature is recognizable in the lower right-hand corner. On the same page Batman looks at a computer-generated array of various visuals of the Joker, one of which is an insert of, or done in the style of, the work of Dick Sprang, Batman's artist in the 1950s. Perhaps more dramatically in the case of characters written out of continuity, but also in the Joker's design, Batman's own history is exposed to be deeply "multiple choice."

The other key moment of reflexivity occurs when Commissioner Gordon is shown adding to his scrapbook of newspaper clippings about Batman. His daughter, Barbara, expresses the difficulty of organizing such a chaos of history: "Some day you ought to let me work out a proper filing system, like we used at the library."[114] Such a system, however, would be impossible when a contemporaneous article was authored by another character practically written out of continuity, Vicky

---

[113] Moore et al., *The Killing Joke,* 10.

[114] Ibid., 12.

Vale. History flows through the whole of *The Killing Joke,* but particularly in this scene of Gordon's bookkeeping. Most revealingly, we are given a moment that reflects on the pastiche quality of Bolland's art mentioned above. Barbara remarks, "Urrgh. Look, you used too much paste! It's all squidging under the edges of the clipping,"[115] exposing the artifice of the pastiche and emphasizing the difficulty of making the pieces fit together nicely. And Gordon literally tries to fit Batman's history into a whole. The first newspaper clipping includes a "photograph" that is a reproduction of Bob Kane's cover art on *Detective Comics* #27 (1939), Batman's debut. Commissioner Gordon remarks of another clipping, "Heh. Look at this one. First time they [Batman and the Joker] met. Now, what year was that?"[116] Of course, he can't remember, because, although the Joker's first appearance was in 1940, the superhero narrative's peculiar chronology, discussed above, makes dating any event all but impossible. The history makes no sense, and a character achieves definition through her reaction to it: Batman's response is to organize the chaos, the Joker's to embrace it, but Commissioner Gordon simply cannot remember. Like the Joker, Moore enjoys these conundrums and allows them to stand exposed in the text. The revisionary superhero narrative is weighed down by overdetermination, and many of its stories are infected by this kind of schizophrenia. An awareness of its own structure marks the first defense of the revisionary superhero narrative. As Bloom writes: "To be enslaved by any precursor's system, [William] Blake says, is to be inhibited from creativity by an obsessive reasoning and comparing, presumably of one's own works to the precursor's. Poetic Influence is thus a disease of self-consciousness."[117]

In the final moment of *The Killing Joke,* Batman offers his help to the Joker, to rehabilitate him rather than lock him up. The Joker's response is an interesting one:

> No. I'm sorry but . . . no. It's too late for that. Far too late. Ha ha ha. Y'know, it's funny . . . this situation. It reminds me of a joke . . . See, there are these two guys in a lunatic asylum . . . and one night, one night they decide they don't like living in an

---

[115] Ibid.
[116] Ibid.
[117] Bloom, *Anxiety,* 29.

asylum anymore. They decide they're going to escape! So, like, they get up onto the roof. And there, just across this narrow gap, they see the rooftops of the town, stretching away in the moonlight. Stretching away to freedom. Now, the first guy, he jumps right across with no problem. But his friend, his friend daren't make the leap. Y'see . . . y'see he's afraid of falling. So then the first guy has an idea . . . he says, "Hey! I have my flashlight with me! I'll shine it across the gap between the buildings. You can walk along the beam and join me!" B-But the second guy just shakes his head. He suh-says . . . He says, "Wh-what do you think I am? Crazy? You'd turn it off when I was halfway across!"[118]

Batman laughs with him. The implication is that the break to sanity, rationality, and order can only be reached by an enabling fiction and that even that enabling fiction—intangible as a beam of light—will not be sustained long enough to reach a final order. The synthesis or suspension of superhero continuity is always doomed to be arbitrary and temporary as drops in a puddle.

Indeed, the idea of a final order is itself an illusion "stretching into the moonlight." The current of sadness that runs through *The Killing Joke* stems from the Joker's metatextual awareness that because of the lateness of this work in its tradition ("Its too late for that. Far too late"), because its tradition has become sufficiently dense with precedent to support this revisionary narrative, the Joker—as emblematic of contradictory tradition and influence, of the madness of oversaturated continuity—can, like the superhero narrative itself, never go back, never find resolution or be rehabilitated. The superhero can never return to some now fantastic period before the anxieties of influence. The revisionary superhero narrative may organize history, but the Joker knows that the imposition of order is just a trick of the light, that for convoluted fictional overdetermination to step into some final rationalization will only result in death. Like Friedrich Nietzsche's paradigm of Apollo and Dionysus in *The Birth of Tragedy,* the revisionary superhero narrative is about the conflict between Batman and Joker, about the dialectic between the arbitrary imposition of order—the arbitrary answer to the question of

---

[118] Moore et al., *The Killing Joke,* 44–45 (Moore's ellipses).

the "multiple choice"—and the eternal recurrence of the chaotic, elemental, fictional repressed.

Alan Moore's revisionary superhero narrative *Watchmen* expresses its anxieties about the recurrence of the fictional repressed in terms of the return of the dead. Before looking closely at this trope, however, we must understand *Watchmen*'s rather different stance on the superhero: its criticism. It begins questioning the assumptions of the superhero with its title, which lures the comic-savvy reader into assuming that it is the eponym of a superhero team around which the book revolves—not in fact the case. The last page of the work reveals that the title is actually taken from the Juvenal epigraph *Quis custodiet ipsos custodes?* ("Who watches the watchmen?"), a phrase that occurs throughout the work in the form of graffiti. The statement contains a kind of a priori destabilization of the assumptions that make superhero comics work: that heroes can simply look after a population without complications. The understanding that the police require police officers ad infinitum questions whether the very foundations of superhero literature can in fact be maintained. *Watchmen* declares that they cannot.

Moore takes on a more complex job than Miller. *Watchmen* is an attempt to make sense of superhero history in all its varied aspects rather than synthesize the history of a single character. A sprawling work much longer than *The Dark Knight Returns,* it engages comic book history through a number of devices including epigraphs for all twelve issues culled from sources as disparate as Jung, Blake, Shelley, Nietzsche, Einstein, Bob Dylan, and the Bible. Each issue, with the exception of the last, is also accompanied by a prose piece from the fictional world of *Watchmen*: excerpts from the autobiography of a retired hero, right- and left-wing newspaper articles, Sally Jupiter's scrapbook, a psychological profile on one of the heroes, a scientific article on Dr. Manhattan's powers, and an essay on bird watching by the alter ego of Night Owl, Dan Dreiberg. An analysis of *Watchmen* cannot simply reiterate points made about *The Dark Knight Returns.* We will look at a few key strains in *Watchmen,* paying attention to where it differs from Miller's work. Observations on *The Dark Knight Returns* placed alongside an analysis of *Watchmen* will give a complete picture of the first phase of the revisionary superhero narrative.

The first thing to note is the difference between Miller's realism and Alan Moore's. As noted above, Miller's realism revises by intensifying the superhero narrative, insisting on its perspective as the answer to the "multiple choice" comic book history in which it participates. Miller's is a movement, in Bloom's terminology, of *tessera*: "A poet antithetically 'completes' his precursor, by so reading the parent-poem as to retain its terms but to mean them in another sense, as though the precursor had failed to go far enough."[119] Alan Moore's realism, on the other hand, performs a *kenosis* toward comic book history, a term Bloom defines in *The Anxiety of Influence*:

> The later poet, apparently emptying himself of his own afflatus, his imaginative godhood, seems to humble himself as though he were ceasing to be a poet, but his ebbing is so performed in relation to the precursor's poem-of-ebbing that the precursor is emptied out also, and so the latter poem of deflation is not as absolute as it seems.[120]

Moore's realism does not ennoble and empower his characters as Miller's realism does for Batman. Rather, it sends a wave of disruption back through superhero history by asking, for example, what would make a person dress up in a costume and fight crime? Dan Dreiberg sees his own adoption of the Night Owl persona as a childish fantasy: "Being a crimefighter . . . was just this adolescent, romantic thing. . . . That's why I sort of regretted the Crimebusters falling through back in sixty-whenever-it-was. It would have been like joining the Knights of the Round Table."[121] He names his airship after Merlin's owl from *The Sword and the Stone*. While endearing, there is something distinctly sad for the comic book reader confronting Dan's realization that "it's all crap dressed up with a lot of flash and thunder. I mean, who needs all this hardware to catch hookers and purse-snatchers?"[122] Here, Moore devalues one of the basic superhero conventions by placing his masked crime fighters in a realistic world where flashy masked villains—albeit with a

---

[119] Bloom, *Anxiety,* 14.
[120] Ibid., 14–15.
[121] Alan Moore and Dave Gibbons, *Watchmen* (New York: DC Comics, 1986–1987), #7, pp. 7–8 (my ellipses).
[122] Ibid., 8.

few pathetic exceptions—simply don't exist. Superheroes only make sense in a world where masked opponents support their fantasy, and masked opponents only exist to fight superheroes. The fictionality of a genre that might appear to have some elements of social relevance because its setting is contemporary urban America rather than medieval times or outer space, is exposed in a particularly tragic way. Moore's *kenosis* is a powerful strategy: to defeat comic book history with superheroes is to take your place at the head of the tradition.

Moore connects the decision to dress up as a masked crimefighter, not only with childhood fantasies and midlife crises of the idle rich, but also with the more disturbing and interesting issue of sexual fetish. Dan Dreiberg (Night Owl) keeps a picture of an old costumed villain, The Twilight Lady—posed on a bed, dressed in leather, and sporting a riding crop. He fails to perform sexually with Laurie Juspeczyk (the second Silk Specter) until they embrace in costume after a night adventuring. Laurie asks, "Did the costumes make it good? Dan . . . ?"[123] To which he replies, "Yeah. Yeah, I guess the costumes had something to do with it. It just feels strange, you know? To come out and admit that to somebody. To come out of the closet."[124] The public is fully aware of the sexual dimension of these self-styled heroes. An interview with Sally Jupiter (the first Silk Specter), asks "How much would you say that it's a sex thing, putting on a costume?"[125] This only makes for all the more disturbing a setting in which to take up crimefighting.

Another prose piece, the autobiography of Hollis Mason, the original Night Owl, includes his observation that "[s]ome of us [became costumed crimefighters] out of a sense of childish excitement and some of us, I think, did it for a kind of excitement that was altogether more adult if perhaps less healthy."[126] We are told one villain dressed up because he took sexual/masochistic enjoyment in being assaulted;[127] Hooded Justice and The Silhouette are revealed as homosexuals, and Rorschach's interaction with Night Owl[128] suggests homoerotic tendencies.

---

[123] Ibid., 28.
[124] Ibid.
[125] Ibid., #9, prose.
[126] Ibid., #2, prose.
[127] Ibid., #1, 26.
[128] Ibid., #10, 11.

Clearly the suggestion of sexual fetish and homosexuality has a strong reverberation with the accusations of Fredric Wertham, discussed above. Moore's exploration of the motives for costumed crimefighting sheds a disturbing light on past superhero stories, and forces the reader to reevaluate—to revision—every superhero in terms of Moore's *kenosis*—his emptying out of the tradition. Miller's Batman is a powerful but realistic figure in his costume. Dan Dreiberg's informing Laurie that the first time he used his prototype exoskeleton suit it broke his arm summarizes Moore's position. "That sounds like the sort of costume that could really mess you up," she says. "Is there any other sort?"[129] he replies. Dave Gibbons's illustration is an underrated part of this project of demystification, but *Watchmen* cannot be appreciated without taking it into account. Miller's moody shadows, reminiscent of film noir, are very romantic and invoke a world as tough and gritty as it is operatic. Gibbons's characters, on the other hand, all have a distinct sadness, and his frumpy characters stand in stark contrast to Miller's very "cool" Batman. Moore's realism does not empower, as Miller's does, but empties out the power of previous superhero narratives to ensure the primacy of *Watchmen* in the tradition. The price he pays for this success, however, is accounted for in *Watchmen*'s anxiety over the return of the dead, the return of the past he has stolen inspiration from, in a sense almost literally deflating. To understand this, the reader must be made aware of exactly where comic book history, though submerged, breaks through.

Unlike Miller, who comes to a Batman already written by many authors, Moore's characters appear, at first glance, to have a clean slate and in this respect should be able to offer little, outside of marginal, commentary on established heroes. As noted in most academic discussions of *Watchmen*, however,[130] Moore's characters resonate certain comic book archetypes in such a way as to suggest other established superheroes. Adrian Veidt's (Ozymandias's) optimism, confidence, and Antarctic headquarters invoke Superman and his Fortress of Solitude.

---

[129] Ibid., #7, 8.

[130] See McCue, *Dark Knights,* 73; Jeffery A. Brown, *Black Superheroes, Milestone Comics and Their Fans* (Jackson: University Press of Mississippi, 2001), 153; Matthew J. Pustz, *Comic Book Culture* (Jackson: University Press of Mississippi, 1999), 147; and Reynolds, *Superheroes,* 107.

His wealth, intelligence, birthday (1939), and perfected human physical prowess recall Batman. His role in his corporation suggests Bruce Wayne and Wayne Corp. Night Owl's wealth, gadgets, costume, mode of transportation, and basement equipment room—and the fact that his predecessor, Hollis Mason, began fighting crime in 1939—also suggest Batman and the Batcave, but equally invoke the Blue Beetle. The second Night Owl's alter ego, Dan Dreiberg, visually suggests an impotent, middle-aged Clark Kent. The Comedian, in one of Moore's more powerful tropes, is a kind of Captain America if Captain America had gone to Vietnam. Rorschach's reactionary, violent, obsessive-loner personality and refusal to compromise suggests the same Batman picked up on by Frank Miller, or Marvel Comics' Wolverine, or the Punisher. Dr. Manhattan, as the only super-powered being, aloof, almost alien, and never aging, suggests Superman. The reference to "Wally Weaver . . . Dr. Manhattan's Buddy"[131] reminds the reader of "Jimmy Olson, Superman's Pal", and indeed, in the graphic for the military complex in which Dr. Manhattan lives is embedded the Superman shield.[132]

This move of referencing in order to shed light on established heroes by invoking certain archetypal comic book signifiers is common to the revisionary superhero narrative's investigation of its own history. The current character, though obviously in debt to its source, can often act as a powerful misprision of that original character, while the fact that it is not actually the original frees the writer from the constraints of copyright and continuity. This is the superhero narrative's revisionary referencing, an idea central to understanding this emerging literature.

Watchmen's revisionary referencing is used to ask questions about the history it absorbs. Is Adrian Veidt a hero? Is his massive hoax, which killed three million people but prevented a nuclear world war, where Batman's foresight and intelligence must lead? Or is Batman more accurately reflected in Rorschach, a violent psychopath whose refusal to compromise will be his downfall? To what degree are Wertham's observations of homoeroticism actually reflected in comic books themselves? How can Superman retain his humanity in light of his power? How can readers accept that Marvel Comics' Captain America still retains his optimism after Vietnam and Watergate? Is the cynical Comedian what he should look like?

---

[131] Moore and Gibbons, Watchmen, #3, 13 (my ellipsis).
[132] Ibid., #1, p. 19, panel 1.

These last two questions are a perfect example of the strategy employed in the revisionary reference. In relation to Captain America, Alan Moore's Comedian performs Bloom's *clinamatic* swerve: "a corrective movement in [the latter] poem, which implies that the precursor poem went accurately up to a certain point, but then should have swerved, precisely in the direction that the new poem moves."[133] The Comedian is this swerve. This strategy of revisionary referencing must be kept in mind throughout this exploration of the revisionary superhero narrative, as it is one of its most common and interesting moves.

In this context of intertextuality, *Watchmen*'s scene juxtaposition is crucial. Again and again two seemingly unrelated scenes are juxtaposed, and the dialogue from one is a running commentary on the other. In one exchange, for example (to select one from scores), Dr. Manhattan is being interviewed while, elsewhere, Dan and Laurie battle a street gang. The host selects an audience member to ask a question and says, "Now, how about you over there. Yes, you, sir. And please [*cut to Dan and Laurie attacking*] let's try and keep it snappy."[134] A reporter claims Dr. Manhattan's friend died of cancer in 1971 and, as the next panel shows Dan striking a thug in the face, says "I believe it was quite sudden and quite painful."[135] The reporter goes on to mention a villain Dr. Manhattan encountered "during the Sixties in battles, conflicts [*cut back to Dan and Laurie's brawl*] whatever it is you super-people do."[136] Throughout *Watchmen* it can be seen that meaning is elsewhere, deferred, and very often unaware of its relevancy. Within the text this takes the form of spatial juxtaposition, but this method also illustrates *Watchmen*'s place among the texts that inform it, and which it informs. It is entirely appropriate in this context that Rorschach's psychological report shows that he has witnessed at a young age his mother engaging in a sexual act; only later could he understand what it was he was seeing. This structure of deferred action, as it is known in psychoanalysis, powerfully informs the reader's understanding of *Watchmen*. The superhero stories read as a child must be entirely reevaluated in light of such later knowledge as the revisionary superhero narrative provides.

---

[133] Bloom, *Anxiety*, 14.
[134] Moore and Gibbons, *Watchmen*, #3, 13.
[135] Ibid.
[136] Ibid.

Like *The Killing Joke, Watchmen* also has many moments of reflexivity, not concerned with the contradictory history of any one character but rather with the difficulty of absorbing such a dense tradition as superhero comic book literature. *Watchmen* betrays an intense anxiety over the return of the dead, the return of the comic book history Moore's *kenosis* disabled, rising for revenge. To situate our thought around the return of the dead and the status of tradition, I would like to quote theorist Slavoj Žižek, from *Looking Awry: An Introduction to Jacques Lacan through Popular Culture*. He writes:

> The return of the dead is a sign of a disturbance in the symbolic rite, in the process of symbolization; the dead return as collectors of some unpaid symbolic debt. . . .
>
> . . . It is precisely for this reason that the funeral rite exemplifies symbolization at its purest: through it, the dead are inscribed in the text of symbolic tradition. . . . The "return of the living dead" is, on the other hand, the reverse of the proper funeral rite. While the latter implies a simple reconciliation, an acceptance of loss, the return of the dead signifies that they cannot find their proper place in the text of tradition.[137]

One recalls, when reading *Watchmen,* that the gravestone marker Rest in Peace (R.I.P.) does not mean "Sleep well" but "Do not return to disturb us." Žižek captures *Watchmen*'s anxieties exactly. To a large degree, *Watchmen* is an attempt to provide the dead a proper burial, making sure its predecessors find their proper place in the text of tradition, and ensuring that *Watchmen* incurs, despite its obvious poetic inheritance, no unpaid symbolic debt that the dead will return to collect. The horror comic, the broken tradition of comic book history within *Watchmen,* allows the reader to see the anxiety of influence in operation.

Watchmen invokes its own history as a superhero narrative, but also makes reference to a host of apocryphal comic book literature: the horror comic books shut down by Wertham,[138] Sally Jupiter's "Tijuana

---

[137] Slavoj Žižek, *Looking Awry: An Introduction to Jacques Lacan through Popular Culture* (Cambridge, MA: MIT Press, 1992), 23.

[138] It should be noted in this context that in the fictional world of *Watchmen,* Wertham did not succeed in harming the comics industry (Moore and Gibbons, *Watchmen,* #5, prose), and superhero comic books died on their own after the emergence of real-life

Bible,"[139] and Adrian Veidt's "Veidt Method [for body building]," which appears in the back of *Watchmen* as a prose insert and recalls the Charles Atlas self-improvement advertising featured in the backs of early comic books. The most noticeable item of comic book apocrypha, however, is the horror/pirate comic book. Throughout issues 3 to 11, the reader continually returns to a boy reading "Tales of the Black Freighter," a story within a story. As a warning for heroes, the plot of "Tales of the Black Freighter" clearly juxtaposes itself against the plot of *Watchmen* as a whole—a man, attempting to save his family and home from destruction, becomes, in his obsession, the very instrument for the force he was trying to stop.

It is the story's imagery, however, that betrays a different reading, in terms of *Watchmen*'s interaction with its own history. In "Tales of the Black Freighter," the dead become an emblem of *Watchmen*'s submerged past that informs, supports, and threatens Moore's narrative. A weighted summary is necessary to gather key images from the various issues throughout which this mini-narrative is spread: our nameless protagonist buries his fallen shipmates after "several of the beached corpses had become inflated by gas,"[140] attempts "matching odd limbs as best [he] could,"[141] and finally sleeps upon the grave; when he wakes, he "conceived of building a raft, although inwardly [he] doubted it would float."[142] The trees are not buoyant enough for a raft, so he exhumes the gas-bloated corpses he has buried and dreamed upon—pausing in his work, "entranced by the startling beauty of a tattoo or the enigma of an old scar,"[143]—and makes a craft of their bodies. "By afternoon, I'd felled enough young palms to build the deck of my conveyance, affixing it to the human float beneath."[144] The craft is a disturbing and

---

masked adventurers. In a world where superheroes really exist, superhero comic books are not necessary, and horror/pirate comics filled the gap they left.

[139] A Tijuana Bible is a subversive form of pornography from the 1930s and 1940s, an illegal pulp comic book featuring established, often copyrighted, comic book characters, along with celebrities and film characters, in sexually explicit situations. Sally Jupiter's copy features her own persona, the Silk Specter.

[140] Moore and Gibbons, *Watchmen*, #3, 22.

[141] Ibid.

[142] Ibid., #5, 8.

[143] Ibid., 9.

[144] Ibid.

powerful emblem of *Watchmen,* sailing on the gas-filled—literally "inspired"—dead history of old comic book literature (*inspired,* from the Latin *inspirare,* "to fill with wind"). After dreaming upon their bodies, *Watchmen* (and our narrator, as an emblem of the revisionist) finds a way to utilize, to hijack, their inspiration, rather than toss another body, its own, on the heap—and cobbles together their ruins, stopping to appreciate unique moments of beauty or question old markings. The utilization of tradition and influence is not an idle game of tongue-in-cheek allusions but is actually necessary for the narrative's survival. Music critic Perry Meisel's remark on a "tradition sufficiently dense with precedent to cause the kinds of self consciousness and anxiety with which we are familiar" (quoted above) takes on a particularly literal twist here. If our "revisionary" narrator or revisionary antihero of "Tales of the Black Freighter" is not supported by a certain number of "inspired," gas-bloated bodies, his craft—the revisionary narrative—will sink.

Watchmen does not stop there if this allegory is to be understood as such. Absorbing more dead, our protagonist consumes a seagull he plucks out of the air and eats raw, but cannot contain it, and vomits.[145] (Note the bird as an especially poignant symbol of poetic inspiration, e.g., Keats's nightingale, Hardy's darkling thrush.) The absorption of the dead, of tradition, requires a certain process or methodology (in this case, gastrointestinal) in order for the corpses of tradition to be properly "incorporated." This failure to incorporate is juxtaposed against the false confidence of the newspaper vendor whose voice often breaks over the kid during his reading of "Tales of the Black Freighter": "I absorb information. I miss nothing. . . . The weight o' the world's on [the newspaper vendor], but does he quit? Nah! He's like Atlas! He can take it!"[146] *Watchmen* is very concerned with being able to handle all of the dead it attempts to ingest and fears being a regurgitation, rather than an organization, of superhero tradition. It fears that the dead it attempts to handle will overwhelm it, and failing control it will perish, sinking down among them to be judged by a stronger vision above the waves, above Miller's "endless spring right beneath," above chaotic comic book tradition.

The eighth issue of *Watchmen* takes place on Halloween and aligns masked crimefighters with the children in costume on the street. The

---

[145] Ibid., #5, 12.
[146] Ibid., #3, 2 (my ellipsis).

epigraph, "On Hallowe'en the old ghosts come about us, and they speak to some; to others they are dumb,"[147] emphasizes that Halloween is the day when the dead tread closest to the living and that *Watchmen* is a text trying to contain a mass of dead souls. Our Black Freighter narrator is disturbingly close to the dead who literally keep him afloat: "[I]t seemed I conversed with my perished shipmates. Their voices spoke from beneath the raft; thick; bubbling"[148] Rorschach's past comes to claim him in the prison riot: "You're alone in the valley of the shadow, Rorschach," says one of his antagonists—referring both to the biblical shadow of death and metatextually to Bloom's shadow of influence—"where your past has a long reach and between you and it there's only one crummy lock. Think about it. . . . Halloween, when the dead things return."[149]

Watchmen is the "one crummy lock" that can hold back and organize the past, keeping the dead from rising while floating on their inspiration. References to the dead abound in *Watchmen*. Rorschach remarks of the Egyptian decor in Veidt's office, "Whole culture death-fixated, obsessively securing their tombs against intruders. . . . Didn't like the thought of corpses interfered with. [Superheroes/*Watchmen*] can't afford to be so squeamish. Disturbing dead our job."[150] He continues to note that the pharaohs "believed cadavers would rise. . . . Understand now why always mistrusted fascination with relics and dead kings. In final analysis, it's us or them,"[151] a very revealing remark in terms of literature's interaction with its own tradition.

Adrian Veidt modeled his life on Alexander the Great and reminds us that "[h]e entered Egypt through Memphis, where they proclaimed him son of Amon, Judge of the Dead."[152] In a drug-induced vision the resurrected dead inspire him. Veidt's perfume, Nostalgia, with its advertisements ("Oh, how the ghost of you clings"), reinforces the connection between the dead and the resurrected influence of the past. The image of the Nostalgia bottle shattering, its contents spilling, takes on heightened relevance in this context: nostalgia, clinging ghosts unable to

---

[147] Ibid., #8, 28.
[148] Ibid., 13.
[149] Ibid., 7, 14 (my ellipsis).
[150] Ibid., #10, 20 (Moore's ellipsis).
[151] Ibid. (my ellipsis).
[152] Ibid., #11, 10.

be contained. *Watchmen* exposes again and again its position as a receptacle for the dead, as being supported on a raft of the dead, and as judging the dead that it receives.

As Harold Bloom notes, one powerful defense against the return of the dead is the rhetorical trope of metalepsis or transumption. It should only be mentioned here, as *Watchmen* only hints at it, and held in mind in case it is of interest in the context of other superhero narratives. Two moments are of primary interest. The first is Adrian Veidt's drug trip in which he communes with the dead while following his pilgrimage in honor of Alexander the Great. He notes:

> The ensuing vision transformed me. Wading through powdered history [cf. "the burnt remains of a crime fighter . . . "], I heard dead kings walking, underground; heard fanfares sound through human skulls. Alexander had merely resurrected an age of pharaohs. Their wisdom, truly immortal, now inspired me![153]

Here Veidt finds his way through the trope of Alexander to an earlyness, a freshness when no ghost or anxiety could have been, to a fantastic fiction of a period before influence. He adopts Ramses II's Greek name, Ozymandias, resolving to apply antiquity's teachings to today's world. Like Joyce's titling his great novel *Ulysses* rather than *Odysseus,* Veidt tropes on a trope, and as Bloom argues, "Transumption murders time, for by troping on a trope, you enforce a state of retoricity or word-consciousness, and you negate fallen history."[154] Thus, as in his drug trip, Veidt is "remarkably freed of the burden of anteriority," because he "himself is already one with the future, which he introjects,"[155] in the form of his utopia-to-be. This is why his Nostalgia becomes Millennium perfume after his master plan succeeds.

As *The Killing Joke* suggests, there is often a connection to be made between the metaphysics espoused in philosophical speeches in a superhero narrative and the construction of the revisionary superhero narrative itself. Alan Moore's use of the revisionary ratio *kenosis,* discussed above, reaches its height in Dr. Manhattan's musings on the universe

---

[153] Ibid.
[154] Bloom, *Map,* 138.
[155] Ibid.

and its depths in Rorschach's understanding of the world. Rorschach takes his name from the psychological ink blot test because it reflects his personal metaphysical views, which a reader may find familiar after our discussion of *The Dark Knight Returns.* It is an example of what Bloom would refer to as a moment of negative transcendence:

> Looked at sky through smoke heavy with human fat and God was not there. The cold suffocating dark goes on forever, and we are alone. Live our lives, lacking anything better to do. Devise reason later. Born from oblivion; bear children, hell-bound as ourselves; go into oblivion. There is nothing else. Existence is random. Has no pattern save what we imagine after staring at it for too long. No meaning save what we chose to impose. This rudderless world is not shaped by vague metaphysical forces. It is not God who kills the children. Not fate who butchers them or destiny that feeds them to the dogs. It's us. Only us. Streets stank of fire. The void breathed hard on my heart, turning its illusions to ice, shattering them. Was reborn then. Free to scrawl own design on this morally blank world. Was Rorschach.[156]

Jon's (Dr. Manhattan's) aloof consciousness of the universe as a giant clockwork machine affords him a similar point of view. Indeed, the issue featuring the bulk of his metaphysical musings ends with a powerful epigraph from Jung, which reiterates Rorschach's observations, though in a friendlier tone: "As far as we can discern, the sole purpose of human existence is to kindle a light of meaning in the darkness of mere being."[157] This is Moore's most powerful act of *kenosis,* his most thorough emptying out of the precursor by insisting on total meaninglessness, total malleability.

Moore protects *Watchmen* from the return of the dead, which threaten to break their bonds by viewing all reality—past and present—as violently empty for interpretation, subjugation, and misprision

---

[156] Moore and Gibbons, *Watchmen,* #6, 26.

[157] Ibid., #9, 28. It dawned on me as I read this epigraph that it must inform the Wallace Stevens poem that shares a title with the ninth issue of *Watchmen,* "Of Mere Being." But as Bernard says to the newspaper vendor on learning they have the same name, "So? Ain't no big deal. . . . Don't signify for nothin' " (Ibid., #11, 23, my ellipses).

(though again, Moore's metaphors, as opposed to Miller's, are textual rather than violent: "free to scrawl design on [a] morally blank world"). Bloom writes: "The poet has, in regard to the precursor's heterocosm, a shuddering sense of the arbitrary—of the equality, or equal haphazardness, of all objects."[158] There can be nothing wrong with looking at human bodies and seeing a raft, or putting the entire history of superhero comic book literature into *Watchmen*'s broad misprision. Moore's "inspiration" is preceded by his *kenosis*-exhalation, which "breathes hard . . . turning illusions to ice, shattering them."

(This study will conclude with the birth of superhero comic books that will be the successor to the silver age. Here we can see the stirrings of a ubiquitous aspect of those narratives, their high level of horrific (sometimes almost comic) violence and use of horror tropes: the severing of Voodoo's legs by a super-powered serial killer in Joe Casey's "Serial Boxes" (*Wildcats* 14–19), the grotesque medical experiments of City Zero in Ellis's "The Day the Earth Turned Slower" (*Planetary* 8), and the almost ridiculous slaughter of Stormwatch by Ridley Scott's Aliens—the transition to *The Authority*—in the *WildC.A.T.s/Aliens* crossover. As a genre, horror is the superhero narrative's diametric opposite: the former portrays the terror of helplessness, while the latter describes a power fantasy par excellence. Moore revives the horror comic book, excised from its production alongside the superhero narrative by Frederic Wertham's *Seduction of the Innocent,* within the superhero comic book. Its appearance in *Watchmen* is merely the "face-hugger" from Ridley Scott's *Alien.* By the time the revisionary superhero narrative outgrows the silver age and finds itself heralding a whole new generation of superheroes, the Alien's monstrous birth will have taken place and the horror comic will be running around as an integral part of the superhero landscape[159] (literally in one instance: see chapter 4). As horror teaches us—and Freud and Jacques Derrida emphasize—the repressed and excised find ways of making their presence felt, and nothing is ever fully or simply erased.)

It is important now to look at Moore's metaphors for the unification of this shattering, his metaphors of misprision. The reader is familiar

---

[158] Bloom, *Anxiety,* 42.

[159] Todd McFarlane's *Spawn* is a perfect example of blending superhero and horror elements; the rest of the narrative, however, lacks interest as far as this book is concerned.

with Rorschach's metaphor of unification from our discussion of Batman: violence and fascism. Adrian Veidt's understanding is perhaps the most interesting. Like Commissioner Gordon's anecdote about Roosevelt, meant to invoke Batman, Veidt will not unite the world through violence but through trickery. As in *The Killing Joke*'s flashlight joke, this unification will be a trick of the light. Facing his wall of television screens Veidt gives a glimpse of the chaos of the superhero narrative: "Meanings coalesce from semiotic chaos before reverting to incoherence."[160] Like Alan Moore's *kenosis*, he must destroy, then reconstruct, in order to build "a unity which would survive him."[161] He succeeds, but—like the unity created by *The Dark Knight Returns*, which is disrupted by *Year One*, "revert[ing] to incoherence"—Jon must ultimately remind him when he asks, "I did the right thing, didn't I? It all worked out in the end?" that "Nothing ends, Adrian. Nothing ever ends."[162] Bloom's definition of *kenosis* understands that "the latter poem of deflation is not as absolute as it seems." Here, Veidt the revisionist confronts the man who has seen the machinery of the universe exposed to him as his father had looked at the inside of watches, and faces the realization of comic book continuity: the chain of revision can never end. One misprision will follow upon another, each as arbitrary an organization as the one that came before.

At this point, the reader may find the continual pointing out of narrative microcosms tedious, but should bear in mind the superhero narrative's high level of interaction with psychoanalysis and the common psychoanalytic theory that every element of the dream represents the dreamer. An entry from Rorschach's journal makes up the opening lines of *Watchmen,* and the journal is thus a synecdoche for it; the journal is ultimately delivered to the *New Frontiersman,* "delivered at last into the hands of a higher judgment."[163] In an example of the textual juxtaposition discussed above, this line is intended to refer back to our Black Freighter narrator, to Rorschach's journal as an emblem of *Watchmen,* and to its judgment by the tradition and the reader. "I leave it entirely in your hands"[164] is the final line of *Watchmen,* as Seymour ("see more")

---

[160] Moore and Gibbons, *Watchmen,* #11, 1.
[161] Ibid., 10.
[162] Ibid., #12, 27.
[163] Ibid., #10, 23.
[164] Ibid., #12, 32.

reaches toward a pile of articles for publication on top of which Ror-schach's journal sits. (Once again, *Watchmen* is supported by a stack of texts.) As the first phase of the revisionary superhero narrative, *Watchmen* will be judged; later phases of superhero narratives—the watchers of the *Watchmen*—will be this judgment.

In Hollis Mason's fictional autobiography, he says he enjoyed the move from the pulps to Superman because "[h]ere was something that presented the basic morality of the pulps without all their darkness and ambiguity."[165] As in *The Dark Knight Returns,* poetic tradition is grasped through allusions: like Bruce Wayne and Zorro, Hollis Mason (the first Night Owl) admits to being inspired to be a crime fighter by reading *The Shadow* and *Doc Savage*—the literature out of which the superhero narrative emerged. *Batman: The Dark Knight Returns* and *Watchmen* return superheroes to their pulp roots, to darkness and ambiguity; and while the second phase of the revisionary superhero narrative will find this atmosphere too dark, never again will the superhero narrative be able to return to the simplicity from which it came without coming to terms with *Watchmen* and *The Dark Knight Returns.*

---

165 Ibid., #1, prose.

2

"It is with considerable difficulty . . ."

THE REVISIONARY SUPERHERO
NARRATIVE, PHASE TWO

This superhero stuff is getting me down, man. I don't
know where it's all going to end.

—*Doom Patrol* 21

It is not possible to step twice into the same river.

—Heraclitus

W here *Batman: The Dark Knight Returns* and *Watchmen* ask, What
would it be like if superheroes existed in our world? *Marvels*
(1994) and *Astro City* (1995) ask, What would it feel like if
we could live in theirs?[166] While the answer to the second question
invokes a much lighter mood, and some portrayals of superheroes that
are less disturbing, these works are no less serious in their investigation
of comic book history, questioning its assumptions and structure. I
would like to quote from Dan Dreiberg's essay on bird watching in
Watchmen to make the transition from the first to the second phase of
the revisionary superhero narrative:

Is it possible, I wonder, to study a bird so closely, to observe and
catalogue its peculiarities in such minute detail, that it becomes
invisible? Is it possible that while fastidiously calibrating the span
of its wings or the length of its tarsus, we somehow lose sight of
its poetry? . . .

---

[166] Kurt Busiek, Brent E. Anderson, et al., *Astro City: Life in the Big City* (New York: DC
Comics, 1995), 9.

Perhaps, instead of measuring the feathered tufts surmount-
ing its ears, we should speculate on what those ears might have
heard. Perhaps when considering the manner in which it grips
its branch . . . we should allow ourselves to pause for a moment,
and acknowledge that these same claws must have once drawn
blood from the shoulder of Pallas.[167]

Alan Moore is the first to become aware of the effect of his *kenosis*.
He has created a superhero narrative that leaves the reader with no
superheroes. *Marvels* and *Astro City* attempt to reclaim heroes and return
to the early days of comic books by way of the lessons of Frank Miller
and Moore. *Marvels* and *Astro City* attempt to re-create—for the new
adult demographic—the wonder of a child reading comic books for the
first time. On another level, however, these two works are a kind of
fantasy. They are an attempt to flee not only the anxieties that informed
The Dark Knight Returns and *Watchmen,* but the anxieties generated by the
works of Miller and Moore—by returning to a time before influence.
Astro City and *Marvels,* as beautiful as they are stylistically, prove that the
superhero can never go home again, never step into the same river—
Miller's "spring right beneath"—twice. The third work of this second
phase of the revisionary superhero narrative, *Kingdom Come,* will establish
the bridge out of this fantasy and into a future that can finally take the
works of Miller and Moore into account.

Kurt Busiek and Alex Ross's *Marvels*

The epigraph to *Marvels*—its opening words—makes its troubling lineage clear. It is from Mary Shelley's *Frankenstein*: "It is with considerable
difficulty that I remember the original era of my being . . . ," a difficulty
imposed by *The Dark Knight Returns* and *Watchmen*. Frankenstein's monster is not the most arbitrary image of artistic creation for a genre cob-
bled together from movies and pulp novels, whose stories now stand as
a curious admixture of science, science fiction, magic, myth, horror,
camp, and the popularity that leads to reinterpretation in other media
such as film and television. These words occur in Shelley's novel when

---

[167] Moore and Gibbons, *Watchmen,* #7, prose (my ellipsis).

the monster attempts to defend his status as a monster. By retelling his recollection of his early days, he will evoke the sympathy of his creator. He insists he should not be abhorred or reviled despite the fact that Victor Frankenstein knows the dark deeds he has already committed. The relation to recent developments in the superhero narrative is clear: Kurt Busiek and Alex Ross's *Marvels* pleads, in an address to a creator or to future creators, that superheroes not be seen as monsters, despite the monstrosities superheroes are exposed to, as in works like *The Dark Knight Returns* and *Watchmen* (and their influences—discussed below). The continuation of Shelley's quote reveals, in part, the difficulty imposed by the work of Miller and Moore; from now on, the superhero narrative must acknowledge its contradictory and convoluted tradition: "It is with considerable difficulty that I remember the original era of my being: all the events of that period appear confused and indistinct. A strange multiplicity of sensations seized me."[168] *Marvels* cannot help but emerge out of a background confused, indistinct, and multiple, as much as it would like to start again at the beginning. The reason that memory is difficult is the same in *Marvels* as it is in *Frankenstein*. Though it would like to be a return to the past, it is instead an all too present recasting of the past. The epigraph begins a story within a story (the monster's story within *Frankenstein*), which is all that *Marvels* can hope to be: a story within the story of tradition, not an authentic return to the origin.

Marvels' interpretative shift is to retell moments from the golden and silver age of comic books from the perspective of New Yorkers who lived through them, specifically, a photographer named Phil Sheldon. Sheldon is publishing a coffee-table book—called *Marvels*—intended to communicate the wonder and majesty of these golden and silver age heroes. Just as in other revisionary superhero narratives, *Marvels* exposes its own construction as its first line of defense against influence. Before understanding *Marvels* in its own right, however, a quick map must be sketched between our first and second phases of the revisionary superhero narra-

---

[168] Mary Shelley, *Frankenstein* (New York: Dover, 1994), 70. Passages from the same paragraph continue to chime with metaphorical weight: "Darkness then came over me, and troubled me; but hardly had I felt this when, by opening my eyes, as I now suppose, the light poured in upon me again. I walked and, I believe, descended. . . . The light became more and more oppressive to me; and the heat wearying me as I walked, I sought a place where I could receive shade. . . . I lay by the side of a brook. . . ." Constructing an elaborate allegory, however, would take us far afield.

tive. The immediate influence of *The Dark Knight Returns* and *Watchmen* was not positive. What superhero narratives learned from the success of these works was that the market was interested in a much higher level of violence and sex than the industry produced at the time. The response was predictable. What resulted in the late 1980s and early 1990s was a proliferation of dark, psychotic, violent loners with sexual dysfunctions who dismembered anyone who looked at them the wrong way. At the time, this was seen as "realism," although the reader familiar with more conventional literature is invited to imagine the history of realism in the novel as being based solely on the distinction between Shakespeare's *Winter's Tale* and his *Titus Andronicus*. In Alan Moore's words:

> obviously, we've [Moore and Frank Miller] to some degree doomed the mainstream comics medium to a parade of violent, depressing postmodern superheroes, a lot of whom, in addition to those other faults, are incredibly pretentious. I stand accused.[169]

Just as Francis Ford Coppola realized that the entire point of the first *Godfather* film had been missed—audiences actually romanticized Michael Corleone, whom Coppola had intended to expose as a horrid monstrosity—Moore was disturbed to find people actually liking Rorschach, and wanting to read more comics that starred characters like him. The superhero market was flooded with poorly written, violent antiheroes who looked like, or actually used to be conceived as, villains: Cable, Wolverine, Venom, the Punisher, Ghost Rider, Spawn, and later Prophet, Supreme, Cyberforce (whose members include Ripclaw and Stryker), Glory, and Pitt. This was the so-called dark age of superheroes, often cited as the successor to the silver age when combined with the works of Miller and Moore: the silver age completely run out of imaginative energy. By reconceiving the earlier days of comics, *Marvels* attempts to usurp the dominance of this kind of superhero literature by an act of returning, a reestablishing of origins. Just as Miller usurps his own Batman through a reimagining of origins, *Marvels* will usurp the field of antiheroes by reminding them where they come from, by insisting on the priority of prior tradition: the establishing days of the Marvel universe.

---

[169] Reynolds, *Mythology,* 117.

As the Shelley epigraph suggests, however, the return to prior tradition is not a simple movement. No objective vision of the past can be achieved without passing through the influence-vision of *The Dark Knight Returns* and *Watchmen*. (Or, in the case of Frankenstein's monster, no sympathetic telling of his early days can be seen except through the knowledge that he murdered an innocent child, knowledge that Victor, his audience, possesses.) Our point-of-view narrator, Phil Sheldon, is disturbed by his city's disillusionment in regard to the Marvels, but this disillusionment is only marginally reflected from the original comic books. The misprisions of Alan Moore and Frank Miller are responsible for the amplification of this particular aspect in the return to the past. In effect, Phil Sheldon provides the only support for the metatextual awareness of the cynicism and violence generated by the first phase of the revisionary superhero narrative.

Sheldon's status as a revisionary narrator must first be seen against the backdrop of *Marvels'* claim to naturalness and objectivity through Alex Ross's revisionary photorealism. In illustrating *Marvels,* Ross breaks new ground with a style unlike anything that has ever appeared in superhero comic books, and *Marvels* was Ross's first major breakthrough into the genre. Ross's major artistic influences include, along with fellow industry professionals Chris Swan and Jack Kirby, Norman Rockwell and Edward Hopper (note his *Nighthawks* tribute in the first issue of *Marvels*).[170] His photorealistic art style is revisionary in the same way as Frank Miller's writing. His portrayals of superheroes are so realistic (to the point of rendering the fabric of the spandex uniform, which he manages to do without exposing the silliness of the garb) that the reader is forced to accept his story as the way it "really happened." The effect of the visual trope is to make the reader feel that Ross's portrayal must be the source of the original issues. The photo-like documentation is only heightened by the fact that he re-renders specific events that occurred in previous comic books. However, the development of Phil Sheldon's character and several key moments in Ross's art expose *Marvels'* as a fantasy of priority, naturalness, and objectivity that cannot be maintained. Cracks appear that expose the work as deeply influenced, overdetermined, and late in the tradition.

---

[170] Kurt Busiek and Alex Ross, *Marvels* (New York: Marvel Comics, 1994), #1 (no pagination).

Marvels emphasizes the act of seeing and sight in its narrator and point-of-view character, Phil Sheldon. The objective photorealistic quality of Ross's art rests upon the fact that everything we see comes through the eyes of a particular subject whom we follow. Sheldon's role as a newspaper photographer places him in a position to generate Ross's images, supported by the fact that he is putting together a words-and-pictures book on the heroes called *Marvels.* Sheldon's subjective vision, however, is not natural but always mediated by the glasses he wears, even in his younger days, and his camera lens through which he captures his world. The key moment occurs when, in the first book, he loses an eye witnessing a battle between Namor and the Human Torch, just at the moment that he feels he has the most natural centralized vision: "It was as if everything that had been brewing since we first saw the Torch burst into flame had broken in one colossal storm—and I was at its eye. I was part of it. I was right where I belonged. I was the witness [*he is hit*]."[171] The excessive use of the word *I* (invoking the crypt term *eye*)[172] makes the meeting between subject and world explicit: "I was at its I." Such conditions mark an ideal moment of objectivity. That he immediately loses an eye for his hubris, and central eye/I of the objective experience, undermines the naturalness *Marvels* seems founded upon.

Batman: The Dark Knight Returns and *Watchmen* metatextually obscure Sheldon's vision. In his quest to write a book glorifying the Marvels, he is met with, and infected by, a growing atmosphere of cynicism and distrust toward superheroes. The resistance places him on the defensive, and he tries to speak for them as praiseworthy. His laments speak not to the portrayal of the heroes in the original comic books (which *Marvels* is only supposed to be showing from another perspective without interpreting) but to the recent misprisions of Miller and Moore: "The Marvels were supposed to be pure. Glorious. Not . . . sordid."[173] Yelling at an apocalypse-prognosticating sandwich board character, recalling Rorschach's alter ego, Sheldon cries at *Watchmen's kenosis* by synecdoche: "Isn't there enough in this world to frighten little girls?! You don't have to go making them scared of heroes on top of it all!"[174] He even ques-

---

[171] Ibid.

[172] For more on the idea of "crypt terms," see John Shoptaw, *On the Outside Looking Out: John Ashbery's Poetry* (Cambridge, MA: Harvard University Press, 1994), 6.

[173] Busiek and Ross, *Marvels,* #3 (Busiek's ellipsis).

[174] Ibid.

tions the legitimacy of his own project ("Marvels") and *Marvels* by association: "My photos showed heroes—but were they accurate? Atomic power had been a shining miracle once, too—before the Cold War. Before it became something to fear. Were we misjudging the Marvels—or were we simply starting to see them for what they really were?"[175] At the end of "Judgment Day" (*Marvels* 3), Sheldon berates a crowd for attacks on the heroes: "Are you so busy digging for garbage you can't even admit to yourselves that you're grateful? Look up, why don't you—Look up for once in your lives—!"[176]

In the final installment of *Marvels* ("The Day She Died," *Marvels* 4), Sheldon looks up—and sees the death of Gwen Stacy. A tragic and serious story, the original "Death of Gwen Stacy"[177] (1973) was the transition between the early superhero stories portrayed in *Marvels'* first three books and more "adult" superhero narratives like *The Dark Knight Returns* and *Watchmen. Marvels* brings the reader from the birth of Marvel comics to this transition, to the narratives of Miller and Moore that inform its vision. The disillusionment with heroes in *Marvels* reaches its height here, when Sheldon witnesses the death of this innocent, ambiguously at the hands of Spider-Man, and internalizes the cynicism he has been confronting. "The Day She Died" builds to this by highlighting several instances of superheroes held in contempt: Spider-Man accused of murder, the trial of the Black Widow for murder, Iron Man striking at student protests, the Falcon (a black hero) accused of selling out, heroes who work for money. "Everywhere, the Marvels were being insulted—degraded. What was wrong with us?"[178]

This is the atmosphere that supported Moore and Miller's work, and sure enough, in the Sub-Mariner's invasion of New York, *Marvels'* indictment of these works is made clear. Among the attacking ships, Alex Ross slips in Night Owl's airship from *Watchmen,* with Dan and Laurie inside.[179] The cynicism toward heroes has been building to the level of *Watchmen*, and now (despite copyright infringement) figures from Moore's work literally arrive. In the face of the calamity Gwen sees the

---

[175] Ibid.

[176] Ibid.

[177] See *The Death of Gwen Stacy* (New York: Marvel Comics, 1999).

[178] Busiek and Ross, *Marvels, #*4.

[179] Ibid.

beauty of the fantastic ships and communicates it to Sheldon, who has lost the feeling: "It's beautiful, isn't it? It's like—like being in a snow globe—so pretty and strange and unreal—as if it's not happening now—it's only a dream of something that happened once."[180] An allusion to *Watchmen* might be implicit here: Laurie Juspeczyk's earliest memory is of playing with a snowglobe as her parents fought in the next room:

> Everything felt secret and enchanted . . . it was like a whole world; a world inside the ball. It was like a little glass bubble of somewhere else. I lifted it, starting a blizzard. I knew it wasn't real snow, but I couldn't understand how it fell so slowly. I figured inside the ball was some different sort of time. Slow time.[181]

It is indicative of the difference between *Watchmen* and *Marvels* that Laurie's globe, connected with the realization that her father was not a good man but rather her mother's rapist, shatters. This allusion betrays *Marvels'* worries over poor parentage, trying to keep the globe and its incipient realization from breaking into the open. In any case, Gwen's statement resonates near the knowledge that *Marvels* is an exploration of the past, of a distinctly fictional past retroactively colored by the present, another world of slow time. When Gwen is killed, Sheldon loses whatever hope he was granted, even his idea to write a book about what the Marvels should mean to the people they protect. His new optimism, his realization that the heroes "weren't here to win the approval of the petty and small-minded. They were here to save the innocent. To save people like Gwen,"[182] ends when Spider-Man fails to save Gwen, and may even be responsible for her death. He gives up.

Matthew J. Pustz offers the following interpretation of the end of *Marvels*:

> Sheldon publishes a book that virtually deifies the Marvels, turning him into a true keeper of the flame, a proselytizer for the

---

[180] Ibid.

[181] Moore and Gibbons, *Watchmen,* #9 (my ellipsis).

[182] Busiek and Ross, *Marvels,* #4.

superheroes, like the fans urged to hook their friends on Marvel comics. When he realizes that the Marvels' battles never end and that the heroes can have little impact on the lives of "real" people, Sheldon abandons his devotion to them. Quitting his job taking photographs of and celebrating the Marvels, Sheldon returns to the family that he has neglected for years to live a normal life. Here, [Kurt] Busiek is also discussing how fans give up on Marvel—how they should give up on superhero comic books—to enter a world of reality, adulthood and normality.[183]

In a footnote, however, Pustz suggests that the final page—and its "nice, normal, ordinary boy," discussed below—might work against this reading: "Perhaps Busiek's point is that fans can never totally escape the world of superheroes, comics and Marvel."[184] The tools with which this book has been working can provide an alternative reading that embraces the difficulty presented in Pustz's footnote.

Infected with the *kenosis* of *Watchmen, Marvels'* culminates in the arrival of the Silk Specter and Night Owl, but Moore's influence has now returned in such a way as to allow Busiek to handle it, to exorcise it. Sheldon passes his work on the heroes to his young assistant, saying:

> You've got to be outside it, to see it for what it is. [Outside] [a]nything. Everything. Whatever. It's the only way to see it right. You've got to have the eye for it, and mine is gone. I've lost it somewhere. I've seen too much. And I'm inside now. Where I can't see anything straight. But you—you're young. You're not tired. You can see what I miss.[185]

Simply put, Sheldon is too far inside Moore's *kenosis* to think outside of it; his vision—both literally and poetically—is too weak to master the heroes. Initially, his admiration made them too big to interpret in any manner other than religious worship, and later he is faced with their failure to live up to his ideal. His assertion that he doesn't "have the eye for it" because he has "seen too much" is clearly a statement about the

---

[183] Pustz, *Comic Book Culture,* 149.
[184] Ibid., 218.
[185] Busiek and Ross, *Marvels,* #4.

weight of tradition, which hampers his ability to see freshly, to see anew without influence. It is also a statement that Sheldon no longer has the personality—the "I"—to master his experience in the manner of Miller's Batman. Sheldon succeeded once with his own work, *Marvels,* but is now the failed poet who cannot bear the weight of tradition, which has worn him away. His retirement can be read in terms of Bloom's revisionary ratio of askesis. Bloom defines the term as follows:

> The latter poet does not, as in *kenosis,* undergo a revisionary movement of emptying, but of curtailing; he yields up part of his own human and imaginative endowment, so as to separate himself from others, including the precursor, and he does this in his poem by so stationing it in regard to the parent-poem as to make that poem undergo an *askesis* too; the precursor's endowment is also truncated.[186]

Sheldon's failure to go on exposes *Watchmen*'s inability to generate anything new. There can be no superheroes after *Watchmen.* After a return to the power of the heroes, Busiek sacrifices Sheldon to the forces of *Watchmen* in order to retire *Watchmen*'s power in the vessel of an old man with poor vision, who can't go on any longer (one recalls those stories where a powerful creature is tricked into the body of something weak, which can be defeated).[187] Busiek returns to an early power of superhero narratives in *Marvels* but ends by retiring a vision of disillusionment before Sheldon can go on to write something like *Watchmen.* Sheldon may have "seen too much," but he will not write about all he has seen.

It is a misprision in the classic comic book spirit. Busiek will travel back in time to sacrifice *Watchmen*'s influence, part of his poetic vision, in the form of Sheldon (writer of *Marvels*), and stop the "dark age" of superhero narratives from ever happening. Sheldon's failure is a failure that retires some of the weight of *Watchmen* with him; his retirement lifts the burden that needs to be cleared to allow the next generation to create anew. This is why the work ends with Sheldon having his retire-

---

[186] Bloom, *Anxiety,* 15.
[187] Moore tells this kind of story himself in *Youngblood* #1 (Los Angeles: Awesome Entertainment, 1998).

ment photo taken with a random newspaper boy—"a nice, normal, ordinary boy"[188]—whose name is Danny Ketch. *Marvels,* which opened with an epigraph about a monster, now closes with a vision of one: as all Marvel fans know, Danny Ketch will become Ghost Rider.

As in *Marvels'* epigraph, the choice is not insignificant: Danny Ketch, like Sheldon, will grow to be a man literally possessed by the violence inflicted upon the innocent. The Ghost Rider will right the wrongs done to them, as Sheldon cannot. The spirit of Ghost Rider has possessed many, and the specific selection of Ketch is a counterpoint. He is the new incarnation of Ghost Rider, influenced by Miller and Moore in just the way described above: violent, dark, gritty, pretentious, and poorly written. This specific Ghost Rider is exactly the kind of antihero Sheldon could have become, written about, or photographed had he allowed his cynicism to consume him, if he continued writing, if he did not retire. Now the reader will look ahead to see what will come next, from Sheldon's assistant and the readers of *Marvels*: to see if *Marvels* was successful in siphoning off some of the negative power of *Watchmen* so that the superhero narrative will not be completely finished.

Kurt Busiek's *Astro City*

Kurt Busiek's Astro City is literally located under the shadow of Kirby Mountain,[189] named for famed superhero creator Jack Kirby. Moments after learning of its "looming bulk," however, our point-of-view character for "Safeguards" (*Astro City,* vol. 1, no. 4) offers the reader her reaction to Astro City superhero Winged Victory, a character clearly in debt to Wonder Woman: "The sight of her, proud and noble, never fails to set my heart racing. The way she sets her own course, free of gravity, of rules . . . without a care for tradition . . . makes me feel like I can do anything."[190] *Astro City* is a work as under the shadow of influence as it claims not to be.

Astro City is a mock-up superhero continuity like that of Marvel's or DC's. It draws on both, creating a kind of amalgam continuity, with

---

[188] Busiek and Ross, *Marvels,* #4.
[189] Busiek et al., *Astro City: Life in the Big City,* 91.
[190] Ibid., 94 (my ellipses).

characters that resonate with echoes of the Fantastic Four (the First Family), Superman (Samaritan), Iron Man (Mock Turtle), Batman (the Confessor), Captain America (the Old Soldier), the Flash (M.P.H.), Spider-Man (Crackerjack), Wonder Woman (Winged Victory), and the X-Men (the Astro City Irregulars). It is a continuity that would like to insist that *The Dark Knight Returns* and *Watchmen* never happened, or rather, as we will see, it is a fantasy that reduces these works to the level of a possible future that can still be avoided. The reader should keep in mind Bloom's definition of fantasy in this context.

> *[F]antasy, as a belated version of romance, promises absolute freedom from belatedness, from the anxieties of literary influence and origination, yet this promise is shadowed always by a psychic over-determination in the form itself of fantasy, that puts the stance of freedom into severe question.* What promises to be the least anxious of literary modes becomes much the most anxious.[191]

Like *Marvels, Astro City* attempts to avoid anxiety by shifting perspective. It often acts as a negative of traditional superhero stories, reversing big and little moments, showing in one panel something that traditionally would take a whole issue, like major battles, and spending time on small moments, like waking up and putting on a costume one leg at a time. *Astro City* is this book's first truly serial revisionary narrative (as of this writing, it is an ongoing narrative), and an analysis can arrive at no specific conclusion of the work as a whole. Here, I want only to hit certain key moments in *Astro City,* concentrating on the moments it differs from the first phase of the revisionary superhero narrative, and especially where it deals, however tacitly, with the works of Miller and Moore.

The first critically important moment in *Astro City* is a special promotional piece published by *Wizard* magazine: *Astro City,* issue 1/2: "The Nearness of You." It is the story of Michael Tenicek, who is troubled by dreams of the same woman every night—not particularly stunning, not even his type—but about whom he knows every detail, and whom he loves. He knows he has never met her, but the fact that he knows everything about her is driving him mad. The moment he considers

---

[191] Bloom, *Agon,* 206 (Bloom's emphasis).

suicide, a mysterious superhero known only as the Hanged Man arrives and explains the reason for Tenicek's obsession. In the aftermath of a huge chronal battle between two time-altering villains (the stuff of major superhero epics like DC's *Crisis on Infinite Earths*), reconstruction of time was not exact, and Tenicek's wife was never born. The Hanged Man says:

> For the most part, the new reality is whole, but close bonds such as yours . . . they create a weakness in the fabric of time . . . one that could let through . . . dangerous things. But the weakness is healed by your understanding. [. . . .] If the pain is too much, I can allow you to forget. . . .[192]

Tenicek chooses not to forget, and learns that no one, given the option, ever does. He sleeps well from then on.

"The Nearness of You" is a story about the effect of a multiple-book crossover on the little characters no one ever sees. This shift of perspective from major to minor characters is Busiek's way of writing a major superhero epic while avoiding influence, staying in the margins of something like *Crisis on Infinite Earths* (the illustration of the chronal battle is clearly meant to invoke the cover of *Crisis* 3).[193] More importantly, however, it is a story about continuity. The traditional inconsistencies in continuity are exactly the kind of discrepancies, endemic to superhero literature, that lead to the madness of Moore's Joker and his "multiple choice" past. Tenicek sees "time and reality fragment from the violence done to it—sees the world thrown into chaos—all eras collapsing, entangling with each other."[194] While Miller's Batman needs to create order, and Moore's Joker finds madness in acceptance, Michael Tenicek finds peace through understanding, not by forgetting, but through memory. "The Nearness of You" establishes, against the horror of mismatched continuity, its beauty and potentiality. The name of the woman whose memory Tenicek will hold, despite its inability to coincide

---

[192] Kurt Busiek, Brent E. Anderson, et al., *Astro City: Confession* (New York: DC Comics, 1997), 184 (Bracketed ellipsis mine).

[193] See ibid., 182–183, and Marv Wolfman and George Pérez, *Crisis on Infinite Earths* (New York: DC Comics, 1985), #3, cover.

[194] Busiek et al., *Astro City: Confession,* 182.

with established reality, is Miranda (from the Latin "wonder"). To once again mark the textual metaphor—peace arrives in the form of the Hanged Man, who "speaks" as writing. Tenicek "does not hear the words. Rather, they simply appear in his mind—not so much spoken as inscribed."[195] The text absorbs what consciousness cannot, and in this way Busiek avoids in his *Astro City* a character like Moore's Joker.

In "Confession" (*Astro City* issues 4–9) Busiek tells the story of the Confessor and Altar Boy, characters who stand in relation to Batman and Robin as revisionary references. The two very clearly suggest the established heroes visually and in their interaction, but Busiek's casting of the elements of Batman is aimed at revising the tradition that includes Miller and Moore. This is why the Confessor and Altar Boy stand as revisionary references rather than tributary ones (by which I mean to invoke the meanings both of homage and derivative status). Altar Boy discovers that the Confessor is actually a vampire, a trope that Busiek uses as an explanation of the host of powers that Batman traditionally displays. As Altar Boy says to the Confessor: "You're prenaturally [*sic*] strong and fast. You can mesmerize people just by looking at them, and disappear into mist. You never come out in the day. Bullets pass through you."[196] This is, of course, an interpretation of Batman's abilities: his strength and speed come from training; the mesmerizing effect—by which Altar Boy means the Confessor's ability to make criminals unburden themselves—is simply the effect of terror in Batman's presence; Batman is always gone when characters turn around; he never wears the costume in the day, and the effect of bullets passing through him is accomplished by moving his cape so criminals shoot the areas of the costume his body is not in. This is Miller's Batman in *The Dark Knight Returns* and *Batman: Year One,* and Busiek transfers some of Miller's monstrous interpretation to the Confessor by literally making him a monster. Busiek's *Astro City* uses the Confessor's death to transfer the "Batman" mantle to his young (nonmonstrous) protégé, Altar Boy. Like Busiek's retirement of Sheldon in *Marvels* after transferring to him the cynicism of *Watchmen, Astro City* transfers the power of Miller's Batman to the vessel of the Confessor and kills him to curtail the power of Miller's text, making room for its own conception.

---

[195] Ibid., 178.

[196] Ibid., 89. *Preternatural* was obviously the word desired in place of *prenatural.*

Ultimately, *Astro City*'s landscape cannot be complete without a Batman figure, and this is the key move of "Confession": to replace Miller's grim conception of Batman, which had become the dominant interpretation, with something a little more hopeful. Altar Boy's deceased parents, Thomas and Martha, recall Batman's Thomas and Martha Wayne. Altar Boy is not a successor—the Confessor's parents are not Batman's Thomas and Martha—but *the* Batman. His taking on the persona of the Confessor is in its lighter tone a reestablishing of a more original vision. The Confessor leaves him a fortune, and just like the young Bruce Wayne, he travels and trains before returning to fight crime in his own city. He narrates:

[T]he voice modulator worked perfectly. [The criminals] were nervous. They'd heard the rumors. And they came prepared. Holy water. Garlic. Crucifixes. And under my mask, I couldn't help but smile. For a while—for a little while, anyway—this was going to be easier than I thought.[197]

Busiek returns a rejuvenated Batman to the reader. He is no longer a monster, literally no longer a vampire; Busiek deals with Miller's Batman by having his chosen successor replace him, a serious Batman but one who still "couldn't help but smile." A later visual of two other heroes against a bolt of lightning[198] confirms *Astro City*'s overall intention to reverse the darkness imposed by Miller and Moore: it is a recasting of *The Dark Knight Returns*' first issue cover, but rather than a dark silhouette of Batman, there is, fully lit, *Astro City*'s more playful heroes.

The two-part story "Serpent's Teeth" and "Father's Day" (*Astro City* 11–12) engages similar concerns from another perspective. The superhero Jack-in-the-Box confronts two of his sons who have traveled back in time from alternate futures. The first, the Box, is a technological monster recalling Cable or the *X-Men*'s Cameron Hodge. The second, Jackson, is the other side of the dark superhero trend discussed above: an organically grotesque creature reminiscent of Venom, Wolverine, and Sabertooth. Each of these violent, deadly monstrosities claims to be a

---

[197] Ibid., 167–168.
[198] Kurt Busiek, Brent E. Anderson, et al., *Astro City: Family Album* (New York: DC Comics, 1998), 26.

hero, and neither would be out of place in the contemporary superhero continuities of Marvel or DC. Their appearance is a discrepancy in *Astro City,* however, where all the heroes are styled more classically, in the direction of the golden and silver ages. Busiek's constructed world has not yet reached the "dark age" of the other major superhero continuities and might never: the time of Cable, Venom, and Sabertooth is only a possible nightmare future. As a third future son of Jack-in-the-Box explains:

> See, we're all the same person, sort of. From your vantage point we're what you'd call potential futures. Right now, we're all possibilities. As time moves on for you, though, you'll make choices, take actions—and that'll narrow down the possibilities to one actuality at any given time.[199]

Like *Marvels, Astro City* handles influence with the very comic book–style trope of going back in time to prevent a terrible future—the influence of *The Dark Knight Returns* and *Watchmen*—from ever happening.

If Astro City truly is back in time, then "In the Spotlight" and "Where the Action Is" (*Astro City* 13 and 21, respectively) contain *Astro City*'s moral injunction to "future" writers on the status of realism in the superhero narrative. The first story follows the life of a cartoon lion named Leo, accidentally brought to life by a villain's "belief ray." This children's character falls into all the traps of the "real world," in a manner reminiscent of the film *Raging Bull*: fame, women, drinking, drugs, and, finally, the death of an underage prostitute and the end of his career as the host of a children's television show. "In the Spotlight" is a fable about the effects of translating childhood heroes onto a realistic landscape, as Miller and Moore did with superheroes. At one point in his life, Leo becomes a supervillain, the Myth-Master, who fights the Honor Guard by conjuring fictional characters to fight on his side (notably, Achilles and D'Artagnan, influences in the creation of superheroes). The Myth-Master finally threatens the Honor Guard with a ray that will reduce them to fictions.

> Can you feel it, heroes? Can you feel reality draining away, as you become insubstantial—no more than brightly colored fanta-

[199] Ibid., 156.

sies out of some comic book? [*The heroes are pictured as taking on the two dimensional form of old four-color comic book characters.*][200]

He fights them by taking them to the extreme but opposite end of the spectrum that he himself is on; if he is destroyed by becoming real, then so they will be destroyed by becoming fiction. "In the Spotlight" suggests the inability of noble childhood characters like Leo to survive in such realistic adult conditions and situates those who would place them in realistic settings as the villains of the story.

"Where the Action Is" is a story about comic book characters taking revenge for literary misprision. Astro City has its own comic book company, Bulldog Comics, that reports on the exploits of the city's heroes. Its real life "stars" come back for revenge when liberties are taken with their stories—liberties like citing racism as a villain's motivation ("Do you know what color I am under this? What color I was before I got turned into a monster?!" screams Glowworm at the publisher of these comics. "Do you know what my mother thought when she read that stinking book of yours?!").[201] Female superhero Nightingale's complaints about her portrayal in Bulldog Comics recall Silhouette in *Watchmen*: "And what is this 'closer than sisters' crap, huh? What are you trying to imply about Sunbird and me?!"[202] Bulldog Comics are intended to be realistic comic books, not in the sense we have been using above to refer to realism in superhero comic books, but in the diegetic sense of accurately portraying the "real" heroes of Astro City. Local heroes are angry at being treated as *Watchmen* treats superheroes. "Where the Action Is" plays with the fantasy of existent core characters for whom misprision is a kind of slander. In the end, Bulldog Comics is vaporized by an unknown source after running a series of comic books on characters of cosmic power, "villains who are so far above us, they don't give a gnat's fart about ordinary humans or what we do."[203] Like "In the Spotlight," it is a story calling for more respectful treatment of heroes. In literary misprision, as well as in crimefighting, great power comes with great responsibility.

---

[200] Ibid., 188.

[201] Kurt Busiek, Brent E. Anderson, et al., *Astro City* (New York: DC Comics, 1995–present), #21.

[202] Ibid.

[203] Ibid.

Astro City is a fantasy, crying to be free of influence, pretending and wishing *The Dark Knight Returns* and *Watchmen* never happened. Perhaps its revisionary status is more playful than powerful, but an understanding of the revisionary superhero narrative would be incomplete without placing it alongside *Marvels*. *Astro City* stands out for another reason: it is the first of our revisionary narratives that is a running series rather than a completed mini-series. The difficulty in analyzing a serial medium, especially comic books, is that it often does not deal with a completed work. *Astro City* cannot have a focused point, as the other works we have looked at, but it is nonetheless an ongoing exploration of the comic book medium. The best that can be done here is to impart a sense of the series, a sense of how *Astro City* deals with *The Killing Joke, Watchmen,* and *The Dark Knight Returns* through the fantasy that those works have not yet happened, have not yet changed the face of the superhero narrative forever. *Astro City* believes that such work can still be averted by a combination of misprision—absorbing and subverting what will come—and moralizing, asking creators to reconsider what they will inevitably create.

Mark Waid and Alex Ross's *Kingdom Come*

The third key work that attempts to deal with *The Dark Knight Returns* and *Watchmen* understands the gift, rather than the difficulties, that Miller's and Moore's works represent for the superhero narrative. *Kingdom Come* advances to a time beyond the already belated present rather than return to a time, or rather the fantasy of a time, before influence. It presents a world in the near future where the classic DC heroes retired and the world is overrun by the next generation of violent, amoral crimefighters (discussed above). The text is quite aware of these determinations: Hollis Mason's fictional autobiography *Under the Hood,* from *Watchmen,* is on sale in a bookstore window;[204] "Who watches the watchmen" graffiti adorns a building[205] as the new generation of heroes battle outside; in a bar where the new heroes gather, Rorschach can even be

---

[204] Mark Waid and Alex Ross, *Kingdom Come* (New York: DC Comics, 1996), 17.
[205] Ibid.

spotted in the background.[206] *Kingdom Come* stages the return of the classic heroes, the return of the powerful origin and inspiration to confront what was done in their name. Superman must confront one of the new "heroes," Magog, who acts as a stand-in for violent, amoral crimefighters like Cable, whom he superficially resembles.

Kingdom Come stands out along with *The Dark Knight Returns* and *Watchmen* as a superhero story in which the characters are advanced by an act of knowledge. It confronts many of the political issues in the superhero narrative raised by Mark Gruenwald's *Squadron Supreme* (though a discussion of both would be redundant), the fascistic politics inherent in the superhero genre. *Kingdom Come* stands as an answer to the graffiti written on the walls of every superhero story after Alan Moore. What Mark Waid and Alex Ross attempt to reply is that the watchers don't need watchmen because it is a mistake to conceive of the watchers and watched as separate groups in the first place. *Kingdom Come* is a simple deconstruction of a simple binary: the split, in the superhero world, between normal humans and superhumans (referred to in other works as metahumans, posthumans, etc.).

In the story, the classic heroes leave retirement to restore order and justice to the world. In typical fascist superhero fashion, they set out to "fix" a world plagued by the next generation of reckless, violent, amoral superhumans. This time, however, their plan backfires, their self-constructed superhuman prison/"reeducation" camp (called the "Gulag") explodes open, and during the free-for-all brawl, the United Nations decides to drop a nuclear bomb on the battleground and finish the whole superhuman conflict before it destroys the country. Superman, whose quest for peace has led to war, must make a decision. He can stop the bomb, saving the lives of the combatants, whose battle might go on to engulf the world, or allow them all to perish, freeing humanity from the danger superhumans threaten, in the form of both anarchy and fascism. He passes the decision on to Captain Marvel because, as a human being who can transform into a superhuman, he straddles the two groups between which Superman must decide. The story ends with a simple moral. "We saw you as gods," says one of the UN council members. Superman replies:

> As we saw ourselves. And we were both wrong. [. . .] The
> problems we face still exist. We're not going to solve them for

---

[206] Ibid., 84.

you . . . we're going to solve them with you . . . not by ruling above you . . . but by living among you. We will no longer impose our power on humanity. We will earn your trust . . . using the wisdom one man [Captain Marvel] left as his legacy. I asked him to choose between humans and superhumans. But he alone knew that was a false division . . . and made the only choice that ever truly matters. He chose life . . . in the hope that your world and our world could be one world again.[207]

If the watchers and the watched are the same, and can enter into dialogue with each other, then there is still room for superheroes to operate after the advent of *Watchmen.*

The fate of Kansas in the narrative is an especially important trope in *Kingdom Come,* pointing to its role as a bridge connecting the post–Miller/Moore heroes, who learned only violence and cynicism, with the more positive tradition from which they emerged. The first major casualty resulting from the new superheroes is one of Magog's battles in which Captain Atom is torn apart, effectively detonating a nuclear device in the middle of Kansas. The destruction of the heart of America is an obvious trope for the loss of moral substance in the new heroes, but more importantly, a nuclear blast in the site of Superman's childhood signals the devastating blasts that occur in both *The Dark Knight Returns* and *Watchmen.* These were the moments that metaphorically severed the new breed of heroes from their predecessors. The land is rendered completely infertile, just as the superhero narrative after these works had no direction.

A superhuman prison is built on the site of the detonation—an emblem of the attempts of *Marvels* and *Astro City*—but the new generation of superhero cannot be contained, through prison or misprision. A site of battle, narrowly avoiding another nuclear blast, it is finally turned into a place of both harvest and memorial: a graveyard and a farm. The dead will only harm, says Diana (Wonder Woman), "if you forget what they taught you."[208] *The Dark Knight Returns* and *Watchmen* made their mark through violence; their successors learned only violence and forgot the transmission of influence contained in those texts. *Kingdom Come* aims at

---

[207] Ibid., 195–196 (bracketed ellipsis mine).
[208] Ibid., 200.

establishing a lineage of influence, a connection, between the texts that Miller and Moore absorbed and their inheritors, who saw only their break with tradition: the graveyard/farm is a resting place for *Watchmen*'s dead and a farm irrigated by Miller's "spring right beneath." It should be noted that this connection goes both ways: Superman's mistake was wishing to exile the new heroes' influence on the future, as much as they wanted to forget his influence from the past. In the end, these two camps acknowledge each other's influence and move toward the future together.

As Superman's childhood home, Kansas is the heart of the superhero narrative. Once fertile, it is blasted by the first phase of the revisionary narrative and becomes only a battleground, a place of violence. *Kingdom Come* makes it a place of fertility for future narratives, but also a memorial, a place where tradition is remembered and incorporated into growth. The setting for the story's epilogue is a kind of Planet Hollywood for superheroes, which includes memorabilia from the comic books, the *Batman* television show, George Reeves' *Superman* serial, and *Superfriends,* whose customers include Mark Gruenwald, Alex Ross, Mark Waid, Jenett Kahn (president of DC Comics), and Phil Sheldon from *Marvels.* The physical atmosphere shows one more instance of the rich and convoluted tradition upon which the superhero draws. The announcement of the new attempt at a second generation—the child to be raised by Superman, Wonder Woman, and Batman—in this setting suggests progeny more aware of the past that is its inheritance. Future superhero narratives will have rich land to draw upon but must keep one eye on the tradition that provides for its growth.

Like every other text we have read, all in some sense serial narratives, *Kingdom Come* ends with imagery of beginning, always pointing toward the future and coming generations. *Kingdom Come* ends by opening itself to the future troping, inevitable in a serial medium: the Reverend Norman McCay reads to his congregation from the Book of Revelation in the final scene and realizes "that the future, like so much else, is open to interpretation,"[209] in this case, literally the act of textual misprision. By reminding future storytellers of the tradition that Miller and Moore carried and synthesized to the same degree that they broke from it, and inviting revision, *Kingdom Come* moves the revisionary superhero narrative forward to the new age.

---

[209] Ibid., 203.

3

America's Best Comics

TRACING THE (RE)VISIONARY COMPANY

. . . tracing the visionary company . . .

—Hart Crane, *The Broken Tower*

In 1999, Alan Moore launched America's Best Comics (ABC), a name that recalls the big boasts of comic book companies from thirty years ago. (Marvel used to plaster phrases like "World's Best Comics" on the top of every issue, and occasionally still does.) Moore regains access to some of the old magic that made superhero comics great and properly closes the silver age in an ongoing, encyclopedic, retro/classic housing. *Marvels, Astro City,* and *Kingdom Come* lead both here and to the future. Moore's ABC universe is the destination of the nostalgic currents that must be properly siphoned off in order for the superhero narrative to move ahead.

Consisting of five titles, all written by Moore, each work under ABC individually examines some grounding of the superhero narrative. Alan Moore's work often functions as a kind of thought experiment that follows a set of premises to their logical conclusions—*Watchmen* might be described as extrapolating the consequences of superheroes on a society—and ABC is no exception. America's Best Comics imagines what the comic book medium might have been like if it was not dominated by the superhero genre and sheds some light on where the superhero came from for just that reason. It is a recasting of the origin story of superheroes themselves by returning to a time before there were any. *The League of Extraordinary Gentlemen* explores the debt the superhero owes to eighteenth- and nineteenth-century literature; *Tom Strong* examines the status of the pulp heroes—and fascist politics—from which the superhero narrative emerged; *Promethea* struggles with the status of a female superhero in a masculine continuity, and attempts to carve a space for a genuinely female superhero narrative; *Top Ten* renders the realism of the genre, the banality of "crime fighting," and the proliferation of superheroes over the years; *Tomorrow Stories* hearkens back to the golden age of comic books—the days when there would be three or four shorter stories in a single comic book—and through its shorts, "Jack B. Quick," "The First American," "Cobweb," "Splash Brannigan," and "Greyshirt," examines the place of a number of superhero building blocks, such as the use of quasi-science that borders on magic, reactionary political discourse, sexual voyeurism, the status of the comic book as a work of art, the pulp/detective novel influence, and the discovery of the "hero that will last." Moore takes a multivectored approach to grappling with the history of the superhero narrative by writing the titles for an entire company. While each title can be read separately, together they achieve an encyclopedic revisionary height: an elephants' graveyard for the golden and silver ages of comic books. In short, Moore enlarges the revisionary superhero narrative into the revisionary superhero company.

One noteworthy element about the company as a whole is its position on continuity, a force that has driven many of the narratives this book has examined. America's Best Comics began with a continuity that was deeply ambiguous: the question of whether Tom Strong shared the same fictional space as Promethea was left open to debate. Moore returned the reader, so hampered by issues of continuity, to an era before it was explicit, before it was closely tracked. As America's Best Comics continued to publish, one title began to make reference to another, clearly suggesting that ABC made up some kind of inchoate continuity. Like the early days of Marvel Comics, the exact nature of this continuity has yet to be defined, but this shift may point to a future toward which America's Best Comics is growing. Moore might be exploring the ground floor of the superhero narrative in ABC simply because the company is young, and in a movement of "ontogeny recapitulates phylogeny" is mirroring the evolution of the medium in the evolution of his company. Publishing spin-off titles like *Indigo Sunset* (a whole series devoted to *Tomorrow Stories'* Greyshirt) and *Tom Strong's Terrific Tales,* America's Best Comics may eventually grow beyond its "retro" texture into the future of the narrative. Only time will tell. For now, Moore playfully plumbs the superhero's depths from five different directions in one of comic books' broadest singular projects.

The *America's Best Comics 64 Page Giant* is in many ways emblematic of Moore's company and serves as a good starting point for investigation. The format is a rarely used classic of the silver age, a large comic book annual containing a host of small stories featuring every title in a company's lineup. In this case *Tom Strong, Promethea, Top Ten, The League of Extraordinary Gentlemen,* and every short comic in *Tomorrow Stories* ("Jack B. Quick," "Splash Brannigan," "The First American," "Cobweb," and "Greyshirt"). The League is represented by a board game and a *Picture of Dorian Grey* color-by-numbers. The format emphasizes America's Best Comics as a massive churning site of silver and golden age refuse (though much loved refuse) and serves to remind the reader that Moore is not engaged in five projects but in one. Moore has certainly created a place where readers may only read what they like (or can afford), but those who take this route should not forget the utter strangeness of a company of titles written almost exclusively by one man. America's Best Comics is a single work of Alan Moore's, an object with five sides that can only be fully appreciated as a whole rather than in parts.

The League of Extraordinary Gentlemen

The League of Extraordinary Gentlemen (1999) follows the structure of most team superhero stories: a handful of members of disparate personality and abilities are brought together from their various fictional narratives to face a threat that could not be faced alone. A well-rounded superhero team often requires certain stock characters—a leader, a fallen hero, an amoral rogue, a powerful female character (love interest for our fallen hero), an outsider, a man fighting inner demons—as well as certain abilities that must be available—fighting skills, tactical planning, a degree of guile, a moral center, a mode of transportation, a strongman. Moore's playful innovation is to discover all of this in the characters of nineteenth-century British literature, then imagine the protagonists existing in a single continuity, as they would in a comic book (or as many of William Faulkner's novels take place in Yoknapatawpha County). As Alan Moore describes in his introduction to a collected edition of his *Swamp Thing:*

The very first thing that anyone reading a modern horror comic [or any comic at all] should understand is that there are great economic advantages in being able to prop up an ailing, poor-selling comic book with an appearance by a successful guest star. Consequently, all the comic book stories produced by any given publisher are likely to take place in the same imaginary universe. This includes the brightly colored costumed adventurers populating their superhero titles, the shambling monstrosities that dominate their horror titles, and the old grizzled cowpoke who's wandered in from a western through a convenient time warp. For those more familiar with conventional literature, try to imagine Dr. Frankenstein kidnapping one of the protagonists of *Little Women* for his medical experiments, only to find himself subject to the scrutiny of a team-up between Sherlock Homes and Hercule Poirot. I'm sure that the charms and the over-whelming absurdities of this approach will become immediately apparent.[210]

The League of Extraordinary Gentlemen composes a *Justice League of America* if the Justice League had to be formed out of the British litera-ture of the previous century. In the order of the qualities listed above: Allan Quatermain (colonialist and opium addict), Hawley Griffin (the Invisible Man), Wilhelmina Harker (née Murray, from *Dracula*), Captain Nemo (with the Nautilus), and Dr.-Jekyll-and-Mr.-Hyde (who Moore casts as a kind of Incredible Hulk character, timid little man one minute, violent hulking brute the next). The supporting cast includes Mycroft Holmes, Auguste Dupin (from Edgar Allan Poe's "Purloined Letter"), and Broad Arrow Jack and Ishmael as members of Captain Nemo's crew ("Call me Ishmael," he says to the captain, "you've known me long enough").[211] For a villain the reader need look no farther than Professor Moriarty himself.

The League of Extraordinary Gentlemen reveals, through its play, not the absurdity of a nineteenth-century Justice League, but that the *Justice League*

---

[210] Alan Moore, Introduction, in *Saga of the Swamp Thing* (New York: DC Comics, 1984), iv.

[211] Alan Moore and Kevin O'Neal, *The League of Extraordinary Gentlemen* (La Jolla, CA: America's Best Comics, 1999), #4.

of America was formed of nineteenth-century British literature, at least to the degree that it is in debt to its influences. As one of Moore's period-piece inside cover advertisements—for the "Young Helpers' League"—tells us, in nineteenth-century font, "Our Motto: Bear ye one another's burdens, and so fulfill the law of Christ."[212] This "Helpers' League" stands between the *Justice League* and *The League of Extraordinary Gentlemen,* making the structure of influence clear: the *Justice League of America* bears the burden of the previous century's influence, and *The League of Extraordinary Gentlemen* will help bear that burden by creating a nineteenth-century *Justice League* for its fictional characters.

The *League of Extraordinary Gentlemen* also exposes, in its playful attitude toward the literature of the nineteenth century, the superheroes' narrative debt to literary history as a whole. As Wilhelmina Murray looks through her team's new headquarters at the British Museum in Bloomsbury (which includes an item labeled "Yahoo Skull"), she discovers a drawing of something that looks like another superhero team whose members include "L. Gulliver, Esq., Mr. & Mrs. P. Blakeny, the Reverend Dr. Syn, Mistress Hill and N. Bumpo, Esq. 1787."[213] The League of Extraordinary Gentlemen is not the first of its kind; the reader knows from the *JLA* it won't be the last. What Moore does is structure the superhero narrative backwards through time, casting previous literature into a form it will engender. The degree to which it works, however strange, is the degree to which the superhero is in debt to its predecessors stretching back to heroes from ancient Greek mythology and the Bible. *The League of Extraordinary Gentlemen* makes laughable the failures of the dominant high-low culture paradigm by reminding us that the high culture of this century was the pop culture of the last; it is no coincidence that the *League of Extraordinary Gentlemen* points toward the future and begins publication in the summer of 1999. It refutes what Raymond Chandler cites as "that form of snobbery which can accept the Literature of Entertainment in the Past, but only the Literature of Enlightenment in the Present."[214]

---

[212] Ibid., #6, inside cover.
[213] Ibid., #2.
[214] Chandler, *Trouble,* ix.

Tom Strong

Tom Strong has all the hallmarks of a classic superhero book from a bygone era: a clean, pure, easygoing hero who always wins, is loved by his city, never plays dirty, and always fights in the sunlight. Its retro feel recalls a simpler time when superhero stories were easier to tell, before the superhero became engaged with politics, sexual dysfunction, and extreme levels of violence and darkness. To paraphrase an exchange in *Tom Strong* (about a villain's clichéd "flooding room" trap): "[I]t's not crude, it's classic."[215] Beneath the book's sunny atmosphere, however, Moore pulls the wool over the eyes of comic book fans making popular a series that is perhaps more like its predecessors than even its fans might realize. *Tom Strong* is the *Starship Troopers* of the comic book world, and anyone that has seen Paul Verhoeven's masterpiece film will recognize the connection immediately. *Tom Strong* brings back the days when superheroes were simpler, and when no one noticed the questionable politics to which they unwittingly assented.

The reader is immediately introduced to young, wide-eyed Timmy Turbo of Millennium City. He has just received his Strongmen of America Introduction Pack ($9.99) that includes a badge, a certificate, and a book on how Tom Strong got started (which, framing story aside, is *Tom Strong* #1). "Holy Socks," cries the boy, as he heads off to school on the bus to Laundry Street Station, signifiers that suggest the kind of cleaning up Tom Strong intends to do to the dirty history of comics. The city itself is streamlined and clean, and Timmy is so innocent that his mother's head always remains off panel, à la the adult characters in *Peanuts*. The reader is invited to follow and identify with this opening character, the wide-eyed child.

Tom Strong's history is important to note as we gather together his political significance: his father cares more about his equipment than the life of a sailor, makes a steam-powered robot programmed with his own voice, and compliments his wife by saying, "You are quite the perfect match for me, combining as you do intelligence with a physique that is

---

[215] Alan Moore, Chris Sprouse, et al., *Tom Strong* (La Jolla, CA: America's Best Comics, 1999–present), #6.

. . . delightful."[216] Tom himself is his father's "experiment" raised "by pure reason, away from society's influence."[217] More specifically, he is raised in a chamber with increased gravity to enhance his strength (cf. the source of Superman's powers). His parents never touch him because they can only enter the chamber wearing protective suits. Tom Strong is styled classically: dead parents (like both Batman and Superman), a villain recalling Lex Luthor ("This town belongs to Paul Saveen!"), a faithful servant like Alfred, and a clean, carefree attitude. There is something unsettling in his upbringing, however, that readers might not notice were it not born out in the narrative as a whole.

The closing pages of the first issue set the project in motion: the reader, along with Timmy Turbo, is directly addressed by the comic in a full-page "poster shot" of Tom Strong and company. "There! Now instead of fighting, let's welcome our newest member to the Strongmen of America, and to the biggest, greatest family on Earth! And don't forget you can read about us every month here in Tom Strong Magazine!"[218] Timmy Turbo, and perhaps the reader as well, is assigned membership number 2059 and addressed as such by Tom Strong himself. "Aztec Nights" (Tom Strong 3) exposes the comic book's true intention through one of the classic superhero tropes: the villain as mirror. A race of technologically advanced imperialistic Aztec warriors invade our world from an alternate Earth, one where the Aztecs were waiting for Cortés with machine guns. The relation between these colonizers and Tom Strong, whose adopted island homeland now has inhabitants that wear Nike T-shirts and Walkmans, is made clear immediately. As Tom Strong describes the Aztec fortress he has entered:

> Intellectually, a high degree of technological advancement is in evidence. Together with the strong aesthetic sensibility displayed, this indicates extreme and purposeful intelligence. Considered psychologically and socially, I'd be surprised if we weren't looking at some form of grandiose, inflated fascism. Emotionally . . . cold. Horrible. No love. In some ways it reminds me of the high-gravity playroom I was raised in.[219]

---

[216] Ibid., #1 (my ellipsis).

[217] Ibid.

[218] Ibid.

[219] Ibid., #3 (Moore's ellipsis).

The connection to the reader is about to be made. Toying with an image of an eagle grasping lightning bolts over alternate earths, the Aztec leader informs Tom, "[Y]ours is the two-thousand and fifty-eighth Earth to be annexed in our glorious lateral expansion."[220] If Timmy Turbo, who read *Tom Strong* #1 along with the reader, is the 2,059th member of the Strongmen of America, then prior to the first issue, Tom Strong had "laterally expanded" to the exact same number as the Aztec imperialists. Returning to the second issue, "Return of the Modular Man" (*Tom Strong* 2), the reader is now apt to see the armbands that Tom Strong's followers wear, with his inverted triangle logo, in a more sinister light. Contrary to the usual superhero narrative, which would involve Tom Strong defeating this fascist menace and freeing the 2,058 worlds under its control, Tom strikes a deal: he will free the intelligent computer running the imperialism, allowing it to retain control of the alternate earths in exchange for letting this one go. "Aztec Nights" is the meeting of two fascists who walk away with respect for one another.

The next plot arc (*Tom Strong* 4–7) brings the politics inherent in *Tom Strong* to a peak. The story, coherent with *Tom Strong*'s classic retro feel, appears to be a superhero story of the early post–World War II type: Tom Strong versus the Swastika Girls!

> He wanted her for war crimes, but she wanted him for love! It's hot as HELL, buddy, but you'll shiver at the touch of this Teutonic torture-goddess and her Luftwaffe of Lust! You'll never forget the hot lead KISS of the SWASTIKA GIRLS![221]

We are immediately given a glimpse of Tom Strong's fortress—The Stronghold—a structure Albert Speer would admire, complete with a golden statue of Tom Strong posing hands on hips, overlooking his city. As with the Aztecs, the connection between Strong and Ingrid Weiss, Nazi Superwoman, is made immediately: they were both raised in similar conditions, and are both in peak physical and intellectual condition. When it is finally revealed that Paul Saveen is behind this plot to break Tom Strong, his new vision of the city as a Nazi paradise looks exactly

---

[220] Ibid.
[221] Ibid., #4, cover.

the same as the Millennium City Tom Strong calls home, with Tom's symbol replaced by a swastika.

Ultimately, both Tom and his nemesis are seen as creatures desperately clinging to the past. Saveen admits his connection to Weiss: "Sentiment's another thing I have in common with Fraulein Weiss. Nazis absolutely wallow in it, you know."[222] Looking through a kind of museum dedicated to their past encounters, Tom notes, "I see you're even nostalgic about your old hardware."[223] Tom's wife notes that "villains are creatures of habit."[224] Tom mocks Weiss:

> Manifest destiny. "Tomorrow belongs to me." All that fascist drivel. Weiss, answer me something. . . . If you Nazis are so certain of the future, why do you cling to the past so desperately? You're obsessed with memorabilia.[225]

Tom Strong and his enemies are given a glimpse into the future through a piece of memorabilia, a time viewer. We learn from this glimpse of the future that it is Tom Strong—who always finds everything vaguely familiar, and approaches fantastic menaces with an air of having seen it all before—who clings to the past. In 2050, the son of one of his companions, King Solomon, speaks like a 1960s hippy, and Tom comes to fight his more technologically advanced opponent in his one-man backpack helicopter, only to be mocked: "Do you know how ridiculous you are? The city beneath us is a boiling mass of constantly changing nano-structures, and yet you turn up in an engine driven heli-pack!" Tom answers, "I'll stick with what I know."[226] Like his enemy, he is "even nostalgic about his old hardware." He is later described as a fossil, clinging to the optimism of the last century. Apparently, all fascists wallow in nostalgia, a fact that explains the book's retro texture.

In *Tom Strong,* Alan Moore plays with the traditional identification of the reader with the hero, exposing the degree to which superhero narratives boil down to a choice among various modes of fascism whose

---

[222] Ibid., #6.
[223] Ibid.
[224] Ibid., #7.
[225] Ibid. (Moore's ellipsis).
[226] Ibid.

biggest differences are the respective logo designs of their dictators. (Note the similarities between Tom Strong's crew and Weiss's: it is the difference between armband symbols.) This is why Tom always confronts rivals who would remake reality in their own singular image: the Modular Man, Imperialist Aztecs, the Swastika Girls, the Pangaean, and an other-worldly fascist school system.[227] By involving readers directly, charming them into the world of Tom Strong and his followers, inviting them to share his perspective, Moore shows how easy it is to simply follow along with our heroes. It is amazing how natural it seems, in context, that Tom Strong refers to his Strongmen of America by number rather than name. Something so obviously harsh should immediately strike the reader, but instead is simply the natural attitude of this benevolent, loving dictator. The superhero narrative has always flirted with fascism, but only Moore would build a full-fledged sexual relationship between Weiss and Strong (albeit against his will) that goes as far as bearing offspring in fascist dress. The accomplishment of *Tom Strong* is that it provides a background for a huge amount of fascist propaganda while still making it, and its title hero, still seem appealing. Only in *Tom Strong* could lines like "I was looking into her eyes when her spirit shattered. She will not be back" or "I have plans for you . . . tests to see what [you're] made of,"[228] lines usually reserved for villains, be delivered by the heroes and still have those heroes appear positive, likeable, and pure. The atmosphere is built to support them as normal, but quoted out of context they stand out clearly as "bad guy" lines. Tom Strong has been praised for reviving dark and depressing comic books with a positive, fresh hero. The real trick, however, is this: Moore has returned us to the early days of the superhero narrative by reminding even the most skeptical and intelligent reader how primed she is for fascist propaganda. The so-called darkness or optimism of the superhero narrative is only a surface phenomenon concealing politics like those of Tom Strong.

Another aspect of *Tom Strong,* unique in the ABC line thus far, is of a piece with its politics. Tom Strong acknowledges, and indeed builds, contradictory continuity. This is an aspect of comic book literature that this book has returned to again and again, but its occurrence here is different enough to merit closer examination. It begins with a look at

---

[227] Ibid., #8.

[228] Ibid., #7 (my ellipsis).

"An Untold Tale of Tom Strong."[229] This set piece claims to be a reproduction of an issue from an earlier decade of *Tom Strong,* even though the comic book was not launched until 1999. It is one of many pseudo-histories of Tom Strong written and drawn to be stylistically in accord with its proposed period of writing: heroes smoking cigarettes, excessive use of thought bubbles, and closing narration like "Is Saveen truly finished? Find out . . . in future issues of—Tom Strong Magazine!!!"[230] In this particular episode, Tom learns that Saveen has discovered Phlogisten, the theoretical liquid form of heat. "There's no proof that such a substance even exists!" cries Tom Strong. Saveen answers, "Ah. Then you have nothing to fear, and nothing shall pour from that spigot above you save pure scientific conjecture."[231] Tom escapes the "liquid heat" and lives to fight another day. Back in the regular story, for which the Phlogisten "reprint" served as a flashback, the reader is privy to this conversation: Tom says, "Incidentally, you know science eventually proved Phlogisten didn't exist?" to which Saveen replies, "Mmm. Isn't that odd? And yet we both know it existed back then. How can that be, I wonder? I've been meaning to write a paper on it, but I never have time."[232] Moore, given the chance to write a new comic book character free of the continuity difficulties that plague established superheroes, artificially creates the contradictory history within his own book. Lacan invites us to consider this more closely: "Discontinuity, then, is the essential form in which the unconscious first appears to us as a phenomenon—discontinuity, in which something is manifested as a vacillation."[233] It is thus at the points of discontinuity that we should pay the closest attention.

It may seem strange that *Tom Strong* is intentionally established upon this shaky foundation, but turning to Moore's earlier work *Miracleman,* the reader can get a clue as to why. Miracleman discovers a tape detailing his true history, not as sunny as he had believed: his history of superhero adventures is an artificial construct designed by his owners to keep him under their control.

---

[229] Ibid., #6.
[230] Ibid.
[231] Ibid.
[232] Ibid.
[233] Jacques Lacan, *Seminar 11: The Four Fundamental Concepts of Psychoanalysis,* ed. Jacques-Alain Miller, trans. Alan Sheridan (New York: Norton, 1978), 25.

[In] order to fully control the thought processes and motivations of these potentially catastrophic creatures, an entirely artificial reality set is constructed. The reality is then fed directly into their unconscious minds while they lay under the effects of powerful sedatives. . . . Some of the fantasies we project contain deliberate contradictions, some contain events to stretch the subject's credibilities to the fullest. We are attempting to determine how our artificial belief-system will endure under stress.[234]

For an example of stretching credibility, the reader need look no further than "Flip Attitude" (*Tom Strong* 9), where Strong's daughter fights Kid Tilt, a villain with magic boots who can "flip" the terrain ninety degrees, causing predicable effects (e.g., cars on the street now "fall" into the faces of buildings on which the characters can now run). If Kid Tilt used her powers again, everything would presumably fall into the sky, and people in buildings would slam into their ceilings. It is immediately obvious to the reader that this doesn't make any sense at all: what exactly is it that she is "tilting"? In the aftermath of the battle, after all has returned to normal, the following exchange takes place between King Solomon and Tesla Strong:

SOLOMON: But however did she tilt it in the first place? I mean, logically, you'd have to tilt the entire bally planet!
TESLA: Magic boots.
SOLOMON: No, but realistically it couldn't be done without . . .
TESLA: Solomon, I said they were magic! Now just drop it, okay?[235]

The relation of the *Miracleman* passage quoted above to *Tom Strong* is clear and powerful. Contradictory history (such as the mutually exclusive existence and nonexistence of Phlogisten) or situations that test credibility (such as Kid Tilt's powers) are intended to test how much a reader, or Strongmen of America member, can swallow. The use of contradictory continuity in *Miracleman* and *Tom Strong* is unlike its appearance in

---

[234] Alan Moore et al., *Miracleman* (Guerneville, CA: Eclipse Comics, 1982), #3 (my ellipsis).
[235] Moore, *Tom Strong,* #9. The fact that this episode is revealed to be a fabrication of Tesla's does not invalidate the point: it is clear that "King Tilt" is a member of Tom's Rogues Gallery, and Tom Strong has encountered his magic boots before.

The Killing Joke. Here the history is deliberately constructed to not fit together. The difference between *Miracleman* and *Tom Strong* is that in the former, the false memories are intended for an outside party to control the hero, whereas in the latter, the contradiction is intended to be believed by the reader, a tacit member of the Strongmen of America. The fact that the reader can be made to believe that Phlogisten both exits and does not exist cannot be far from the kind of thinking that forces a person to accept that two and two equal five: the reader has been compromised by *Tom Strong* in the same way Winston Smith is broken by O'Brien and made to love Big Brother in *1984*. As Richard Rorty comments on Orwell's novel:

> The *only* point in making Winston believe that two and two equals five is to break him. Getting somebody to deny a belief for no reason is a first step toward making her incapable of having a self because she becomes incapable of weaving a coherent web of belief and desire. It makes her irrational, in quite a precise sense: She is unable to give a reason for her belief that fits together with her other beliefs. She becomes irrational not in the sense that she has lost contact with reality but in the sense that she can no longer rationalize—no longer justify herself to herself.
>
> Making Winston briefly believe that two plus two equals five serves the same "breaking" function as making him briefly desire that the rats chew through Julia's face rather than his own.[236]

Superhero literature already primes its avid readers to accept these kinds of contradictions and impossible situations because they have already assented to the contradictory continuity of many given superheroes. Moore aligns this with the reactionary politics of the superhero, suggesting the reader is completely compromised from the beginning. If They can make you believe in Kid Tilt's powers or the simultaneous existence and nonexistence of Phlogisten, then They have you completely under their control. If you are a reader of superhero narratives, then you have

---

[236] Richard Rorty, *Contingency, Irony, Solidarity* (Cambridge: Cambridge University Press, 1989), 178.

probably already assented to such nonsense. Welcome to the Strongmen of America: the Superheroes love you.

Promethea

Promethea may be immediately set against the only (token?) female member of her city's other "science hero" team, The Five Swell Guys. Roger, as she is called, wears a suit and sports super strength; at one point it is revealed that she was once a he.[237] She is literally a man in a woman's body. *Promethea* is an attempt to write a genuinely feminine superhero narrative, reversing a trend in superhero literature that sees a female hero as a male character, a male mentality, drawn with a stereo-typed female body. Women superheroes traditionally are, or were, sim-ply objects of sexual voyeurism, more pinup girls in capes than genuine characters. Jeffery A. Brown describes the women of Image Comics as "uniformly illustrated as impossibly sexy, silicone injected, and scantily clad babes wielding phallically obvious swords."[238] He further comments:

> [S]uperhero comics are one of our culture's clearest illustrations of hypermasculinity and male duality premised on the fear of the unmasculine other. Since the genre's inception with the launch of Superman in 1938 the main ingredient of the formula has been the dual identity of the hero. While the superhero body represents in vividly graphic detail the muscularity, the confidence, the power that personifies the ideal of phallic mas-culinity, the alter ego—the identity that must be kept a secret—depicts the softness, the powerlessness, the insecurity associated with the feminized man.[239]

This particular vein of America's Best Comics is an attempt to ad-dress this dismal situation and to provide a truly feminine hero. *Pro-methea* is the story of Sophie Bangs, a student writing a term paper on a

---

[237] Alan Moore and J. H. Williams III, *Promethea* (La Jolla, CA: America's Best Comics, 1999–present), #8.
[238] Brown, *Black Superheroes,* 176.
[239] Ibid., 174.

fictional character that appears in eighteenth-century poetry, comic strips, World War I legends, pulp novels, and superhero comic books. What she discovers is that Promethea is an eternal story that can become real, that can be projected onto the real world from the realm of imagination (where all stories live) if someone believes strongly enough. Sophie, of course, becomes the mythical Promethea and, in some ways, the first truly "female" superhero. Even visually *Promethea* is an indictment of traditional women in superhero comic books; she stands as a full-bodied woman against the traditional depiction of female superheroes as huge-breasted figures with slim hips. Promethea is Wonder Woman as Wonder Woman could have become, a powerful heroine in her own right rather than something for young male readers to ogle. And in the methodology of America's Best Comics—a tremendous version of the way Moore's heroes in *Watchmen* reverberate with larger superhero archetypes—*Promethea* encapsulates not only a line of disenfranchised short-lived female superhero comics, but also superhero writers from Margaret Brundage to William Moulton Marston to Grace Gebbie Drayton, all coded into the book in some form or another. (Note the letter, in the back of issue three, from Trina Robbins, author of *Great Women Superheroes.*) Even Mary Shelley, author of "The Modern Prometheus," is not left out of the mix.

Promethea's city is grim and gritty: a dirty city filled with sex shows, angst-filled rock concerts, and celebrity serial killers like Painted Doll ("Over One Million Killed" reads a T-shirt sporting his picture). A mayor with multiple personality disorder (forty-two of them) cannot help but be seen in this study as another example of overdetermination of the superhero narrative. Most interestingly here, however, is the billboards that pepper the city for the popular comic book company Weeping Gorilla. Each advertisement for the apparently depressing comic book series (we are never given a glimpse of the kind of stories Weeping Gorilla actually tells) features an image of a weeping gorilla with a different thought bubble: "I have some unresolved childhood issues . . . ,"[240] "If I only understood what women wanted . . . ,"[241] "That Tamagochi trusted me . . . ,"[242] and "We probably expect too much of George

---

[240] Moore and Williams, *Promethea,* #2.
[241] Ibid., #3. Though not an advertisement, this is clearly meant to be in line with adds for Weeping Gorilla comics.
[242] Ibid., #5.

Lucas . . . ,"[243] to cite from dozens of examples. As discussed above, Moore's *Watchmen* spawned a huge number of pointlessly depressing imitators; what can the images of the Weeping Gorilla comic book company suggest more than the angst-filled clumsy "aping" of *Watchmen's kenosis* embodied in the so-called dark age of superheroes? (*Tomorrow Stories* features a "First American" story based on *A Christmas Carol*: the "spirit of comic books' future" is an ape, and the blasted landscape where he is from—note the blast metaphor of *The Dark Knight Returns* and *Watchmen* in *Kingdom Come*—ends with a vision of the San Diego comics convention as a stand-in for the Statue of Liberty in *The Planet of the Apes*.[244]) That Weeping Gorilla is produced by Apex Productions is a simple statement that this trend has reached its peak. The silver age is over, and it ends here: Moore's "house of magic" is built over the apex of the late silver age, as the final page of *Promethea* 1 suggests. To some degree, the optimistic style of America's Best Comics is intended as a kind of apology for *Watchmen* and its negative effects, and *Promethea* specifically emphasizes the split by casting its beautiful, powerful, optimistic heroine in what appears to be a futuristic version of New York circa 1985.[245] Promethea stands as a beacon of imagination and light (which, of course, she literally is) at the dead center of the most uninspired and depressing period in comic book history: the landscape blasted by *The Dark Knight Returns* and *Watchmen*. *Promethea* is a savior, not only of her world but also of the dark trends in the superhero narrative itself.

One aspect of this role is that *Promethea* is also the site, in America's Best Comics, for radical stylistic experimentation and innovative storytelling techniques. "Rocks and Hard Places" (*Promethea* 7), for example, takes the "photorealism" of Alex Ross to another level by incorporating actual photographic images. This device communicates that the "material reality" is approaching the Immateria, the realm of imagination, whose morphing Daliesque landscape stands as yet another image of the convoluted fantasy space that supports the superhero narrative. "Under

---

[243] Ibid., #7.

[244] Alan Moore et al., *Tomorrow Stories* (La Jolla, CA: America's Best Comics, 1999–present), #5.

[245] It should be noted that, although the city appears futuristic, it is in keeping with Alan Moore's beliefs about how to keep superhero comics "realistic." The understanding is that a world populated by decades' worth of science heroes would be affected by their presence and inventions and develop accordingly.

Attack" (*Promethea* 11) is written like a film, complete with a cover that looks like a film poster, opening credits, and "widescreen" rectangular frames intended to be read with the spine of the book horizontal. "Mercury Rising" (*Promethea* 15) features a sequence where Promethea and a guide walk on a mobius strip: the page is designed to be rotated by the reader following their walk, with parts printed upside down. *Promethea* is also the site of the innovative art of J. H. Williams III, who brings a particularly intriguing style to *Promethea*'s visuals by conceiving of the page layout, the page spread, and even whole issues as a single organic whole, rather than discrete parts. Recent issues of *Promethea* (12 and 14) might have been published as a continuous scroll effectively presenting twenty-two pages as one large piece of tapestry with panels read from left to right.

Promethea is perhaps too young to fully comment upon, but I hope these remarks will give a hint as to how the book might be appreciated within the space of Moore's work. Its omission would not allow the reader to fully appreciate the multiple perspective quality that ABC achieves as the revisionary superhero company.[246]

Top Ten

Top Ten is another instance of how far realism can go in a superhero narrative, telling an *NYPD Blue*–style ensemble drama about the super-

---

[246] Almost fully outside the scope of the present book, but worth mentioning, and worth understanding, is the role of mysticism in *Promethea* and such mystical systems of understanding as the Kabbalah. Moore seems to have created in *Promethea* a story whose main purpose is to educate readers about the various mystical systems and related theories of the universe. Recent issues have left behind any sense of plot or narrative in favor of various expositions of mystical theory, including a whole issue in which Promethea learns the meaning behind each of the major tarot cards (*Promethea* 12). The connection of the superhero to this realm is little more than one of the many archetypes that Moore describes as interlocking into various systems of mysticism and mystical archetypes. While the argument could be made that in the America's Best Comics lineup *Promethea* acts as the encyclopedic and exhaustive reservoir of all those interpretations that fall under the Jung–Campbell–Lévi-Strauss triad, a tedious interpretive structure that future superhero narratives need to leave behind to move forward into something like Morrison's *Marvel Boy,* such a reductive statement seems to do *Promethea* an injustice.

powered police force in a city populated entirely with superheroes. The prose piece at the end of the first issue establishes the landscape clearly:

> Built shortly after World War II, Neopolis was first conceived as an attempt to circumvent the social problems posed by an alarmingly expanded population of science-heroes, heroines, and villains that seemingly ballooned into existence during the pre-ceding decade. . . .
>
> Given that most former science-types tended to have problems adjusting to an ordinary existence and often were perceived as a disruptive influence by their conventionally human neighbors, the creation of a city in which all the forms of costumed life could live amongst each other in productive coexistence seemed an elegant solution.[247]

Top Ten responds to superhero trends in realism and continuity and incorporates the metatextual knowledge of the superhero "population" booms that occurred after World War II, in the early 1960s and 1980s. Everyone in Neopolis was once some kind of superhero and still has both a superhero name and alter ego in his or her day-to-day life. Even the hot dog vendor on the street wears a cape and cooks hot dogs with heat beams from his eyes, and a local clothing store is called the Phone Booth. Beyond the opening premise, everything that happens (considering the city) is ordinary street crime.

Though all of the comics in the ABC lineup are a resting place for a huge number of golden and silver age tributaries, *Top Ten* is the most emblematic of this role. With flat allusions to hundreds of comic books littered everywhere, its closest literary model would be Samuel Beckett's *Happy Days,* with its litter box of references to fragments of Shakespeare, Milton, Keats, and Browning. Within its tradition, *Top Ten* is an erratic but encyclopedic collection of allusions to various aspects of superhero tradition brought to the most quotidian level. "I have a giant-size man thing"[248] (an allusion to Marvel's enigmatic monster, Man-Thing) and "Who Watches the Simpsons"[249] read two examples of graffiti. There

---

[247] Alan Moore, Gene Ha, and Zander Cannon, *Top Ten* (La Jolla, CA: America's Best Comics, 1999–present), #1, prose.

[248] Ibid., #1.

[249] Ibid., #2.

are superhero prostitutes (Immune Girl; Annette "Neural 'Nette" Du-valle, whose powers affect pain or pleasure centers of the brain; M'rrgla "Vigilante from Venus" Qualts: alien porno queen/prostitute/serial killer) and a form of superhero AIDS ("S.T.O.R.M.S. is what happens when you have a whole city of genetically unstable or alien individuals interacting sexually with each other").[250] Local cop Duane "Dust Devil" Bodine finds his mother's apartment (she has lie-detecting powers) in-fested with superpowered rodents, complete with capes. He has to hire Ex-verminator (whose van advertises that he kills "Radioactive Spiders" [Spider-Man's origin] and "Career Defining Bats" [Batman's]), who brings in superpowered cats (in capes as well). Both of these examples, as well as being wonderfully clever and imaginative, also resonate with Wertham's objections already quoted above:

> What is the social meaning of these supermen, superwomen, superlovers, superboys, supergirls, super-ducks, super-mice, super-magicians, super-safe crackers? How did Nietzsche get into the nursery? . . . Superheroes undermine respect for the law and hardworking decent citizens.[251]

Wertham's rhetorical exaggerations—superlovers and supermice—become part of the literal landscape of *Top Ten*. The important thing to note is that these aspects are not present in the narrative as a spoof or parody subplot but a real, if strange, part of a serious narrative. The supermice plot becomes a full-scale supermice versus supercat crossover. As the Ex-verminator explains:

> See, Ultramice, they behave sorta like regular science guys. Get enough science animals together, it's a big event. Next thing, it escalates. You get a whole secret crisis-war crossover thing going. . . . Inevitably cosmic powers get involved. You know how it is. It's difficult keeping up with the cross continuity, but I think Cosmouse just gave the Saturnian Scraphunter his Ultimate Pac-ifier to use against Galactapuss. . . .[252]

---

[250] Ibid., #7.
[251] Wertham, *Seduction*, 15.
[252] Moore et al., *Top Ten*, #9 (Moore's ellipses).

Ex-verminator's speech exemplifies *Top Ten*'s rich allusion-laden prose and rhetorical strategy. In Neopolis, a mouse infestation is imbued with references to no less than three major superhero epics: Marvel's *Secret Wars*, DC's *Crisis on Infinite Earths*, and the most famous adventure of Marvel's Fantastic Four, the battle with Galactus (*Fantastic Four* 48–50).

Top Ten emphasizes the way all of these incredibly strange elements of any superhero narrative have become very normal and banal to the average reader, just part of the landscape. *Top Ten* communicates the feeling of a veteran comic book fan walking into a comic book store: hundreds of references to fantastic ideas and weird concepts that have lost the newness that made them great. In the Marvel universe, Thor is a superhero: the gods of Asgaard can walk among mortals because their realm is connected to ours. In Neopolis, the gods separate themselves from mortals by frequenting a bar that serves only deities. Time travel, space travel, and parallel universe hopping, once fantastic ideas, have become so commonplace in both the superhero narrative and science fiction as a whole that the "Grand Central Station" of Neopolis is filled with bored references to these kinds of travelers: the alternate-universe X-Men (from "The Age of Apocalypse"), Captain Kirk and Spock, the Mirror Master (a *Flash* villain), the cast of *Lost in Space,* the cast of *Stargate: The Television Series.* Underneath a poster that reads "Vacation on Infinite Earths," a rider is instructed to check cloths for insects before boarding a teleport beam, an allusion to the monster produced in *The Fly* by an accident of this sort.[253] All of these fantastic products of science fiction and the superhero narrative are just part of its landscape now, just part of an *NYPD Blue*– or *Homicide*-style story. The whole mess of superhero overdetermination appears here: its quotidian status is ABC's way of dealing with the huge amount of superhero tradition continuously trying to make itself felt.

Top Ten, like *Promethea,* is still in its formative days, but an analysis of America's Best Comics would not be complete without at least sketching out its relation to other superhero narratives. In the issues to come, it will be a reservoir of very well written and engaging, but pedestrian, superhero literature.

---

[253] Ibid., #8.

Tomorrow Stories

Tomorrow Stories uses an early comic book format—the anthology book—which features five separate narratives, each of which explores an aspect of the early days of comic books. Each short forces the reader to confront, perhaps, some less than noble concepts that were on the ground floor when the superhero emerged. Because the anthology book was the original home of characters like Superman (*Action Comics*) and Batman (*Detective Comics*), it is also an especially useful frame in exploring how superheroes emerged from other forms of literature and art.

Tomorrow Stories' first short is "Jack B. Quick." Jack is a middle-school-age boy genius living on a farm and performing various outlandish science experiments. His use of quasi-scientific theory as an explanation for various fantastic effects exposes the shaky relation between the science hero and science. As Richard Reynolds notes:

> Scientific concepts and terms are introduced freely into [the superhero narrative] and used to create atmosphere and add background detail to artwork—but the science itself is at most only superficially plausible, often less so, and the prevailing mood is mystical rather than rational.[254]

Jack makes cats fly by buttering their backs, combining "two well-known scientific principles! Firstly, cats always land on their feet. Secondly, toast lands buttered side down."[255] He removes all light from his hometown by arresting photons for traveling above the local speed limit,[256] and creates a mini-sun with a homemade "quantum vacuum cleaner" because "Einstein suggests that a sun can expand from a point in a quantum vacuum."[257] The theories are, of course, utterly ridiculous but hardly more so than the fact that the Flash received his power to travel at speeds close to light from chemicals being spilled on him, that Peter Parker got superstrength, agility, the ability to sense danger before it happens, and the power to stick to walls from the bite of a spider

---

[254] Reynolds, *Mythology,* 16.
[255] Moore et al., *Tomorrow Stories, #*3.
[256] Ibid., *#*2.
[257] Ibid., *#*1.

exposed to radioactive material, or that the Incredible Hulk was created when Bruce Banner was caught at ground zero during the testing of an experimental "gamma bomb." A reader unfamiliar with superhero comic books would quickly tire of "Jack B. Quick's" stupidity; its success is that it leaves those in debt to superhero literature unable to scoff at its nonsense science, science they have already unwittingly accepted in other contexts.

"The First American" highlights the superhero narrative's reliance on reactionary political discourse in the same way "Jack B. Quick" highlights its foundation on nonsensical science. In "The 20th Century: My Struggle" (*Tomorrow Stories* 7), we see the skewed impressions of how the arrogant First American, a Captain America figure, affected the course of history. In "The Bitter Crumbs of Defeat!?!" (*Tomorrow Stories* 4), the reader sees our patriotic hero exposed as an immoral degenerate sellout, and later (*Tomorrow Stories* 6) as a shallow sex fiend. Each one of these incidents is saturated with his patriotic rhetoric and moral "lessons." In "The Curse of the Reverse" (*Tomorrow Stories* 5), a time-altering villain regresses the First American (along with his sidekick, U.S. Angel) decade by decade, revealing how little sense a Captain America figure can make given America's changing stance over the years, and how each decade defines the politics he spouts. "Omigosh!" cries "F.A." "Comic books past were completely lame! I never realized before!"[258] "The First American" points out the large part political rhetoric plays in the foundation of the superhero, the way it shifts to reflect the reactionary concerns in various periods in history, and casts Captain America as a buffoon. This too, says Moore, stands at the origin of the superhero.

"Cobweb" highlights another rather embarrassing quality that defined the emergence of the superhero: sexual voyeurism. We uncover that each one of Cobweb's adventures, classy as many appear, is really just an excuse to hint at a forbidden level of sexuality. Her costume—made of a kind of mauve gauze—is clearly intended to reveal more than it covers, and Cobweb always seems to find herself in positions that reveal the top of her stockings and garter belt. In one episode, Cobweb gives mouth-to-mouth resuscitation to a young woman who has fallen, and the rather purple dime-store novel prose reveals the less than subtle sexual connotation: "Cobweb crushed the hot, encarmined fruits of her

---

[258] Ibid., #5.

lips against those of the fugitive, forcing the air back into the stilled lungs until once more Eurydice's breast swelled and dropped with life's slow tidal rhythm."[259] The status of Cobweb's relationship with her scantily clad "female assistant," from whom Cobweb is once seen receiving a nude massage,[260] is kept tantalizingly ambiguous. Alan Moore's published notes for *Glory* (a character intended to be a very close reworking of Wonder Woman) are worth quoting in this context:

> [M]y central idea is to prime the story with plenty of open spaces for the readers' filthy, disgusting thirteen year old minds to inhabit . . . which is only natural . . . without doing anything that is anything other than entirely innocent and in keeping with classic comic tradition. I think the word for our best approach is "disingenuous." [. . .]
>
> [. . .] As an example, I don't think we should ever do anything to state that the Isle of Thule [the all female society from which Glory comes, like Wonder Woman's Paradise Isle] is a lesbian Pornotopia, but I don't think we should state that it isn't, either.[261]

As in *Glory,* Moore has a conscious intention to make the reader accountable for voyeurism simply by reading the book's stories, and also plays with the fact that in a genre of literature involving strikingly unrealistic women running around in spandex, sexual voyeurism needs to be acknowledged as another rather embarrassing part of its origin. In another story, "*La Toile dans le Chateau des Larmes*" ("Cobweb in the Castle of Tears," *Tomorrow Stories* 5), he identifies as a comic book origin the even earlier French collage novels, of which this story claims to be a reprinting. Once again, the sexuality at the heart of early comic books is emphasized: the "collage" is composed of censored shots of early pornography.

"Splash Brannigan" toys with the relation of comic book literature to "higher" forms of art, specifically painting. "Splash Brannigan" tells the adventures of a creature made of "four-dimensional ink" created by

---

[259] Ibid., #3.

[260] Ibid., #6

[261] *Alan Moore's Awesome Universe Handbook,* vol. 1, #1 (Los Angeles: Awesome Entertainment, 1999) (bracketed ellipses mine).

a disgruntled, insane, comic book professional forced to work in inhumane conditions. The comic book industry is presented as pure uninspired drudgery. ("Sarcastic Thug" is one of the works published in Brannigan's fictional world by Kaput Comics; a plot summary reads "pages 8–19: Guys fight in space. Pages 20–24: Everything works out okay.")[262] "Splash Brannigan" sets itself against "high art" when Splash thwarts a "snobbery robbery" by the criminals Mom and Pop Art (the farmer and wife from *American Gothic*). The reader is left to ponder the relation, if any, between the silly adventures of this character and the history of art. The fact that his second adventure leaves Brannigan making "high art" (the snobs at the gallery admire the inkblots he splatters when he moves) playfully rides the fence on whether a connection between comic books and high art should be made.

"Greyshirt" looks at the origin of comic books from the status of the early dime-store detective novels, from which the superhero emerged (the early masked detective/crime fighter figure). "Greyshirt," whose title character is reminiscent of the Shadow or Will Eisner's Spirit,[263] tells pulp-style stories, emphasizing that the superhero and the detective were once one, making the bridge between the two genres, now lost, a little clearer. More importantly, however, is that, unlike every other work in *Tomorrow Stories,* "Greyshirt" is not a parody, does not fit the pattern of playfully deriding ground-floor aspects of comic book tradition: quasi-science, bad politics, sexual voyeurism, or comic book's (recent) claim to the status of high art. "Greyshirt," then, earns its place as the gold in an otherwise "trashy" anthology comic book. The fact that Greyshirt is the only character in the book that is at all "cool" reminds the reader of Batman's context in *Detective Comics* or Superman's in *Action Comics*: the fact that he has now been given his own title in America's Best Comics "Greyshirt" spin-off *Indigo Sunset* suggests Superman's and Batman's graduation into their own titles. Are readers privy, in this way, to a character that will endure? "Greyshirt" is the readers' chance to spot that new Batman or Superman, before the character reaches the status that these other characters have achieved.

---

[262] Moore et al., *Tomorrow Stories,* #6.

[263] It should be noted that Alan Moore and Dave Gibbons composed the first issue of *Will Eisner's The Spirit: The New Adventures* and that it is an extremely close stylistic match for Moore's "Greyshirt," which premiered only two years later. Alan Moore and Dave Gibbons, *Will Eisner's The Spirit: The New Adventures* (Northampton, MA: Kitchen Sink Press, 1997), #1.

4

Pumping Up the Volume

THE REVISIONARY SUPERHERO
NARRATIVE APPROACHES THE NEW AGE

And it takes a very open mind indeed to look beyond
the unnecessarily gaudy covers, trashy titles and barely
acceptable advertisements and recognize the authentic power of a kind of writing that, even at its most
mannered and artificial, made most of the fiction of
the time taste like a cup of luke-warm consommé at
a spinsterish tearoom.

> —Raymond Chandler, Introduction to *Trouble*
> *Is My Business*

Beside it everything else seems pale and stale and repetitive. Be honest. . . . At a stroke The Authority has
endowed the tired superhero archetypes with vigorous new meaning pumping up the volume until noses
bleed and bass patterns register deep on the Richter
scale in Norway.

> —Grant Morrison, Introduction to *The Authority*

Grant Morrison's *Justice League of America* and Warren Ellis's *Authority* hedge away from the realism of the works we have looked at and extend themselves into the realm of operatic storytelling. These works focus on coming to terms with the huge degree of power inherent in the superhero narrative, and access this power to overcome influence, achieving the sheer momentum toward an authentic break from the silver age. Harold Bloom anchors us into the next phase of the revisionary superhero narrative when he writes:

Conceptually the central problem for the latecomer necessarily is *repetition,* for repetition dialectically raised to re-creation is the ephebe's road of excess, leading away from the horror of finding himself to be only a copy or a replica.[264]

Morrison is already aware of the status of repetition inherent in the storytelling codes of his genre:

The way I look at it, comic book superhero stories are pretty simple. There's one guy who's got one set of powers and he's got to fight another guy who's got another set of powers, or else he's got to deal with a natural disaster or something. But instead of seeing that as a limitation, I looked at it as if you're a blues musician and you've just got three chords: C, G and D. That's it. But if you add two minor chords you've got every Beatles song. So you go in there and you start to really improvise, add in those minor chords. If, say, Superman has got to come in and this baddie beats him up a bit, then Superman rallies and comes back, then what I have to do is disguise that enough so the readers don't realize they've been reading the same story all their life. That's where the creativity comes in.[265]

Morrison knows that his stories are repetitions of others and, needless to say, repetitions of themselves, but will raise (or perhaps raze) repetition by a "road of excess" like none other. The creativity is in raising/razing the repetition, raising/razing the influence he is bound in debt to repeat, making his vision clear as the most glorious repetition possible—the repetition that reduces the predecessors to so much ash. What Morrison will accomplish in his rhetoric, Ellis will achieve as the very terms of his story. They will achieve the escape velocity necessary to propel the superhero narrative out of the silver age and into something altogether new and strange. The *WildC.A.T.s/Aliens* crossover, one of the most thoroughly perverse comic books ever produced, will eventually vanish, leaving as its trace the twisted origin of the new age.

---

[264] Bloom, *Anxiety,* 80 (Bloom's emphasis).

[265] Grant Morrison, interview in *Writers on Comics Scriptwriting,* ed. Mark Salisbury (London: Titan Books, 1999), 222.

Grant Morrison's *Justice League of America* and the Dialectic of the Sublime

Like most of Grant Morrison's work, the *Justice League of America* (or *JLA*) presents the reader with a dizzying array of metaphysical realms and dimensions, any one of which might determine the metaphysics of a given fantasy continuity. Morrison exploits comic books' contradictory sixty-year buildup of, and reliance upon, a myriad of metaphysical realms, and brings them all to bear upon a single text, a single site, in a process I am going to call the dialectic of the sublime. Morrison's reader, and more importantly his text, is forced into overload by a variety of alpha metaphysics: the vast extremes of outer space, including the realm of Jack Kirby's New Gods and Wonderworld, heaven and hell, the Still Zone (also called the Ghost Zone and Limbo), the Phantom Zone, Olympus (home of the gods of Greek myth), the fifth dimension, Earth 2 (our antimatter counterpart, which is also separated by a "moral membrane," i.e., the bad guys always win there), the vanishing point at the end of time ("the atto-second before the last exhausted electron loses its charge to meaningless, unending entropy"),[266] the magic realm of Shazam, the Quintessence, the realm of the Flash's speed force, the realm of Sandman and the Endless, the land of dreams, and a wide variety of possible and possibly inevitable futures (which, due to time travel, influence the present), ranging from the domination of Darksied over Earth fifteen years in the future to the 853rd century (which would place contemporary comic books around issue #1,000,000). To quote a (surprisingly) relevant passage from Joseph Campbell, "As in a dream, the images range from the sublime to the ridiculous. The mind is not permitted to rest with its normal evaluations, but is continually insulted and shocked out of the assurance that now, at last, it has understood."[267]

To appreciate Morrison's *JLA,* the reader must understand the status of metaphysical ideas in comic books and how they differ from those in other fantasy continuities. The first thing to keep in mind is that in superhero narratives, metaphysical concepts like heaven are more than a language game, or in Richard Rorty's words, a final vocabulary: they are

---

[266] Grant Morrison, Val Semeiks, and Prentis Rollins, *DC: One Million* (New York: DC Comics, 1998), #2, 14.

[267] Campbell, *Hero,* 270.

real. If a superhero story wished to draw upon Plato, then the realm of the Forms would be an actual place where a visitor could meet an indigenous population and find sources of power. These might possibly make sense in a given story, but because a company's superheroes operate in the same continuity, any writer on any title who invented such a realm for a single character was adding to the architecture of a given superhero continuity. After sixty years and hundreds of titles, the DC universe, for example, stops making sense. On a micro-reading, which is expected for any given title, the text functions normally. The *Batman* titles are about fighting realistic crime, and no place is given for heaven and hell as actually existing, even though Batman works with an angel superhero, Zauriel, on the Justice League. In a macro-reading, however—one that looks at the DC universe as a whole—massive contradictions spring up: why would anyone fight crime when faced with at least some kind of external proof in a Christian afterlife where earthly wrongs are righted? The *Justice League of America* stands as Grant Morrison's macro-reading, macro-misreading, of the DC universe. It is a crosshatching and interweaving of the DC universe's mutually exclusive metaphysical determination, the first of its kind.

As a point of reference, I would like to place the *JLA* against two textual foils: the *Star Trek: The Next Generation* television series and Neal Gaiman's *Sandman*. Like most contemporary science fiction, *Star Trek* presents a somewhat believable world where known science is simply more advanced than our own, rather than entirely imaginative. The technology is always explained to the viewer to make it more palatable, more "realistic." The antimatter core that is supposed to power the ship on *Star Trek* is a relatively realistic piece of technology that, on a small scale, has already been achieved: antimatter, made by manipulating a proton to orbit an electron, is kept from touching matter by a magnetic field; when antimatter comes in contact with matter, it releases huge amounts of energy, and the magnetic field simply controls the rate of matter/antimatter contact, the rate of energy being released. This energy powers the ship. Compare this to Morrison's "scientific" explanation of the origin of the Mageddon warhead. Scott Free says:

> Before the birth of this universe there was Urgrund—the world of the Old Gods. We don't know much about our predecessors, but we do know this: they manufactured weapons beyond our

comprehension and tore infinity apart. Unfortunately one of those weapons survived, imprisoned for 15 billion years in a gravity sink on the outer curve of spacetime.[268]

Here is Metron's "explanation":

Here on the ultimate rim of all things [Wonderworld], these legions met to defend the cosmos against the archaeo-technology buried in the primal pit which encircles the universe.[269]

Aztek describes the same creature as "rising up from *beneath* our solar system."[270] None of these descriptions makes any sense individually, and together the situation is even more obscure. Morrison, though drawing as heavily on science as *Star Trek* does, lets the chaotic stand in his text, which is not a weakness, but a strength of his poetics, as we will see.

Sandman is the other text worth viewing as a counterpoint to Morrison's metaphysics in the *JLA*. *Sandman* is a "Dungeons and Dragons"–type text that involves a richly complex but organized fantasy world of gods and monsters. One of the main strategies of this kind of text is to explain disparate phenomena as aspects of a single source (e.g., all the world's religions are merely aspects of the one true God). *Sandman* has as many metaphysical realms as Morrison's *JLA,* but they are organized according to a clear hierarchy. Any one of the realms Morrison draws upon could take the top link of the "chain of being," as it were, but none is allowed primacy. Morrison's *JLA* could never be supplemented with the kind of map one might find in an appendix to Dante, for example.

Morrison allows mutually exclusive metaphysics to stand in relief in the same way a text like *Batman: The Killing Joke* suspends Batman's fictional continuity. On the field of the *JLA* he is able to play one realm off the other, never placing them in any kind of hierarchy, allowing rival superhero metaphysics to engage in dialectic. Each one of these realms is so ridiculously huge and any one on its own would seem to encompass a universe, even in a world of absurdly huge heroes they stand as markers

---

[268] Grant Morrison, Howard Porter, John Dell et al., *Justice League of America* (New York: DC Comics, 1996–2000), #36.

[269] Ibid.

[270] Ibid., #39 (my emphasis).

of the sublime. This insanely massive and conflicting background stands in relation to the heroes as the heroes' contradictory continuity stands to the reader. In accounting for the overdetermination of superhero metaphysics through its grand paradoxical status, Morrison's work on the *JLA* accomplishes a sweeping rhetoric that serves to handle the over-determination of influence as well.

To appreciate how Morrison handles the "realism" of his predecessors, I would like to quote from theorist Slavoj Žižek's essay on David Lynch's *Lost Highway, The Art of the Ridiculous Sublime* (a title very appropriate to Morrison's *JLA,* and invocative of the Campbell quote above):

> The final conclusion to be drawn is that "reality," and the experience of its density, is sustained not by A/ONE fantasy, but by an INCONSISTENT MULTITUDE of fantasies; this multitude generates the effect of the impenetrable destiny that we experience as "reality." . . . Against this "multiple reality" talk, one should thus insist on a different aspect, on the fact that *the fantasmatic support of reality is in itself necessarily multiple and inconsistent.*[271]

Žižek's Lacanian musings, crossing as they do with popular culture, should often be kept in mind when approaching superhero texts. His understanding of *Lost Highway* is clearly relevant to much of the work put forth here on continuity and consistency. In this regard, the superhero narrative is much more literal about its inconsistent, but nonetheless strong, support. The *JLA* is paradoxically more "realistic" than a series with more consistency because, according to Žižek, reality, like the superhero narrative, is supported by an inconsistent base (Miller's "spring right beneath"). Žižek will be our first hint that the *JLA* can stand (amazingly) as a realistic text: one that finds a way to be totally fantastic while participating in a tradition that includes revisionary realism as its poetic inheritance. Morrison's own biographical claims will solidify this paradoxical stance.

Before moving on, however, it should be noted that this is why the members of the JLA have such a casual self-consciousness, as opposed to the tortured self-consciousness of Moore's Joker. Green Lantern

---

[271] Slavoj Žižek, *The Art of the Ridiculous Sublime: On David Lynch's Lost Highway* (Seattle: The Walter Chapin Center for the Humanities, 2000), 41 (Žižek's emphasis).

complains, "What is it with supervillains nowadays? What happened to crazy jewel heists and dumb traps? Now they murder your girlfriend and stuff her in the fridge for kicks."[272] Wonder Woman is exasperated with Aquaman for using phrases out of comic books: "Oh, stop posturing, Arthur. 'The sea is my responsibility?' What a ridiculous thing to say."[273] They make fun of each other's names: " 'Armek' 'Zenturion'! They sound like a line of cheap toys! Why don't they get themselves regular names like every other Joe in spandex?"[274] Superman laments at the low turnout at a fellow superhero's funeral, because, as the priest explains: "The sad fact is, normal people aren't very interested in metahuman funerals anymore, Superman. Everyone knows you people come back all the time."[275] This self-consciousness is Morrison's inheritance coming after the works we have already read, but his particular troping leads into Morrison's personal beliefs on reality and the return of the classic silver age villain, the Key.

Many of the works we have looked at have been in part distinguished for their realism—their realistic take on the codes of the superhero narrative—which takes on a peculiar twist for Grant Morrison. At first glance, Morrison's work is the most unlikely candidate for a realistic superhero narrative, but this needs to be seen against the fact that, in his mind, the split between fiction and reality is not as absolute as it seems. The rhetoric of his interview for the nonfiction *Writers on Comics Scriptwriting* is as wonderfully overblown and encompassing as his superhero stories. At his best he reads like an amalgam of Ralph Waldo Emerson, William S. Burroughs, and Stephen Hawking.

> I met these entities from the fifth dimension or something like it. . . . I was taken to a place that seemed to be made of pure information. The way I describe it is the way dolphins swim in the sea and have complete freedom, complete three-dimensional movement within the medium in which they swim. These beings lived in liquid information, and they swam about in it. It was

---

[272] Morrison et al., *Justice League of America,* #3.
[273] Ibid., #2.
[274] Ibid., #1.
[275] Ibid., #5.

outside space and it was outside time and you could look at spacetime as an object.[276]

I finally figured out what my agenda is with *The Invisibles,* and with the superhero stuff as well. Within a year we'll see man's first contact with a fictional reality, seriously. That's what magic's all about. Fiction and reality are going to become interchangeable. . . .

. . . It's a technology. . . . I've already done it in *Animal Man,* but I went in as myself. I realize now you can go into any comic or any piece of fiction wearing a Fiction Suit.[277]

Later in the same interview, however, he says:

If you want fame and people to know you and your stuff, they need to think of it as an extension of you; so if they meet you it's like meeting your character. So you create personas, make stuff up, make yourself into something people would want to be.[278]

Morrison's prose, his rhetoric in both fiction and life, is so sprawling and insane as to be able to contain the mass of signification endemic to the superhero narrative; his accomplishment on the *JLA* is to discover rhetoric appropriate to the sweeping superhero continuity. If Miller imagines contradictory superhero tradition as a "spring right beneath," then Morrison incorporates this spring (this "liquid information") into the very rhetoric of his narrative. He is able to write a superhero story in a classic mode after Miller and Moore—without making the awkward poetic swerves of *Marvels, Astro City,* or *Kingdom Come*—because he has found a rhetoric that is so utterly fantastic and contradictory that it absorbs previous signification, most powerfully collapsing the poles of the fantastic and the real. Morrison reconciles the superhero narrative's history of the fantastic with its more recent emphasis on "realism" by writing the most absurdly fantastic texts—filled with "silver, morphing hyper-dimensional gels,"[279] "genetically targeted atomic bullets,"[280]

---

[276] Morrison, *Scriptwriting,* 209.
[277] Ibid., 212–213.
[278] Ibid., 218.
[279] Morrison et al., *Justice League of America,* #3.
[280] Ibid., #1,000,000.

four-dimensional batteries, and telepathy that operates across "the infra-sombre bands of the mood spectrum"[281]—and then claiming that this is reality.

The effect of this success of rhetoric is that the *JLA* achieves the appearance of freedom from influence and is able to participate in classic superhero stories without the tortured anxiety experienced by its predecessors. After the entrance of realism into the superhero narrative, Morrison cannot simply write fantasy without taking it into account: rather than asserting the common explanation that the fantastic is good because it is an escape from reality, he claims that reality itself—from quantum physics, quarks, and curved spacetime to his own contact with higher dimensions—is fantastic.[282] Because Morrison claims these experiences actually happened to him, because of the *art* of his own interview, because Morrison engages that myth or metaphor of the author on which Bloom tells us our experience of literature partly depends, he is able to both completely deny and participate in the realism of Miller and Moore. He embraces this paradox as a bridge to more classically written superhero stories. *Marvels* and *Astro City* attempted this, but they were too hampered by the conflicting determination of both absurd continuity and realism to create the kind of free environment necessary for a suc-

---

[281] Ibid., #38, 14.

[282] Morrison's work on *Animal Man* offers a different angle on a similar theme: Animal Man (the character) meets "Grant Morrison" (the creator) and realizes his status as fiction. When he asks that his murdered family be brought back to life, "Morrison" tells him "It wouldn't be realistic." Grant Morrison et al., *Animal Man* (New York: DC Comics, 1988–1990), #26. Matthew J. Pustz writes:

> [*Animal Man*] is certainly grounded in the peculiar realism of superhero comics, where reality is created out of continuity and specific formal rules. In part, Morrison seems to be responding to some of the other peculiarities of mainstream comic book realism, including those that declare that violence, not compassion, is "realistic." The realism that he creates in issue 26 is, finally, a more authentic version where Animal Man is a fictional character in his world as well as our own. (Pustz, *Culture*, 129)

This is not realism in quite the same sense, but it is worth noting nonetheless. This operation of superhero comic books across several levels of reality is important in paving the way to *Planetary* and the Snowflake. In Morrison's own oeuvre, however, this theme is fully achieved outside the codes of the superhero genre in his tremendous, mind-boggling, drug-crazed *Invisibles*.

cessful classic superhero narrative. By collapsing fiction and reality, Morrison's fantasy is his realism.

It seems important to turn now, with this understanding, to some specific plot arcs of the *JLA*. "Imaginary Stories" and "Elseworlds" (*JLA* 7–8) feature the return of the classic JLA villain, the Key. In another example of Morrison's playfully convoluted rhetoric (it is indicative of Morrison's success that this has to be noted, but this is the Key in the pages of *JLA* rather than Morrison in an interview), the Key says:

> The Justice League always wins. So I had to make them win for me; I had to turn my problem into a solution. I created the world's first programmable psycho-virus. A kind of dream flu, which takes over the central nervous system and produces structured hallucinations. . . . Recently I discovered negative space and I realized what might happen if I projected myself into it. Problem 2: my mind, unbound as it is, lacks the necessary power to crack open the negative space doorway. So I thought, "Why not steal the energy from these superminds to boost my own?" I dosed them with the virus and trapped them in curious little dream realities. And I'm waiting. I'm waiting for them to realize they're dreaming. I'm waiting for that inevitable Justice League victory. Because the accompanying psycho-electric surge will give me the means to take control of everything. . . . When I enter negative space, the entire universe will fit around me like a glove! I'll be in complete control![283]

The Key's plan seems to reiterate much of the movement of Morrison's *JLA*. Using a standard superhero convention, that the JLA always wins, the Key will propel himself from a weak second-string villain to a position of mastery and control, which we know from our reading of *The Dark Knight Returns* is often a metaphor for authorial mastery of the chaotic elements of the superhero narrative (and "negative space" might be a trope located near Bloom's—and *Watchmen*'s—negative transcendence). The Key will gain the power for this move to centrality by trapping each member of the JLA in a "curious little dream reality," distinct realms that resemble variations on the individual comic books

---

[283] Morrison et al., *Justice League of America,* #9.

that star each member of the JLA (*Batman, Superman,* etc.). The Key's dream reality allows interaction across a single continuity, as the DC universe does. When the members of the Justice League realize their status as fiction, as just a dream, the Key will have the energy for mastery; power will result from the achievement of self-conscious fiction. Self-conscious heroes are a source of power, and power is exactly what is needed to overcome overdetermination and influence, to propel the Key and Morrison to the center of the creative vision. This is Morrison's troping of the power that has been bequeathed to him by the revisionary superhero narratives we have looked at thus far. The resulting upshot is that the writer's burden transfers directly onto the characters, resulting in the playful nature of Morrison's approach, his seeming freedom from the anxieties of influence.

Because of this switch of responsibility from author to character, a new demand is put upon the League to juggle the intricacies of their own narrative. Text, overdetermination, and the limits of handling information overload become forces the JLA must confront. Evil angelic hosts actually conceive of the mortal world as a text, and threaten our heroes with the command to "[s]tand aside or be erased from the Book,"[284] by which they mean obliterated from the world. For both Morrison and his characters, writing and reality are one and the same. Prometheus, a supervillain who is the antithesis of Batman, is actually defeated when the computer that downloads data directly into his brain overloads with the information of the battle with the JLA, overloads under the burden of the JLA's signification. Prometheus is the weak rebel poet, who lives to fight authority but cannot handle determination, and lives in a "subdimension" that looks to the reader not unlike a blank page (and may recall the white energy that obliterates whole universes in *Crisis on Infinite Earths*).[285] Yet another villain, Starro the Conqueror, infests the dreams of the world with its presence, and replaces the waking world with the

---

[284] Ibid., #6.

[285] Morrison's *Animal Man* includes an exchange between Animal Man (who in the course of Morrison's run will discover he is a fictional character) and the alien being who gave him his power in a realm of undifferentiated white: "The great light you see is a manifestation of the vast absence that lies behind what you call 'reality.' From that light unfolds the continuous process of creation and destruction." Morrison et al., *Animal Man,* #12. Morrison clearly understands this white background in terms of both the comic book page and energy.

totalitarian vision dreamed. In order to win, a boy must believe that fictional heroes are real; relevant to the "dream realities" of the Key, the metaphor for dreams as text is made explicit when we meet the Sandman, referred to as both the "King of Dreams"[286] and the "King of Stories."[287] In *DC: One Million,* the height of civilization, the 853rd century, is an entire culture that "organizes itself around the processing of information,"[288] the ultimate galaxy-wide organization of superhero continuity; the JLA must face a villainous computer that is also a living star. In "Crisis Times Five" (*JLA* 28–31), the reader is shown that the fifth dimension looks upon the third dimension as we look upon two-dimensional four-color comic books, and that here on Earth, fifth-dimensional beings live in ink. These examples serve to illustrate how the *JLA* becomes a text about text: the *JLA* is entirely supported by and revolves around the invention of its own rhetoric.

Bloom conceives of the rhetorical struggle as a struggle for priority, an agon against being a latecomer, but the superhero narrative—a very cheerful late text, or middle one—operates in strange relation to this schema. Morrison obscures what it would mean to be early or late by placing the JLA in a world where no notion of either earliness or lateness can be conceived. The *JLA* is filled with images of agon against various foes for priority, including much that Bloom would find significant (e.g., Superman wrestling an angel). Morrison's world turns any notion of priority on its head. In Morrison's final story arc, the oldest worlds in the DC universe—from the New Gods to the angels—find themselves trumped by an even older force: Mageddon, a weapon from the universe that preceded this one. Conversely, the far future of the 853rd century is so remarkably free of influence, or perhaps so accomplished at dealing with influence, that heroes turn villains just for something to do. Starman says:

> In the end, what made me turn [back to good] was remembering the light in old man Knight's eyes. The costume. The heritage. Like it was all still new and meaningful. In the System [the 853rd century], nothing meant anything because everything was

---

[286] Ibid., #22.
[287] Ibid., #23.
[288] Morrison et al., *DC: One Million,* #1.

possible. So I sold my soul to Solaris because I couldn't think of anything better to do; that's the honest truth. I couldn't buy it back, I knew that. But I could look good trying.[289]

In one of the strangest motivations for villainy in the history of superhero comics, Morrison plays with Bloom: freedom from influence is evil; only tradition, inheritance, debt, and agon create superheroes. Morrison's *JLA* is one of the first modern superhero texts that is truly joyful in overdetermination and thus leads the superhero narrative into its next incarnation. Here, he demonstrates that the superhero narrative only exists as a latecomer, as belated, from its initiation drawing so heavily on—bastardizing, even—classic heroes, pulp novels, and film as to bring it near smothering. The superhero narrative exists only because of overdetermination: Miller and Moore brought it to bear, Busiek and Waid struggled with it, and America's Best Comics gives it a place to come home. Grant Morrison and his successors remind us that the insanity that is the superhero narrative's heritage is all the fun. In the final issue of Grant Morrison's *Justice League of America,* after Superman is able to absorb the cold, the sick, and the horror of the antisunlight, at the heart of the Mageddon warhead, Jack Kirby's New Gods bid the team farewell. Metron, a New God whose name derives from the Greek word Bloom would translate as *misprision,*[290] says:

> The future was saved. When the Fourth World Universe of us New Gods is made complete and put away, the gods of the Fifth World will arise from this planetary cradle. This planet no longer requires our presence. We have shown you the shape of the world to come. Now you must find a way there. Farewell.[291]

"Dude," mumbles Green Lantern as they teleport away, "I thought they'd never leave." Metron's (misprision's) injunction that "you must find a way there" might also be rendered "you must find a trope there," as *trope* derives from the ancient Greek word for "way" or "direction."

---

[289] Ibid., #3.
[290] Bloom, *Agon,* 38.
[291] Morrison *Justice League of America,* #41.

Here begins the true successors to the silver age, the shape—or trope—of things to come.

Warren Ellis: *Stormwatch, The Authority,* and the Origin Story that Never Happened

Shall not the judge of all the earth do justice?

—*Genesis 18:25* (quoted as the epigraph of Alan
Moore's *Watchmen, #3*)

In the final plot arc of Warren Ellis's *Authority,* before he handed the writing of the title to his friend Mark Millar, the Authority defeat God, not the Judeo-Christian God but an immense, uncommunicating, pyramid-shaped being who formed Earth from the primal stuff of the universe. Returning from an eon-long exploration of the cosmos, it now returns to the planet it formed as its final dwelling only to find what appear to it as billions of ants swarming on its doorstep. It sends "heralds" (in the words of the Doctor)—giant amoeba-like creatures—to terra-form the Earth's atmosphere back into the environment of its early days, a climate toxic to human beings. Jenny Sparks, leader of the Authority, defeats "God" with a massive electrical charge to its brain, and dies, on midnight, December 31, 1999. Her electrical powers are only the manifestation of her role in the Wildstorm universe as "the spirit of the twentieth century," a century she cannot outlast. (In Mark Millar's run, she will be reborn, as an infant, as the spirit of the twenty-first century.) Fellow Authority member Swift comments: "The century doesn't click over til 2001, anyone with half an education knows that," to which Sparks replies, "Don't blame me, blame the planet that counts it. Consensus reality. Entire bloody century's been run by the fish-head majority."[292] This "consensus reality" is exactly what comic book continuity amounts to, as Ellis's Authority are more than aware. It is an important realization at the moment they defeat what is essentially a trope of Jack Kirby's most famous villain, the world-devouring Galactus,

---

[292] Warren Ellis, Brian Hitch, Paul Neary, et al., *The Authority* (La Jolla, CA: Wildstorm, 1999–2000), #12.

whose arrival is one of the silver age's definitive moments (*Fantastic Four* 48–50).

What is the meaning of *these* supermen, superwomen, superlovers? *Stormwatch* commands respect only in light of the fact that from its ashes rises the more important *Authority,* but neither work has the overt critical faculty of the works we have looked at in earlier chapters: at least in relation to Bloom. Like the *JLA,* of which *The Authority* will be a trope, its value lies in a more stylistic aspect, its unfathomable usurpation of the raw power of the superhero narrative. Surprisingly, it is not through Bloom the reader will be able to grasp how *The Authority* achieves this potency, this freedom from influence, but through Lacan (or, more specifically, Lacan through Žižek). Every superhero narrative after Moore's opus is defined by its answer to the question "Who watches the watchmen?" In *Stormwatch,* the seeds are planted for *The Authority*'s resounding "Fuck off."

The Authority gleefully embraces the questionable politics entailed by the terms of the superhero narrative. As noted above, the question of democracy and politics in comic books is tied to issues of power. Superheroes could impose worldwide "justice" rather than combat day-to-day battles—rather than fight for the status quo—with no fear of retaliation. In *Stormwatch* and *The Authority,* this threat becomes explicit: Jack Hawksmoor says to the representative for the United States,

> Do you know what twenty superhumans working in concert are capable of? Stormwatch could expunge all life in this city in under an hour. Given a day, twenty superhumans could destroy all life on earth. Stormwatch is the only real superpower of the late twentieth century.[293]

Stormwatch and *The Authority* impose their vision of "a finer world," and no one will stand in their way. These works assert that the superhero catchphrase "with great power comes great responsibility" (Spider-Man) is more often a justification to maintain the status quo than an impetus

---

[293] Warren Ellis et al., *Stormwatch: A Finer World* (La Jolla, CA: Wildstorm, 1999), no pagination. Although this statement occurs in one of the Wildstorm universe's parallel timelines, it nevertheless reflects the political situation of Wildstorm's central characters.

for positive change. Grant Morrison's JLA defends their own status as keepers of the status quo in the final pages of his first story arc:

> SUPERMAN: [The Hyperclan, villains posing as heroes] said they would fix the world. It doesn't work that way.
>
> WONDER WOMAN: Then where does that leave us? Are we doing too much or too little? When does intervention become domination?
>
> SUPERMAN: I can only tell you what I believe, Diana: humankind has to be allowed to climb to its own destiny. We can't carry them there.
>
> FLASH: But that's what she's saying. What's the point? Why should they need us at all?
>
> SUPERMAN: To catch them if they fall.[294]

The Authority accepts, along with their almost sublime levels of power, the responsibility to change the world and carry humanity where they believe humanity should go, rather than "catch them if they fall." *The Authority* is the zenith of the superhero qua power fantasy, and the degree to which readers enjoy the title is the degree to which they participate in the genre for precisely this reason.

Before making the transition from the position of the conservative JLA's "catch them if they fall" to the radical statement that Earth now has to answer to "a higher Authority," Stormwatch must confront a foe that will shadow their later superhero career, and will follow them when the team becomes the Authority: a creature called Father, the product of a German scientist trying to engineer supersoldiers. Father walks the countryside killing anything he sees while spouting passages from Nietzsche's *Thus Spake Zarathustra.* He is eventually destroyed when he is shot with the medallion that the Stormwatch team uses for teleportation. With the medallion embedded in his chest, Stormwatch uses it to teleport away the lower half of Father's body. "All I wanted to do was change the world," are his final words, words that echo with the new direction of the team as put forth by Henry Bendix to Jenny Sparks: "Didn't you ever want to change the world?"[295] The final image of Ellis's

---

[294] Morrison et al., *Justice League of America,* #4.

[295] Warren Ellis et al., *Stormwatch,* vol. 1, #37–50 (La Jolla, CA: Wildstorm, 1996–1998), # 37.

first issue of Stormwatch is devastatingly clear. This creature, whose face is torn to reveal his skull, is seen dead, with the *Stormwatch* insignia (from the teleport medallion) visible where it might be located on a team uniform. "Behold I teach you the superman" are the final words of the issue. "He is this lightning. He is this madness."[296] Father the Superman, who kills out of joy and "joins" the team at the moment of death by "appropriating" their insignia, is the figure of Lacan's obscene father-of-enjoyment. As Žižek writes of this phenomenon:

> [W]e have the father at whose core there is the Real of the unconstrained violence: after we dismantle all protective fictions that surround him, we see him as what he is, the brutal *jouisseur* [he-who-enjoys].[297]

> This figure of the obscene rapist father, far from being the Real beneath the respectful appearance, is rather itself a fantasy formation, a protective shield—against what? Is the rapist father from the False Memory Syndrome not, in spite of his horrifying features, the ultimate guarantee that *there is somewhere full, unconstrained enjoyment?* And consequently, what if the true horror is the lack of enjoyment itself?[298]

This is the specter behind Stormwatch, the transition between the superego/superhero as responsibility (*Spider-Man*) and superego/superhero as obscene enjoyment (*The Authority*). Ellis formulates his superhero narrative as Miller and Moore do by exposing some submerged aspect of the literature. Here, it is the realization of the subtle figure of the father-of-enjoyment hiding under the traditional benevolent, paternal ascetic superhero, or as Žižek would have it (and I think rightly) the fantasy projection that meets the reader's power fantasy identification and "guarantees" full unconstrained enjoyment. To state this in other terms (and it is a Žižekian method to state the same complex idea from several points of view), earlier superheroes were an ethical power fantasy

---

[296] Ibid. It should be noted that Ellis's image draws heavily on the final page of Alan Moore's first installment of *Marvelman,* which quotes the same passage, while also zooming in on an image that fades to black.

[297] Žižek, *Lynch,* 29.

[298] Ibid., 31 (Žižek's emphasis).

that concealed the fear of powerlessness. *The Authority,* on the other hand, is a different kind of fantasy. It accesses the "enjoyment of power" embedded in the ethical power fantasy and exposes unconstrained enjoyment to conceal the true horror that unconstrained enjoyment exists nowhere. While Superman as a fantasy is a protection against the idea that the power fantasy father figure is an obscene monster like the Authority, *The Authority* is a protection against (the real horror) that full unconstrained enjoyment does not exist. What allows for the father-of-enjoyment, Žižek tells us, is "an inconsistency of the socio-symbolic Other, the positive side of which is obscene enjoyment."[299] In other words: *The Authority* is the positive figuration of the inconsistent/contradictory status of superhero continuity. If it was under Miller's narrative, and fused with Morrison's rhetoric, the "inconsistent socio-symbolic Order" (in a strange way) actually *is* the Authority in all their obscene glory.

This obscene glory of the superhero/superego is positioned in *The Authority* as the rejection of the superhero's traditional moral constraints, a state particularly clear in Mark Millar's continuation of *The Authority* after Ellis (*The Authority* 13–20, 22, 27–29).[300] Richard Reynolds writes in *Superheroes: A Modern Mythology:*

> [The superhero] pays for his great powers by the observance of this taboo of secrecy—in a manner which is analogous to the process in which warriors in many societies "pay" for their strength in battle by abstaining from sex, eating special foods, and other taboos designed to isolate the "masculine" in their characters.[301]

The Authority, in contrast, are pop stars: smoking, having casual sex with other superheroes, with each other, drinking. ("Can you smell

---

[299] Slavoj Žižek, *The Sublime Object of Ideology* (London: Verso, 1989), 79.

[300] Mark Millar's run on *The Authority* was interrupted by a fill-in issue, a change of artist and accidental circumstances that delayed the book for eleven months. What should have been issues 13–24 became issues 13–20, 22, followed by a fill-in plot arc by another writer and artist team that covered issues 23–26. Mark Millar then finished his run with issues 27–29. This fill-in arc was entirely inconsequential, and issues 13–20, 22 and 27–29 can be read as a single unit without interruption.

[301] Reynolds, *Mythology,* 15.

alcohol off these clowns?" asks a villain confronting Apollo. "What kind of superpeople show up for a fight stinking of booze?" "The dangerous kind,"[302] Apollo replies, as he blows the villain's head off.) During "Earth Inferno" (*The Authority* 17–20), the Doctor is out of commission due to a heroin overdose. (The opening page of the third part of "Earth Inferno" is perhaps one of the most terrifying shots of a superhero ever: the Doctor preparing to shoot up.) The Midnighter's obscene revenge upon a villain who raped his boyfriend (fellow superhero Apollo)—the vision of his carrying a jackhammer, menacingly, toward the Soldier lying prostrate and crippled below his waist—is perhaps the best illustration of the atmosphere of *The Authority*. This description should not elide the fact that at no point are the Authority really presented as reprehensible for their behavior. The Midnighter's grim though unillustrated (i.e., "offscreen") revenge is clearly not intended to detract from his heroism. Readers may have some misgivings about these heroes, but the overall impression is one of enjoyment, celebration, power, and superheroism. Žižek writes: "THIS is respect at its purest: respect for the figure of authority [respect for the Authority] even when he is disrespectful, embarrassing, obscene."[303]

One effect of this "disrespectful, embarrassing, obscene" Authority is a perverse response to the many "soap opera" plots that have become staples of superhero team books, the most prominent example being Chris Clairmont's run on the *X-Men*. His work on that title is an important foil for *The Authority,* because Ellis and Millar overturn not only *The X-Men*'s angst-filled teenage morality ("Oh, but how can I even think of kissing him, when he is with her?") but its impenetrable continuity as well. In shedding the "superhero soap opera," *The Authority* writes whole new terms for the team superhero comic book. A single issue, even one in the middle of a plot arc, can be enjoyed by itself, picked up and put down. Clairmont's *X-Men,* in contrast, can barely be followed by new readers unfamiliar with the vast network of unresolved tensions among a huge cast of characters spanning decades. The Cyclops—Jean Gray—Wolverine love triangle, for example, develops into a structural convention for the *X-Men*. For a quarter of a decade readers have been

---

[302] Mark Millar, Frank Quitely, et al., *The Authority* (La Jolla, CA: Wildstorm, 2000), #14.

[303] Žižek, *Lynch,* 30.

subjected to the angst-filled thought bubbles of a woman loved by two men: the upright team leader she knows she loves and the mysterious animal bad boy to whom she cannot deny being attracted. Relationships of this type stand for decades in superhero comic books, unresolved for dramatic reasons. Compare the angst of unrequited love between X-Men with the postcoital, lit-cigarette conversation of the Doctor and fellow Authority superhero Angie:

> THE DOCTOR: The only thing I don't understand is how I ended up in bed with the one person on the team who genuinely hates my guts.
>
> ANGIE: I'm as confused as you are, Doctor. Maybe I just get turned on by people who single-handedly save the world.
>
> THE DOCTOR: What about Jack [Hawksmoor, team leader]? I thought you two were . . . ah . . . [dating]
>
> ANGIE: Having regular sex? Oh, we are. But he's up in the showers with two of those alternative [universe] Wildcats girls [other superheroes] and I can't stand women with tattoos.[304]

Problem solved. Another subject of many didactic superhero stories, tirades on the evils of drug use (Captain America Goes to War Against Drugs!),[305] becomes, in *The Authority*, the semiresponsible use of illegal drugs by the heroes themselves. Jack Hawksmoor dismisses the Doctor's heroin use in a media interview: "The Doctor's drug-problem hasn't affected his work so far and, frankly, that's all I'm concerned about."[306] Again, the Authority have the audacity to gloss over the personal angst—particularly prevalent among the X-Men—when a hero is even marginally responsible for killing an enemy even in mortal combat. In the "X-cutioner's Song,"[307] Archangel, an X-Man fighting for control of his newly received razor-sharp metal wings, which seem to have a mind of their own, finds that his wings severed the head of a man he didn't even know was trying to kill him. A killer has died, and Archangel's responsi-

---

[304] Millar et al., *The Authority,* #20.

[305] Cited in Reynolds, *Mythology,* 76.

[306] Millar et al., *The Authority,* #22.

[307] Peter David and Jae Lee, *X-cutioner's Song,* chapter 6 (*X-Factor* 85) (New York: Marvel Comics, 1994).

bility in the matter was minimal at best; he is nevertheless a broken man. The Authority, on the other hand, understand themselves as soldiers and act accordingly. Morality aside, the Authority "resolve" a number of clichéd comic book stories in their sweeping acceptance of all that comes with being the "only superpower of the late twentieth century."

In *The Metastases of Enjoyment,* Žižek discusses the Slovenian "post-punk" group Laibach: "an aggressive inconsistent mixture of Stalinism, Nazism and *Blut und Boden* ideology."

> Their public (especially intellectuals) is obsessed with the "desire of the Other"—What is Laibach's actual position? Are they truly totalitarians or not [are they being ironic]?—that is, they ask Laibach a question and expect an answer from them, failing to notice that Laibach themselves *function not as an answer but as a question.* By means of the elusive character of their desire, of the undecideability as to "where they actually stand," Laibach compel us to take up our position and decide upon *our* desire.[308]

The Authority parallels this situation exactly. A discussion of whether the Authority are heroes or villains who think they are heroes misses the thrust of the work altogether. *The Authority* accepts every aspect of the superhero, no matter how questionable, and forces readers to "decide upon their desire." The obscene underside of the classically heroic JLA forces the reader to confront the whole of comic book tradition.[309] This is the fulfillment of the promise in *The Dark Knight Returns* of a collapse between hero and villain, the point at which Adrian Veidt (Ozymandias from *Watchmen*) becomes the main character. Reading *The Authority* and reading the works of Miller and Moore are vastly different experiences, characterized by the fact that *The Authority* is the beginning of a genuine

---

[308] Slavoj Žižek, *The Metastases of Enjoyment: Six Essays on Causality and Women* (London: Verso, 1994), 71–72 (Žižek's emphasis).

[309] The obscene underside of traditional heroes is a theme of Ellis's work and accounts for the generally high libidinal value of his stories: note his portrayal of the dark side of *Gen-13* in *DV8* (an underside linked by the "T-and-A" quality of both works), his villainous *The Fantastic Four* in *Planetary*'s Four Voyagers (chapter 5), and his nauseous and sickening version of *Marvels* in *Ruins*. Individual stories present us with the dark side of an American political figure (the serial killer nephew of Kennedy: Ellis, *Storm-watch,* #43), and religion's obverse in an incestuous cult (*DV8* #2).

break with the silver age. *The Dark Knight Returns* and *Watchmen* were an examination of superheroes from the end of the silver age; *The Authority* is the first glimpse we have of a perspective from the outside, a sketch of things to come.

The Authority's status as a troping of the *JLA*—figures of the *JLA*'s obscene enjoyment—is made clear in "A Finer World," the first appearance of Apollo and the Midnighter. These founding members of the Authority first appeared in *Stormwatch* as the only surviving members of a team of seven characters intended to invoke the Justice League: the woman warrior with superstrength (Wonder Woman), the speedster (the Flash), a creature who creates shapes of light (Green Lantern), the alien (Martian Manhunter), and a woman who resembles the Black Canary. Apollo and the Midnighter are clearly Superman/Batman analogues. Apollo possesses sun-powered superstrength, flight, and heat vision; the Midnighter, grim and efficient, has peak fighting ability, wears all black, and has arm buckles where Miller placed fins. Along with Ellis's liberal heroes of enjoyment arises a significant statement of power: the open homosexuality between the two masculine powerhouses of the team, Apollo and the Midnighter. *The Authority* takes the homosexual subtext that Miller and Moore brought to the fore and brings the volume all the way up, openly troping it as the foundation of superhero literature in the figures of Superman and Batman. Ellis embraces his inheritance and insists that homosexuality functions at full volume, rather than as concealed subtext. This is not a subtle homoeroticism that may or may not be there: this is the two most powerful men on the team making out with each other and swapping playful banter with the rest of the team about their sexual orientation.

Warren Ellis's *Stormwatch* and its narrative transformation into Ellis's *Authority,* continued by Mark Millar, have been discussed across their similarities as something akin to a single body of work. It is the transition between *Stormwatch* and *The Authority* that is most remarkable, however, and stands in many ways as the origin story of the successors to the silver age. A few remarks about the state of *Stormwatch, WildC.A.T.s,* and Wildstorm in the early 1990s are necessary to fully understand the *WildC.A.T.s/Aliens* crossover.

After *The Dark Knight Returns* and *Watchmen, Stormwatch* and *WildC.A.T.s* represented, in many ways, the stale repetition of a late silver age whose time had ended with Miller and Moore, but which persisted because nothing had yet replaced it. *Stormwatch,* which began publication in 1993, was the story of a large-scale, United Nations–funded, international police force that amounted to a superhero book in the vein of Marvel's *Avengers. WildC.A.T.s* followed the story of a covert team of alien hybrids fighting a secret war with another race of aliens that had infiltrated Earth, unbeknownst to the bulk of the population. Both books were created by "Mr. X-Men" himself, fan favorite Jim Lee, and *Wild-C.A.T.s* amounted to little more than an *X-Men* rip-off he could use to siphon off fandom from his popularity on that Marvel title. This was Image Comics.

When Image Comics launched in the early 1990s, it was a genuine break with the big publishing houses (particularly Marvel) into creator-owned work. At DC and Marvel (the only big publishers on the block), a work-for-hire situation meant that any characters or concepts created were the copyrighted property of the company. When Frank Miller created Elektra for Marvel Comics, for example, he was paid for his work but received no royalties for action figures or shirts based on the character, and was not paid or consulted when the character appeared in other Marvel titles. Image Comics defied all expectations when popular writers and artists left the big companies to do creator-owned work and competed successfully with DC and Marvel. These now independent creators, free of the limitations imposed by corporate-owned characters, ushered in a new kind of comic book.

Image, however, was not so much a company as a loose conglomeration of creator-owned projects. Continuity among titles was strange, as some clearly went together (*WildC.A.T.s* and *Stormwatch*), whereas others had a distinct feel (Sam Kieth's *The Maxx* and Erik Larson's *Savage Dragon*). The early days of Image featured a host of "guest appearances" in which Savage Dragon appeared in *The Maxx* and Spawn interacted with the WildC.A.T.s. Crossing such continuities, creators of one title were able to introduce new fans to the work of a fellow Image creator. Eventually, Image separated into studios, as some creators needed their characters to exist in an entirely separate continuity from the other Image creations.

Todd McFarlane brought *Spawn,* basically the "dark age's" *Batman,* to Todd McFarlane Productions. Though completely uninteresting in the terms this book has set forth, McFarlane did achieve a great deal of success with his creator-owned character, taking him past a landmark no one thought any Image comic book would reach, 100 issues. Dale Keown's *Pitt* was *The Incredible Hulk* for the "dark age," and typified that trend by being dark, violent, and dying off fairly quickly. Erik Larson remained under his own banner with his *Savage Dragon,* little more than torch-bearing for Jack Kirby, and succeeded in surpassing the seventy-five-issue mark. It is especially remarkable that Erik Larson writes and pencils every issue himself, rather than hiring others to take over his successful work, as Todd McFarlane did.

Rob Liefeld, famed for his X-Men spin-off *X-Force* (he was "Mr. X-Force" to Jim Lee's "Mr. X-Men"), started Maximum Press. His *Supreme* and *Glory* were Superman and Wonder Woman rewritten for the "dark age" of superheroes and, like Lee's *WildC.A.T.s,* Liefeld's *Youngblood* was written as a substitute for his work on Marvel's *X-Force.* Marc Silvestri, creator of *Cyberforce,* started Top Cow Productions. A great exemplar of the kind of comic books Kurt Busiek and Mark Waid were trying to break away from in *Marvels, Astro City,* and *Kingdom Come, Cyberforce* told the story of a group of characters whose names alone suggest the dark, angst-filled tone of the book: Ripclaw, Styker, Impact. Accepting the failed thesis that the so-called dark age was the proper successor to the silver age (a thesis this book presents an alternative for, conceiving of the dark age as merely late, redundant silver age), Silvestri now writes for that age. Again, the titles express his attempt at a "dark age": *Witchblade* and *The Darkness.* Jim Lee's *WildC.A.T.s* and *Stormwatch* and Silvestri's *Cyberforce* were at the same company when it was called Homage. When Silvestri left, the company was renamed Wildstorm, derived from the company's most important titles, *Stormwatch* and *WildC.A.T.s.* With all pretensions to the "dark age" (late silver age) fallen away, *WildC.A.T.s* and *Stormwatch* were free to follow another direction.[310]

Wildstorm Rising was an intracompany crossover designed to make a coherent space out of titles like *Gen-13, Union, Stormwatch, WildC.A.T.s,* and *Wetworks* (and, to a much lesser extent, *Deathblow, Backlash,* and *Grifter*). What is interesting is how the title *Wildstorm Rising* would become deeply auspicious. Soon after the events of the crossover firmly established their continuity, everything changed. As a direct result of the narrative events resulting from the crossover, the WildC.A.T.s returned

---

[310] For this historical overview of Image and its fragmentation, I am deeply indebted to conversations with Brad Winderbaum.

to the alien civilization that was the foundation of their identity as a team. Discussed in more detail below, this was Alan Moore's run on the title in *Homecoming* and *Gang War,* and when he returned the WildC.A.T.s to Earth, they would never be the same. Warren Ellis, a figure who later transformed the company, entered Wildstorm with *Stormwatch,* and found the company offered the perfect environment to support the kind of life he would grow. It all came to a head in the *WildC.A.T.s/Aliens* crossover. It is startling that such a lengthy analysis of a single comic book is necessary (or indeed possible), but the sheer strangeness of this single moment, on both narrative and formal levels, cannot be emphasized enough.

Stormwatch and *The Authority,* while similar enough to discuss together in terms of the obscene rapist father, were not the same team, and Stormwatch could not simply become the Authority. Ellis first presents Apollo and the Midnighter in *Stormwatch* but doesn't make them members of a team until *The Authority.* "Bleed" (*Stormwatch,* vol. 2, issues 7–9) featured the discovery of a parallel universe inhabited by alternate versions of Wildstorm heroes about to be destroyed by an alien invasion. Stormwatch leader Jackson King could not bring himself to take the responsibility to interfere, beyond the smallest hint, with another timeline. While disaster for that timeline was avoided to a degree, the message was clear: in a universe of parallel realities, Stormwatch was too small to be a major force. The *WildC.A.T.s/Aliens* crossover proved they were too small to even survive in the growing conception of the Wildstorm universe. Because of their role as an international, UN-sponsored, superpowered police force, Stormwatch was too tied up with conventional notions of morality and responsibility to make a genuine break with the past. There is a sense that the WildC.A.T.s participate in the moment Stormwatch becomes the Authority because *The Authority* represents a synthesis of the original conception of *Stormwatch* and the *Wild-C.A.T.s.* The Authority emerge with a sense of planetary (and beyond) responsibility, but unlike Stormwatch and like the WildC.A.T.s, they are willing to reach beyond conventional ethics in making their presence felt and answer to no one.

The *WildC.A.T.s/Aliens* book is the vanishing mediator between *Stormwatch*'s full transition to *The Authority,* which can only exist with the powerful foundation this remarkable crossover provides. We cannot grasp the significance of this moment without understanding the usual status of an intercompany comic book crossover. Intercompany crossovers are works that stand outside the run of a series (e.g., *WildC.A.T.s* publishes every month and is numbered accordingly, but the *WildC.A.T.s/ Aliens* crossover is a "one shot," i.e., numbered 1 without any subsequent issues). These crossovers are unlike the common meetings of intracompany characters, which happen all the time; they are cross-company, dual published events between characters that do not usually share the same fantasy space. They are often more of a gimmick than a story (a kind of "What if so-and-so met so-and-so" scenario), usually scripted and drawn by artists unknown to the titles involved. Since the events that happen in them can never be mentioned in the regular run of the comic book (e.g., *WildC.A.T.s*) because of copyright infringement issues (*Aliens* is trademarked to Dark Horse Publishing), crossovers are, as a rule, totally irrelevant to the ongoing storyline of the characters that they cross.

WildC.A.T.s/Aliens is maneuvered by Ellis in such a way as to break the conventions of the crossover while at the same time adhering to them strictly. Even on the smallest scale, the typically irrelevant nature of crossovers usually means commissioning less than the best talent to produce the book. Sprouse's art, though quite good in its own right (e.g., *Tom Strong*), is wildly inappropriate here. A glance through *Wild-C.A.T.s/Aliens* in the store only serves to confirm (incorrectly) suspicions that it is not worth buying. The prelude to the crossover is established in "No Reason" (*Stormwatch* 10): an asteroid headed toward Earth is discovered, and an anonymous team is sent to blow it into the sun. Discovering that the rock contains signs of building, probes are sent to investigate. Radio contact is ominously lost, but the charges go off, the rock is sent into the sun, and the ship returns to base still not answering communications. The story continues in the *WildC.A.T.s/Aliens* crossover where something has gone wrong on board the space platform; thinking Stormwatch is in trouble, the WildC.A.T.s investigate and discover that the Aliens (yes, from the Ridley Scott movie of the same name) have already killed three core members of Stormwatch and countless space platform employees. Once the survivors are safe, Winter gives his life piloting Stormwatch's space station into the sun, on full burn, to ensure that the Aliens will not survive. The final words of the work are Weatherman Jackson King's report to the UN:

> For a few days, code-name Winter—Nikolas Kamarov, born in Russia—was the fastest human ever to live. The Storm Door

[forcefield] went down a few hours before Skywatch struck the sun's photosphere. It didn't matter.[311]

The final words are deeply ironic and horribly true. When even one member of a major superhero team dies, it is always treated as a major event, both inside the book and on the level of marketing: a funeral or "death of a friend" issue is almost always published. What Ellis has done here is to kill off, not just one, but four key members of a superhero team, in a space that has important ramifications for *The Authority*. The first feature to note is that the deaths of three major heroes occurs "offscreen" (and as Scott McCloud writes in his treatise on the fundamentals of comics, "To kill a man between the panels is to condemn him to a thousand deaths").[312] The reader did not see them die in an even vaguely heroic or dramatic context. By the time we arrive, they are already dead. We have missed the full battle, missed the last words of these heroes, missed the event. Stormwatch member Fugi, for example, was a fairly popular Wildstorm character, often making guest appearances in the company's other titles, when he was brutally killed off here. Fans did not even witness Fugi die fighting. When the WildC.A.T.s arrive, there are only bodies. Even more devastating is that the title characters of *Stormwatch* were killed, not in their own book, or even in someone else's book, but in someone else's crossover. For reasons mentioned above, crossovers are likely to be irrelevant to the characters involved, existing in a space almost outside continuity. The horrible thing to realize is that on at least one level Ellis does not break with convention: *WildC.A.T.s/Aliens* is completely irrelevant to the degree that it does nothing to advance the story of either the WildC.A.T.s or the Aliens. To *Stormwatch,* however, it is vitally relevant, as the team cannot continue minus four members and a headquarters. The Stormwatch issue after the release of *WildC.A.T.s/Aliens* involves the dissolution of the team within the book and the cancellation of the *Stormwatch* title altogether. "No Direction Home" (*Stormwatch* 11) makes explicit what Ellis has done in killing off these main characters in this manner.

[311] Warren Ellis, Chris Sprouse, et al., *WildC.A.T.s/Aliens* (La Jolla, CA: Wildstorm–Dark Horse), 1998.
[312] Scott McCloud, *Understanding Comics* (New York: A Kitchen Sink Book for Harper Perennial, 1993), 69.

Because of the cross-company nature of the crossover—because both companies receive royalties for use of the characters they own—within the crossover there is no difficulty in telling the story. It is upon returning to the main title that the reader discovers the problem. The characters cannot be remembered in any way—the manner of their deaths can only be recounted in the most abstract manner—because any mention of the Aliens, any flashback showing the final moments of their death, for example (which the reader was denied, even when it was legally possible), would violate copyright law. What happened on board Skywatch can only be referred to as the "xenobiological infestation," and never shown. The issue is housed in a kind of intentional awkwardness that makes this painfully obvious. There is something distressingly embarrassing about the death of heroes unable to be properly commemorated in the space of their own book.[313]

Ellis's strategy has ramifications on the level of publishing as well. Because crossovers are often irrelevant, significantly fewer issues are printed than, say, a regular issue of the running title: *WildC.A.T.s/Aliens* sold out completely. To alleviate the difficulty of finding his other popular, sold out issues, Wildstorm has collected Ellis's work on *Stormwatch* and *The Authority* into trade paperback reprints. But the central moment between the two works is opaque to many readers. The death of *Stormwatch* and the glimmerings of *The Authority* in *WildC.A.T.s/Aliens* cannot be collected in a trade paperback because of the intercompany nature of the central issue, a printing of which is almost impossible to find,[314] due to the later popularity of *The Authority*.[315] Because Stormwatch is destroyed in another book's crossover, and because its own continuity is

---

[313] To make a loose analogy with another kind of literature, the non-comic book reader is invited to imagine an episode of *The X-Files* spin-off *The Lone Gunmen,* airing at 2:00 A.M. on a Tuesday and killing off Mulder and Scully one episode prior to *X-Files'* cancellation. Thanks to comedian Eddie Izzard for inspiring this comparison.

[314] This author had to rely on the loan of a copy of a friend. Thanks again to Brad Winderbaum.

[315] Just before this manuscript was completed, a trade paperback collecting *Stormwatch* 10, *WildC.A.Ts/Aliens,* and *Stormwatch* 11 was released. The point above still stands, however, as it is recognized that Ellis's crossover changed the industry. The crossover was written at a time when the comments above still stood, and Ellis was drawing on the atmosphere and its meanings when he wrote *WildC.A.T.s/Aliens.* He had every reason to think that it could not be reprinted. His presence, however, caused the reprint to be possible.

prohibited from mentioning the occurrences of that crossover, a kind of positive objectified void becomes the foundation for *The Authority*. This void, which is highly significant when regarded in the context of the work of Jacques Lacan, as we will see, is mirrored in the collections of many readers who have every issue of *Stormwatch* and *The Authority* but lack the central transition, the origin story of the Authority.

The significance of *WildC.A.T.s/Aliens,* the justification for spending so much time explicating a single issue, lies in Ellis's completely innovative move to block revision. He founded *The Authority,* his troping of the Justice League, on a kind of nonevent, the death of a team in another's totally irrelevant crossover. Stormwatch's destruction occurs in a space that cannot be returned to, a story that can never be retold, a realm of darkness and obscurity on both the level of the narrative and the level of publishing. Against the often reimagined and reinterpreted origin of various superhero books, the misprisions of successors upon the founding moments of a book, Ellis has installed a kind of block (possibly unique to the functioning of comic books) against ever returning to the site of the battle that founded his opus. In *The Sublime Object of Ideology,* Slavoj Žižek comments upon the film *Alien* in terms of Lacanian psychoanalysis and Lacan's *objet petit a.* That the same Aliens appear here in a kind of objectified void at the origin of the most powerful of superhero teams points to the relevancy of that passage. Žižek writes:

> The "alien" . . . is an object which, being nothing at all in itself, must none the less be added, annexed as an anamorphic surplus. It is the Real at its purest: a semblance, something which on a strictly symbolic level does not exist at all but at the same time the only thing in the whole film which actually exists, the thing against which the whole reality is utterly defenseless.[316]

Lacan's *objet petit a* is "this coincidence of limit and excess, of lack and surplus . . . [it is] the leftover which embodies the fundamental constitutive lack."[317] *The Authority* is founded upon this "leftover," this "fundamental constitutive lack," in the form of the *WildC.A.T.s/Aliens* crossover origin story. This key issue stands outside the numbering of

---

[316] Žižek, *Ideology,* 79.
[317] Ibid., 53.

Stormwatch and *The Authority*—it is their leftover—but it is also the void between *Stormwatch* and *The Authority*: the transition that wasn't there. When Žižek writes that the Aliens are the Real, he refers to Lacan's "traumatic kernel," the Thing, the event that cannot be symbolized, cannot be brought into the "symbolic order" of the social reality. For *The Authority,* and most specifically, for "No Direction Home" (*Stormwatch* 11), the relevance of the *WildC.A.T.s/Aliens* crossover to this schema is clear: the events of the crossover, for the reasons of copyright discussed above, are retroactively structured as the Real event because upon return to *Stormwatch* proper they cannot be integrated into the symbolic order of comic book continuity. The social reality is, as Žižek writes, utterly defenseless against this traumatic event: Stormwatch is destroyed, and the book is cancelled as a direct result of the crossover. This is the form in which the excised horror comic book makes itself felt, its entrance into the superhero narrative as adumbrated in chapter 1.

But how does the Lacanian formulation of the *objet petit a* relate to Bloom's theory of influence and the argument put forth here? According to Lacan, the Real itself contains no necessary mode of symbolization,[318] that the symbolic order, the truth of reality, is always constituted by "misrecognition" (*meconnaissance*). Bloom himself notes that this is synonymous to his concept of literary "truth" being the result of "misprision" and "misreading."[319] The unique status of the superhero narrative, specifically *The Authority,* gives us a key to understanding this connection more fully. The *objet petit a* is "both the object of anxiety and the final irreducible reserve of libido,"[320] a conception that seems to mirror Bloom's understanding of tradition as an object of anxiety and as a reserve of poetic power. (The point of coincidence is obvious: both Bloom and Lacan are strong misreadings/*meconnaissances* of Freud.)

Armed with this information, we can ask, What happens in *The Authority*? After its foundation on the "traumatic kernel" of the *WildC.A.T.s/Aliens* crossover, *The Authority* is seemingly unburdened from the anxieties that affected other superhero narratives, and it reads as something distinctly different—the future of the superhero narrative. Grant

---

[318] Žižek, *Ideology,* 97.

[319] Bloom, *Agon,* 109.

[320] Dylan Evans, *An Introductory Dictionary of Lacanian Psychoanalysis* (New York: Routledge, 1996), 125.

Morrison describes it as "the first great superhero team book of the 21st century. Beside it everything else seems pale and stale and repetitive. . . . *The Authority* has endowed the tired superhero archetypes with vigorous new meaning, pumping the volume until noses bleed."[321] The connection between *The Authority*'s achievement and the *WildC.A.T.s/Aliens* crossover is in the space of overlap between Bloom and Lacan. Bloom writes that, in his schema, the meaning of a poem can only be another poem,[322] but according to Lacan, there is always a surplus in signification (i.e.,'X means Y' always entails a leftover), the object–cause of desire, the "unattainable something that is in the object more than itself." The *WildC.A.T.s/Aliens* crossover allows *The Authority* to function at "full volume." Ellis's *Authority* appears to be free of the burden of anxiety and tradition because it embraces, at its origin, precisely the gap between itself and its tradition: the surplus X, the constitutive lack, the leftover in the signification "the meaning of a given poem is always another poem." In other words, to quote Žižek again, "The lack in the Other [Ellis's crossover] gives the subject [the Authority]—so to speak—a breathing space, it enables him to avoid the total alienation in the signifier not by filling out his lack but by allowing him to identify himself, his own lack, with the lack of the Other."[323]

This move gains a poetic "breathing space," and its success can be measured by the experience of reading *The Authority*. The book's breathtaking intensity—its status as the obscene father-of-enjoyment—is the direct result of this founding space, this inscrutable origin story, the *objet petit a,* that never happened, and was at the same time too much to bear. Lacan writes, "Is it not remarkable that, at the origin of the analytic experience, the real should have presented itself in the form of that which is *unassimilable* in it—in the form of the trauma, determining all that follows, and imposing on it an apparently accidental origin?"[324] This "accidental origin" is quite remarkable indeed, and the trace it leaves behind is the beginning of the modern age.

---

[321] Grant Morison, "Introduction," in *The Authority: Relentless* (La Jolla, CA: Wildstorm, 2000).

[322] Bloom, *Anxiety,* 95.

[323] Žižek, *Ideology,* 122.

[324] Lacan, *Seminar 11,* 55 (Lacan's emphasis).

5

The Superhero as Critic

THE BIRTH OF THE MODERN AGE

Jakita Wagner: We gather information on the hidden
wonders of the world.
Elijah Snow: Mystery archeologists. There's a
hundred years of fantastic events that the
Planetary intends to excavate.
Jakita Wagner: We're mapping the secret history of
the twentieth century.

—Warren Ellis, *Planetary*

Criticism is the art of knowing the hidden roads that
go from poem to poem.

—Harold Bloom, *The Anxiety of Influence*

When the Fourth World Universe of us New Gods is
made complete and put away, the gods of the Fifth
World will arise from this planetary cradle.

—Grant Morrison, *Justice League of America*

*P*lanetary is the apex toward which this book has developed. It is
the height of the revisionary superhero narrative. *Planetary* is the
comic book as literary critic, the superhero narrative that knows
the hidden roads that go from poem to poem, from issue to issue. It
transubstantiates those spandex fistfights that are a convention of the
genre into a staging of Bloom's generational agon: "Revisionism, as
Nietzsche said of every spirit, unfolds itself *only in fighting*. The spirit

portrays itself as agonistic, as contesting for supremacy, with other spirits, with anteriority, and finally with every earlier version of itself."[325] The superhero narrative follows exactly this pattern. It begins as agonistic spandex fistfighting, the contest for supremacy between superheroes. The revisionary superhero narrative battles anteriority, the past, by coming to terms with its own fictional history and narrative overdetermination. *Planetary* shows comic book history as a battle with an earlier version of itself—pulp novel characters struggling with the golden age superheroes, silver age heroes killing off golden age icons. *Planetary* culminates this lineage, and places the revisionary superhero narrative in its proper context, with an antagonism between the four-member Planetary team and their most present imaginative debt: the royalty of the silver age, the Fantastic Four. *Planetary* presents the structure of misprision within the superhero genre as the perfect superhero narrative. As the Fourth Man asks Ambrose Chase in "Planet Fiction" (*Planetary* 9):

THE FOURTH MAN: You know what Planetary is? It's this mirror. Look into it.

CHASE: It's warped.

THE FOURTH MAN: No. The mirror's fine. It's the world that's warped. This is the mirror we holdup to it.[326]

Planetary is the misprision (the warped mirror) that is powerful enough that the world itself appears warped.

Planetary is the story of three superpowered individuals, Elijah Snow, Jakita Wagner, and The Drummer. They are the foundation of the Planetary organization and work for an unknown "fourth man," uncovering mysteries across the globe. *Planetary* asks, What if all the superhero literature, all the monster and kung-fu movies, all the sci-fi and pulp adventures, were true? Each issue is a separate event, the revelation of a new secret about the real history of superhero literature: the connections between works that appear unconnected, the battles for literary priority, the murders that allow a given tradition to survive over its fallen predecessors and influences. To quote again the most fantastic issue of *Plane-*

---

[325] Bloom, *Agon,* vii (Bloom's emphasis).
[326] Warren Ellis, John Cassaday, and Laura Depuy, *The Planetary* (La Jolla, CA: Wildstorm, 1999–2000), #9.

tary, "Planet Fiction," this time the words of the villain unveiling what he and his team of scientists have done:

> We're in a strange relationship with our fiction, you see. Sometimes we fear it's taking us over, sometimes we beg to be taken over by it . . . sometimes we want to see what's inside it. That was the initial project profile. To create a fictional world, and then to land on it. A sample return mission. To bring back someone from a fictional reality.[327]

Planetary is this investigation of fiction through fiction, on the plane of fiction. It is an investigation of fiction that is as real as the characters examining it: bringing back characters from a fictional reality into the space of the Planetary, to investigate the inside of each narrative, and discover the connections among them. Each of the Planetary's discoveries is a powerful revisionary reference to the history of the superhero narrative, and each issue stands up to a close reading. And as one could get an education in the humanities by following every reference in James Joyce's *Ulysses,* the popular culture scholar could do worse than track *Planetary*'s source material.

In the first issue, "All Over the World," Elijah Snow is recruited, and a cave under the Adirondack Mountains is explored. Dr. Axel Brass, incapacitated for fifty-four years, is discovered and tells the story of how he came to be crippled there. He and his associates created an absurdly powerful supercomputer to put a stop to World War II: "This quantum brain would perform each calculation across universes, each possible answer being processed in a different world—each alternative universe vanishing, one by one, until the answer made itself real."[328] Doc Brass describes what went wrong:

> The snowflake [the structure of alternate universes] grew. Universes spun into life, their spans measured in seconds—by our reckoning. But time moved differently in there. Within each newborn universe, billions of years span out in those few seconds we perceived. And, at the end of those few seconds, in the

---

[327] Ibid. (Ellis's ellipsis).
[328] Ibid., #1.

last thinnest splinter of time—a group of people in a mountain hideaway looked across that gulf of realities at us, knowing that their universe was on the verge of decoherence, destruction—and went for us.[329]

Brass's people and the superbeings from this other reality duel for survival in a massive battle. Everyone is destroyed except Brass, who stays behind to make sure nothing else slips through this fissure in reality. The Planetary leave with Brass and the computer. Snow remarks, "It's a strange world," to which Wagner responds, "Let's keep it that way."[330]

To the attuned reader, the significance of the story is even more fantastic than its ostensible content. (And let one aspect of the snowflake be noted now: unlike the snow globe trope from *Watchmen* and *Marvels*, we now look at the snow as fast time, rather than slow—we are now in the globe looking out.) An analysis of the members of both Brass's people and the alternate Earth superbeings is necessary and instructive. Although the names have been changed, there is enough left of their appearance and manner to identify the allusions. Doc Brass himself is clearly pulp hero Doc Savage, the Man of Bronze. From left to right: the Asian gentleman with the six-inch fingernails is clearly Fu-Manchu; the man in the blue suit, called "the Operator," is Operator 5, a kind of proto–James Bond; the Aviator is G-8, World War I pilot hero; the man in the lab coat, referred to as "Edison," is the inventor Tom Swift; the man in the purple suit with the leopard-skin cravat, who did not travel from England as the Operator assumes, but from Africa ("visiting childhood haunts"), is Tarzan, all grown up; and the man in black is the Spider (from the company who brought you the Shadow), described by Warren Ellis as "Batman with guns and no mood stabilizers."[331] These are the classic pulp novel heroes of the 1920s and 1930s—the direct predecessors of the superheroes who would be created in 1938—in a kind of JLA of pulp heroes.

---

[329] Ibid.

[330] Ibid. In marked contrast to Alan Moore's *Top Ten, Planetary* is intended to make texts that most readers know achieve a strangeness and newness again. Like many great superhero comic book writers, Ellis accesses the essential idea that made the original works great, and strives to present that idea in his work.

[331] www.warrenellis.com/brass_people.htm.

The alien superbeings, or, more specifically, their allusions, can be identified by their appearance, their presence in a group, and their powers. They recall the classic Justice League of America. The red cape with the glowing red eyes is Superman; the woman warrior is Wonder Woman; the crouching figure in the dark cape is Batman; the figure in blue who can create glowing structures is the Green Lantern; the runner in yellow is the Flash; the creature with the gills suggests Aquaman; and the figure with the oddly shaped forehead is J'onn J'onzz, the Manhunter from Mars.

The battle between the groups reveals Bloom's structure of misprision. Each member of Brass's people battles the "JLA" member most in debt to their pulp influences. "Doc Savage, the Man of Bronze" (whose name is Clark) fights "Superman" (the Man of Steel, also Clark); the shadowy detective the "Spider" takes on "Batman, the Dark Knight Detective"; "Tarzan," the noble savage, struggles against "Wonder Woman," the Amazon warrior; "Tom Swift," the science-based hero, obliterates the "Flash," created by a chemical spill; the Aviator (World War I pilot) takes out "Green Lantern," whose alter ego, Hal Jordan, was a pilot; and alien meets alien when "Fu-Manchu," the enigmatic Chinaman, clashes with the Martian Manhunter.

Ellis stages the battle in which the contemporary superhero replaced these classic pulp heroes, all but forgotten in the world of contemporary comic books. It is a staging of the battle that will determine literary primacy within the field of superheroes. The Planetary emerges from this background as a recorder of this battle, as witnesses to the anxiety of influence struggle that took place between the pulp novel heroes and the superheroes. When the Planetary walk away from what, for the reader, is their first encounter, with Doc Brass's universe-generating supercomputer, they are walking away with the structure of misprision, discussed in more detail below.

The trope of the Four Voyagers is central to *Planetary*'s mapping of the hidden roads behind the superhero narrative. The Four, the Planetary's enemies and counterparts, are a clear and powerful misprision of Marvel's *Fantastic Four*. Stan Lee and Jack Kirby's 1961 creation, which Robert C. Harvey describes as "the astonishing first of the new generation of superheroes—the characters that would change the nature of superhero comics,"[332] rang in the silver age of comic books with a different kind of hero. Unlike golden age icons, such as Superman, Batman, and Wonder Woman, the Fantastic Four are science heroes: inventors, explorers, and adventurers. Their superpowers emerged when their experimental rocketship failed to shield them from "cosmic rays." Ellis exploits the knowledge that American rocket technology after World War II came from ex-patriot Nazi scientists (like Wernher von Braun)— that if the Fantastic Four were real and if they went up in 1961, then their rocket technology would be deeply in debt to Nazi science—and refigures the Fantastic Four as self-interested Nazi villains, each member clearly suggesting a counterpart from the Fantastic Four. Richard Dowling, the team's leader, is the Fantastic Four's Reed Richards if he had kept his scientific breakthroughs to himself. Like Johnny Storm (The Human Torch) and Sue Storm (Invisible Woman), William Leather and Kim Suskind have fire and invisibility powers, respectively. The Four keep the bodies of three creatures under glass in a trophy room labeled "Subterrans" (a clear allusion to the first issue of *The Fantastic Four,* in which the team meets the Molemen) and have a window in their lab to a place that might be akin to the negaverse or the microverse, realms discovered by Reed Richards. As the Johnny Storm of the group, William Leather, describes the Four:

> Remember what we four are. We were reborn in the exploding heart of the multiverse. We are optimal humans. We are explorers, scientist gods, the secret heroes of a world that doesn't deserve us. We were given the world in 1961. We know all the things that you've struggled to uncover for decades. We are all those things. We are the secret history of the planet—for we are its secret chiefs.[333]

The significance of troping characters emblematic of the silver age of superhero narratives into the main archrivals of the Planetary, into ever-present Nazi agonists, reveals the anxiety of influence structure. The Planetary and their mysterious "fourth man" are themselves explor-

---

[332] Robert C. Harvey, *The Art of the Comic Book: An Aesthetic History* (Jackson: University Press of Mississippi, 1996), 45.
[333] Ellis et al., *Planetary, #*6.

ers, investigators, who from their first issue are in possession of a computer that is the "exploding heart of the multiverse"; Ellis displays *Planetary*'s imaginative debt to established heroes like the Fantastic Four, not through the passive tributary references of *Astro City,* but by utilizing the superhero convention of the villain-as-mirror and literally staging the agon with tradition, representation, and literary history. The four-member exploratory Planetary team are clearly in debt to Stan Lee and Jack Kirby's Fantastic Four, so the Fantastic Four are reconceived as the Planetary's Nazi foes.

Much of *Planetary* yields to this kind of reading, staging again and again various battles for priority between distinct periods of the superhero narrative. Having already seen *Planetary* emerge from the background of the agon between an otherworldly Justice League and their counterparts in a gathering of pulp novel heroes, the reader is witness to "Magic and Loss" (*Planetary* 10). This issue stages the suppression of the golden age characters at the hands of their silver age successors, Ellis's villainous Fantastic Four. In the story, Elijah Snow confronts three artifacts: a cape, a pair of golden bracelets, and a lantern. The narrative tracks the history of the items, which clearly allude to the origin stories of Superman, Wonder Woman, and the Green Lantern, respectively. It ends by describing how the Four cut each of them down before they could take their roles as heroes. Snow is struck by the realization of what the Four have cost the world, and the issue's cover—filled with a mass of unmarked graves—hints at the larger losses of which these three examples are the only ones known.

The issue has a clear meaning on the level of a fantastic *X-Files*–style conspiracy, but it is on another level completely true: the emergence of a new kind of hero in the silver age, teams like the Fantastic Four, meant that golden age heroes like Superman, Wonder Woman, and the Green Lantern could no longer be written. The silver age of comic books suppressed the golden age heroes as surely as the hard-boiled detective novel replaced the classic Sherlock Holmes stories, or the "modern" novel made writing "psychological realism" impossible in the 1920s. *Planetary* stages the repression of the old, the "impossibility" of writing the earlier form, when the new form literally kills the old. The Fantastic Four eliminate Superman, Wonder Woman, and the Green Lantern as surely as they replaced them. This is the kind of "hidden road"[334]

---

[334] Bloom, *Anxiety,* 96.

(Bloom) that the Planetary are trying to make a part of their "mapping [of] the secret history of the twentieth century"[335] (Ellis).

In "To be in England, in the Summertime" (*Planetary* 7), the Planetary attend the funeral of Jack Carter, who finds a clear analogue in the Vertigo character John Constantine (*Hellblazer*). The issue examines DC's incarnation of the darker, horror side of comics, and their connection to hybrid superhero-horror characters in such titles as *Swamp Thing* (written by Alan Moore), *Hellblazer* (written by Garth Ennis) *Doom Patrol* (written by Grant Morrison, who also wrote *Animal Man*), and, to a lesser extent, *Shade the Changing Man* (written by Peter Milligan) in DC's Vertigo ("for mature readers") line. Moore, Ellis, and Milligan, along with Neil Gaiman, the creator of Vertigo's most popular title, *Sandman,* are from England, Morrison is from Scotland, and Ennis is from Ireland. Ellis suggests a connection between the socioeconomic conditions in 1980s England and the angst-filled narratives those creators produced. Ellis's own contribution to this line was a stint on *Hellblazer,* the source character of the man whose funeral the Planetary (along with Swamp Thing, Doom Patrol, Shade the Changing Man, Sandman, Animal Man—and Grant Morrison) attend. What the Planetary discover is that Jack Carter has faked his own death to avoid being hunted down by a disgruntled superhero, who appears to be an allusion to Alan Moore's *Miracleman,* angry that he has been sullied by the kinds of things with which the "for mature readers" line would sully a superhero: pedophilia, split personalities, nervous breakdowns. What Ellis shows is the hidden road that connects socioeconomic depravity with the resurgence of horror and the critique of the clean, noble, perfect superhero. In the end, Jack Carter walks off to start another life. "The Eighties are long over. Time to move on. Time to be someone else,"[336] he says as he walks off, revealing another hidden road. Trench coat, shirt, and tie removed, head shaven, tattoos revealed, he is the spitting image of Warren Ellis' Spider Jerusalem (the lead character of his *Transmetropolitan*). *Planetary* exposes the road of influence between the two comic book characters by hinting that they are one and the same.

Wildcats and the *The Authority* participate in this structure as well. "The Nativity," a plot that appears in *The Authority* (13–16) after Ellis

---

[335] Ellis, "The Planetary Preview," in *Gen-13* (La Jolla, CA: Wildstorm, 1998), #33.
[336] Ellis et al., *Planetary, #7.*

left the writing of the title to Mark Millar, has a similar construction, very relevant in this context, and one can easily imagine the Planetary being witness to the conflict presented therein. In the story, the Authority—emblematic of the newest kind of superhero at the same time playing a role as a trope of the JLA, discussed above—confront the machinations of the villainous Dr. Krigstein. Krigstein manufactures superbeings in a secret government complex and is using them to gain power over the reborn superhero Jenny Sparks, whose "superpower" is to be the spirit of the twenty-first century:

> The chance to capture the very spirit of an age, and fashion the 21st century into whatever shape we desire. . . . If she's raised on a diet of Karl Marx, the next hundred years belong to the Communists. Tattoo a swastika on her head and they'll be goose-stepping down Broadway. Our concerns about the future are negligible so long as we've got the spirit of the 21st century in our arms. Tomorrow [will belong] to us.[337]

To further this end, Krigstein sends his superbeings against the Authority in separate groupings.[338] The powers and appearance of each group, interestingly, suggest a different silver age Marvel construction: the Avengers (a supersoldier, Captain America; a Norse lightning wielder, Thor; a hulking juggernaut, the Hulk; a tiny woman with wings, the Wasp; a giant, Giant Man; a man in superpowered armor, Iron Man; a man with a bow, Hawkeye; and an android, Vision), the X-Men (a team of visually bizarre teenaged superheroes), S.H.I.E.L.D. (the military team led by a cigar-smoking captain), The Fantastic Four (an elastic man, a man of flames, a man of rock, and a woman who manipulates light), along with a supporting cast (a man on a flying surfboard, the Silver Surfer) and a host of assorted silver age Marvel creations in the final battle spread, including a blind man with billy clubs (Daredevil), a flyer with a British chest emblem (Captain Briton), a creature with a flaming skull (Ghost Rider), and a giant spider-humanoid (Spider-Man). Krigstein is connected to one of the key creators of Marvel's silver age,

---

[337] Millar et al., *The Authority,* #14 and #15.
[338] Ibid., #16.

Jack Kirby:[339] a short, acerbic, cigar-smoking Jew (Kirby was born Kurtz-burg), Krigstein is described in *The Authority* as "the kind of man who would have created all your favorite comic book characters if he hadn't been snapped up by Eisenhower at the end of the war."[340] He is offered a unique defeat, asked to surrender and join the Authority because, as Swift says, "I'm fed up fighting people who either die or disappear so they can bug us eternally. It's just a waste of everyone's time."[341] Follow-ing the structure of agon given in *Planetary*, *The Authority* confronts its influence and successfully absorbs it, by incorporating the creator of the silver age, not simply a character from that period, as a member of their team. In short, almost every superhero created after 1960 has some influence-debt to Jack Kirby. Only on *The Authority* does he work for them. This symbolic movement beyond Jack Kirby is necessary, as War-ren Ellis's comments on Walter Simonson make clear:

> I know Walt Simonson is as happy as a clam working the Jack Kirby Fourth World stuff, and I have to admit that his ORION is a beautiful book . . . but it kills me to see one of the most progressive storytelling artists in comics actively forgoing his own creations to keep the Kirby creations alive.[342]

In effect, something must be *done* with Kirby in order to keep comics moving toward the future, and Mark Millar's handling of *The Authority* is an attempt at a response. In the words of John Ashbery, "Him too we can sacrifice / To the end progress, for we must, we must be moving on."[343]

An examination of Elijah Snow's first name is the penultimate analy-sis before revealing the true role of the revisionary narrative. The con-cept of the superhero has an obvious debt to messianic urges in the larger culture, of which the story of Christ stands as the prototype. An

---

[339] See Harvey's argument that it was Jack Kirby, rather than Stan Lee, who was the major creative force behind Marvel Comics' silver age boom (Harvey, *Art of the Comic Book*, 45–47).

[340] Millar et al., *The Authority*, #15.

[341] Ibid., #16.

[342] Warren Ellis, *Come in Alone* (San Francisco: AIT/Planet Lar, 2001), 17.

[343] John Ashbery, *Self-Portrait in a Convex Mirror* (New York: Penguin, 1975), 51.

Edenic state is disrupted by the intrusion of evil; the endemic forces supposed to deal with it cannot because they are either inept, corrupt, or both; a figure enters the scene from the outside, fixes everything, then leaves. It is a formula that describes a number of texts from *Superman, The Lone Ranger,* and *Star Trek,* to *Mary Poppins, Jaws,* and even *Playboy.*[344] According to Malachi, Elijah is the prophet who will perform the final miracle (and what are superhero powers if not biblical miracles?) before the coming of the Messiah; in superhero literature, he must be the figure that ushers in a new kind of superhero, a new superheroic age after the golden age and silver age of comics. For this analysis, so reliant on Harold Bloom's theory of the anxieties of "sons" in relation to powerful influential poetic "fathers" (Bloom's terms), it cannot be insignificant that the founder of the superhero team that investigates poetic debt (e.g., of the JLA to the pulp heroes) carries the name of the biblical figure who "shall reconcile the hearts of fathers to sons and the hearts of sons to fathers" (Malachi 3:24).

(As a way of returning to where we began, it should be noted that *Batman: The Dark Knight Returns* was heavily influenced by Frank Miller's reading of Kazuo Koike and Goseki Kojima's *Lone Wolf and Cub* (*Kozure Okami*). This manga samurai epic tells the story of a ronin who travels with his toddler son. The son is often used to distract or lure targets as the father makes his living as an assassin for hire. Falling prey to this ploy, one of his target's dying words are "M-monster . . . to the very end you use your own child . . . risk his life," to which the assassin answers in words very similar to those used to describe Elijah:

> Did not I say? A father knows his child's heart, as only a child can know his father's. Father and child walk through life, hand in hand! This is *seikan,* the bond of life. When father and son rely on their bond to do what they must to survive. . . . This is

---

[344] The relation of *Playboy* to this schema may require a gloss: before the reader is a "good girl" who has become sexually insatiable. It is the role of the male reader, in fantasy space, to swoop down, satisfy her through his prowess, then leave. Like the *Lone Ranger, Star Trek,* and *Mary Poppins,* this "savior" should not stay, but must move on. Marrying the woman and starting a life together is not part of the equation. Thanks to Professor Robert Gurland for pointing out the ubiquity of this schema in his lectures at New York University.

how it must be. [He] and I are inseparable. Such is our des-
tiny.[345])

Harold Bloom's theory is based on an irresolvable conflict at the
base of the act of writing; Žižek bases reality around a fundamental
irresolvable antagonism. Jewish folklore says that when a dispute cannot
be resolved, discussion will be suspended until "the time of Elijah." This
is the focus of *Planetary*'s powerful, and radical, reading of history. Žižek
writes:

> What the proper *historical* stance (as opposed to historicism)
> "relativizes" is not the past (always distorted by our present
> point of view) but, paradoxically, *the present itself*—our present
> can be conceived only as the outcome (not of what actually
> happened in the past, but also) of the crushed potentials for the
> future that were contained in the past. In other words, it is not
> only—as Foucault liked to emphasize, in a Nietzschean mode—
> that every history of the past is ultimately the "ontology of the
> present," that we always perceive our past within the horizon of
> our present preoccupations, that in dealing with the past we are
> in effect dealing with the ghosts of the past whose resuscitation
> enables us to confront our present dilemmas. It is also that we,
> the "actual" present historical agents, have to conceive of *our-
> selves* as the materialization of the ghosts of past generations, as
> the stage in which these past generations retroactively resolve
> their deadlocks.[346]

Planetary is, in part, a construction of this "time of Elijah," where the
past will retroactively resolve their deadlocks, and the present is understood as the outcome of the crushed potentials for the future contained
in the past, as in "Magic and Loss" (*Planetary* 10). The prophet Elijah
also captures precisely the sense of contradictory continuity so inherent
to the superhero narrative. His warmhearted folklore persona is abso-

---

[345] Kazuo Koike and Goseki Kojima, *Lone Wolf and Cub,* vol. 1—*The Assassin's Road*
(Milwaukee: Dark Horse, 2000), 68.
[346] Slavoj Žižek, *The Fragile Absolute—or, Why Is the Christian Legacy Worth Fighting For?*
(London: Verso, 2000), 90–91 (Žižek's emphasis).

lutely at odds with the furious, impassioned, uncompromising figure found in the biblical Book of Kings, perhaps—suggests Rabbi Joseph Teluskhin[347]—because, like comic book superheroes, it is implied that he never dies (2 Kings 2:11).

Planetary presents us with a structure, a way of conceiving of the stages of past superhero literature. The silver age's replacement of the golden age is represented by a physical defeat *within* the ostensible narrative: the Four stand in for the Fantastic Four and the silver age, killing figures of the golden age—Superman, Wonder Woman, and the Green Lantern. If this is how we are to understand, retroactively, the birth of the second age of superheroes, then recognizing the third age should be relatively simple: the third age of superheroes will establish themselves by defeating the silver age. This is the structure that the Wildstorm universe has given us. The strong writing here retroactively reconfigures history to set itself up as the inheritor of the new age of superheroes. *Planetary* and *The Authority* (and *Wildcats,* as we will see) are the apex of the study addressed in this book not because every work cited culminates here, but because these works are strong enough to make it look that way. The Planetary's nemesis is the Fantastic Four. Defeating the Four will put the Planetary in relation to them as they were to the golden age characters they eradicated: the Planetary will represent an entirely new age. The Authority has already defeated a mass of silver age icons and absorbed a figure of their creator, Jack Kirby, as a member of the team. Joe Casey's *Wildcats* (this different spelling is indicative of volume 2 of that series) will participate in this structure in an interesting manner.

As mentioned above, *WildC.A.T.s* was launched in 1992 by Jim Lee and Brandon Choi as an attempt to siphon the popularity of Marvel's *X-Men.* Initially, *WildC.A.T.s,* really just an *X-Men* copycat, typified the waning imagination of late silver age comics. When Alan Moore wrote a stint on the title (*WildC.A.T.s: Homecoming* and *Gang War*), he completely undermined their raison d'être: a battle unit in an immense intergalactic struggle with an alien race, the WildC.A.T.s found themselves soldiers without a war. Moore's twist was to "reveal" that the war had been over for centuries; Earth was such an obscure battleground that no one bothered to tell the WildC.A.T.s their side had won. Without a purpose, and

---

[347] Joseph Teluskin, *Jewish Literacy* (New York: William Morrow, 1991), 87.

discovering the alien empire they had served for so long was less noble than they had been led to believe, the team soon broke up. The book was relaunched as something completely different. Although it still carried the name *Wildcats,* the book simply followed the relatively normal lives of characters that were once teammates. It presented its characters not as larger than life superheroes but as frail human beings. In Joe Casey's "Serial Boxes" (*Wildcats* 14–19), the grandson of an old supervillain returns for revenge, but this clichéd superhero story is turned completely on its head. The villian's only power is something like the eye blasts of the X-Men's Cyclops, and having a single power that defines his character certainly links him with those silver age creations. Casey realistically renders the sheer destructive power of having even one of the X-Men's abilities. This uninspired silver age power severs the legs of Voodoo (who, in the traditional *X-Men* copycat role, would be the sex appeal), destroys Ladytron (the team's cyborg), and blinds Maul. Maul is an Incredible Hulk figure that can transform from a mild scientist to a hulking brute at will. He uses his power here for the first time in the new series, now sixteen issues deep, to no avail. The "supervillain" is finally defeated in an anticlimax reminiscent of the final scene of David Fincher's film *Seven* (1995). He is shot in the head when a clear line of sight presents itself to Grifter, the team's marksman. A strange moment passes between Grifter and Spartan. These characters have changed since their creation, and there is a certain ambivalence, a certain strangeness, in them now that suggests they know they are no longer their old selves. Sean Phillips's art, for example, has completely eliminated the flashy "T and A" quality the women of WildC.A.T.s once had, presenting in its stead a neon-lit film noir look and women obviously not intended to entice male readers. The Planetary will defeat the Fantastic Four, the Authority defeats Jack Kirby and all his creations, and the Wildcats destroy their only silver age influence/nemesis: no longer a team, or even superheroes, they have obliterated their old selves as bad, late silver age, X-Men rip-offs. The WildC.A.T.s take their place in the modern age: *Planetary* set the structure, *Stormwatch* became *The Authority,* and the *Wild-C.A.T.s* become the *Wildcats.* Casey's work might go unnoticed were it not published simultaneously with *Planetary,* at the same company and in the same continuity, but Casey is quick to answer the question of where the Wildcats fit into a universe with *The Authority* and *Planetary.*

That *Planetary* gives us the schema for understanding the new age of the superhero narrative is evidenced by the way the schema *fails* the first time it appears, in "All Over the World" (*Planetary* 1). If the paradigm exists as I have suggested, shouldn't the "Justice League of America" have defeated the "Pulp Heroes" since the golden age heroes surely replaced those dime-store novel protagonists? The fact that the only survivor was Doc Brass is not, as may first appear, paradoxical. Doc Brass's source character is Doc Savage, the Man of Bronze. *Planetary*'s role, as has already been discussed, is to uncover the "bronze age," the successor to the golden and silver ages of the superhero, in their archeology of mysteries. The first issue of *Planetary* appears to be about the birth of the superhero comic books out of the pulp novels, but it is actually about how looking at anxiety of influence relationships birth the "third movement" of the superhero narrative.

Returning to *Planetary* with this understanding, what, then, is the significance of the Snowflake, the network of interconnected parallel universes? As Hark describes it, in its first appearance, the supercomputer under the Adirondacks:

> This is the shape of reality. A theoretical snowflake existing in 196,833 dimensional space. The snowflake rotates. Each element of the snowflake rotates. Each rotation describes an entirely new universe. The total number of rotations are equal to the number of atoms making up the Earth. Each rotation makes a new Earth. This is the multiverse.[348]

It might have been responsible for the monsters on Island Zero (*Planetary* 2: "Island"). It appears to be connected to the Chinese phantom cop (*Planetary* 3: "Dead Gunfighters") as a kind of ghost computer, and the shiftship from "Strange Harbours" (*Planetary* 4) is designed to sail it, to sail between universes. It gave the Four Voyagers their fantastic powers and appears to have replaced a man's brain in "The Day the Earth Turned Slower" (*Planetary* 8). As the artificially aware shiftship explains:

> Your universe hangs within a structure of universes, a thing almost like a snowflake. Channels course between the countless

---

[348] Ellis et al., *Planetary*, #1.

alternative earths, keeping them separate. This we call the Bleed.
I was designed to sail the Bleed; a trading ship between universes.[349]

The Bleed is the hidden road that connects the various alternate
earths that make up, not a single comic book continuity, but the multiplicity of all of them, existent and possible. The shiftship (and, incidentally, the Carrier that serves as the base for the Authority) is designed to
sail the Bleed, to explore that place between continuities, the misprisions and tropes that would make up the superhero multiverse, the
parallel existence of all of the various comic book companies, real or
imaginary. In a traditional comic book continuity, various disparate
characters from various titles interact in the same fantasy space. The
snowflake is a way for any imagined character from any company, or any
misprision of any character thereof, to interact across the gulf separating
their separate fantasy continuities.

To play off Alan Moore's humorous explanation of comic book continuity explained for those readers of more traditional literature (quoted
in chapter 3), it is as if the Planetary discovered that the universe of
Samuel Beckett characters hung in a structure that contained the universe of Tom Stoppard's *Rosencrantz and Guildenstern Are Dead,* a world
where all of Shakespeare's stories really happened, and the universe of
Laurel and Hardy, Keaton and Chaplin. The connections among those
works, the path of influence and debt, could be traced on the level of
the fictions themselves, by a work that was itself a tremendous piece of
fiction. With the breakdown of a belief in an objective metalanguage,
this is the space of literary criticism that is as much literature as the
works it confronts (note its "enabling fictions"), participating in the
same anxiety of influence relationships: Bloom, Derrida, Žižek, Rorty.
Can it not be said that they operate in the "Bleed" between various
works of literature, art, and philosophy? That they write as if works of
fiction, philosophy, poetry, criticism, and psychoanalysis existed in a
single continuity, across which they can interact? Does Harold Bloom
not place Milton, Keats, Whitman, Stevens, and Ashbery in a single
space where they may interact in an experiment not unlike *Planetary*? Is
the crystalline Snowflake of *Planetary* not Grant Morrison's dialectic of

---

[349] Ibid., #4.

the sublime? Or Žižek's traumatic kernel of the Real that forever resists symbolization? Jung writes:

> [F]or the more the libido is invested—or, to be more accurate, invests itself—in the unconscious, the greater becomes its influence or potency: all the rejected, disused, outlived functional possibilities that have been lost for generations come to life again and begin to exert an ever-increasing influence on the conscious mind, despite its desperate struggles to gain insight into what is happening. The saving factor is the symbol, which embraces both conscious and unconscious and unites them. For while the consciously disposable libido gets gradually used up in the differentiated function and is replenished more and more slowly and with increasing difficulty, the symptoms of inner disunity multiply and there is a growing danger of inundation and destruction by the unconscious contents, but all the time the symbol is developing that is destined to resolve the conflict. The symbol, however, is so intimately bound up with the dangerous and menacing aspect of the unconscious that it is easily mistaken for it, or its appearance may actually call forth evil and destructive tendencies. At all events the appearance of the redeeming symbol is closely connected with destruction and devastation. If the old were not ripe for death, nothing new would appear; and if the old were not injuriously blocking the way for the new, it could not and need not be rooted out.[350]

Operating in the space of the Bleed, the Planetary see from between the worlds rather than from inside any single one and finds the anxiety of influence connections between various superhero narratives. "As literary history lengthens" writes Bloom, "all poetry necessarily becomes verse-criticism, just as all criticism becomes prose poetry."[351] I would add that all prose poetry becomes something like a comic book continuity: this effect of winter-lateness is clearly invoked by Elijah's Snow, and the Snowflake. Within its own tradition, this conception of a multiverse, the vision that sees the structure of all converging and disparate superhero

---

[350] Jung, *Psychological Types,* 264.
[351] Bloom, *Map,* 3

narratives, is the final overturning of the continuity, the universe, established by creators like Stan Lee, and events like *Crisis on Infinite Earths*. As in *Crisis*, Ellis splinters reality by investigating origins. The idea of a multiverse, the idea of huge numbers of slightly or radically altered earths parallel to this one, is the vision of misprision, of trope. In the world of *Planetary*, we see a Nazi Fantastic Four that keeps their scientific discoveries to themselves, elitists who quest for power, an Incredible Hulk who is the true monster Stan Lee and Jack Kirby might have conceived without the comic book code (*Planetary* Preview issue, "Nuclear Spring"); and a reading of the Authority as sadistic Lovecraftian monsters (*Planetary/The Authority: Ruling the World*).[352] Alternate earths are misreadings of each other, and the Bleed is the space where the connections are traced, where one can see among several texts. The hidden road, the road that the critic knows, is the hidden road of influence, the backroad connecting the superhero narrative with its own history, its tradition, its influences and effects. This is why *Planetary* covers not simply superhero history but also the places where the superhero narrative intersects with other media and stories: the Godzilla monsters of Island Zero (*Planetary* 2: "Island"), the Cantonese action movie (e.g., John Woo's *The Killer*) (*Planetary* 3: "Dead Gunfighters"), 1950s sci-fi (e.g., *Them*) (*Planetary* 8: "The Day the Earth Turned Slower"), *The Matrix* (*Planetary* 9: "Planet Fiction")[353], DC's alternative horror line Vertigo, spy comics and films (*Planetary* 11 "Cold World"), the *X-Files* (*Planetary* 14: "Zero Point"), and the fantastic literature of the nineteenth century from which the modern heroes and villains emerged: *The Invisible Man*,

---

[352] Note Ellis's joke in the *Planetary/The Authority* crossover: the *WildC.A.T.s/Aliens* crossover, which had every reason to be completely without point, had disastrous effects on *Stormwatch*. Readers expecting something similar here find a complete nonevent: the teams involved never even meet. "Ruling the World" was almost a perfect expression of the usual feeling engendered by comic book crossovers—that for all crossovers accomplish, the characters involved might as well never meet. In a very telling moment, the closest the Planetary comes to actually meeting the Authority is an alternative-universe version come through the bleed: that is, the Planetary met the Authority only in misprision.

[353] Ellis writes in his online column, "Its true that 99% of the audience for THE MATRIX really didn't know that what they were seeing was at the root of the superhero genre. And that film showed that the tropes of the superhero genre can be made accessible to a mass audience." Ellis, *Come in Alone*, 143).

Dracula, Sherlock Holmes, Frankenstein, and *20,000 Leagues under the Sea* (*Planetary* 13: "Century").[354]

This, then, is *Planetary*: the record of the battles for priority, the hidden roads that were not the agon in each issue between superhero and supervillain, but the secret history of the twentieth-century super-hero narrative: the combat to determine the shape of the superhero to come, the future of the superhero narrative. As the example of "The Nativity" (discussed above) suggests, it is a battle to control the reborn Jenny Sparks, the combat to determine the spirit of an age. And in all its maneuverings to witness the emergence of the superhero narrative, *Planetary,* of course, becomes that narrative: the new superheroes are the witnesses of agon, the makers of secret maps, the critics who know the hidden roads that go from superhero to superhero.

'Nuff said.

---

[354] The difference between the influences exposed in *Planetary* and the return-of-the-dead trope in *Watchmen* is striking. *Planetary* invokes an entirely different return of the dead: Bloom's revisionary ratio of *apophrades* might be premature, but it is still worth noting:

> The later poet, in his own final phase, already burdened by an imaginative solitude that is almost solipsism, holds his own poem so open again to the precursor's work that at first we might believe the wheel has come full circle, and that we are back in the later poet's flooded apprenticeship, before his strength began to assert itself in the revisionary ratios. But the poem is now *held* open to the precursor, where once it *was* open, and the uncanny effect is that the new poem's achievement makes it seem to us, not as though the precursor were writing it, but as though the later poet himself had written the precursor's characteristic work. (Bloom, *Anxiety,* 16, Bloom's emphasis)

Pop Comics, Harold Bloom at Harvard, and the Oedipal Fallacy

A lthough the argument presented in this book is encompassed in chapters 1 through 5, the serial nature of the superhero comic book calls for at least an adumbration of ideas emerging in comics too early in their runs to be analyzed fully. I present here observations for future study, the superheroes that emerge after Elijah's presence announces something new.

The largest new trend emerging in superhero comic books at the time of this writing is the pop comic. Though many superheroes have been quite popular in their fictional continuities before now, this new trend is the cathexis of several strands of intra- and extratextual material. The modern incarnation began with *The Authority,* which, while raising the bar on high levels of violence and so-called wide-screen storytelling, also accessed the strain of attention and popularity that is a subset of the superhero as adolescent power fantasy. The superhero becomes a kind of sexy pop icon. What separates this emerging trend from its predecessors is the conscious intention on the part of the creators themselves—now making appearances in *Entertainment Weekly*—to make comic books a kind of sexy, popular medium. Matthew J. Pustz describes the world of the average comic book fan in *Comic Book Culture*: a close-knit group of a relatively small number of consumers whose medium of choice is mostly frowned upon by the general public, who still believes that comic books are for children. Some, however, see hope for the comic book to become the next big thing and enter mainstream popular culture alongside novels, films, television, and that especially peculiar emergent storytelling medium, video games. Grant Morrison and Warren Ellis are the most vocal proponents of this movement to make comic books more varied (i.e., no longer 90 percent superhero stories) and accessible to a mainstream audience. Combine this sensibility with the popularity of what amount to thinly disguised superhero stories—*The*

Matrix and *Unbreakable*—along with more obvious superhero films like *X-Men*, *Spider-Man*, and *The Incredible Hulk*, and you have the birth of the pop comic in such titles as *Ultimate X-Men* (Mark Millar), *Marvel Boy* (Grant Morrison), *New X-Men* (Morrison), and *X-Force* (Peter Milligan and Mike Allred). Mark Millar and Adam Kubert's *Ultimate X-Men* is a streamlined superhero story that reads like a James Bond movie with an unlimited budget. For the fan, there is a continuity with the superhero genre, but these stories are designed for a mainstream audience aware of the stigma superhero comic books carry. In Morrison's words on the pop comic:

> My ideal comic is the one which perfectly expresses its moment and makes you want to dance like your favorite records do. The ideal comic is a holographic condensation out of pure zeitgeist. Pop is my god and goddess . . . and I believe comics should strive to be popper yet than Pop itself.[355]

Morrison identifies this (interestingly, I think) with the separation of comic books from other mediums:

> As for Marvel Boy. Not only am I working with one of the best comics artists ever, the coloring gauntlet has been thrown down once again with the most incredible video game lighting and atmospherics. The whole thing really becomes something new with issue 3, however, which I'm unusually proud of. Apart from the fact that the potentially impenetrable central idea (HEXUS, THE LIVING CORPORATION) wound up beautifully simple, original and ridiculous all at once, that was the issue I really began to utilizes J.G. Jones' preposterous genius to its best effects and decided to rethink the prevailing vogue for cinematic/ money shot panel structures and page layouts. Marvel Boy's visual style becomes more like MTV and adverts; from #3 on it's filled with all kinds of new techniques; rapid cuts, strobed lenticular panels, distressed layouts, 64 panel grids, whatever. We've only just started to experiment but already MARVEL BOY looks like nothing else around. Some of the stuff J.G. is doing is like

---

[355] Ellis, *Come in Alone,* 124.

an update of the whole Steranko Pop Art approach to the comics page. Instead of Orson Welles, op art and spy movies, J.G's using digital editing effects, percussive rhythms, cutting the action closer and harder, illuminated by the frantic glow of the image crazed hallucination of 21st century media culture and all that. Comics don't need to be like films. They don't need to look like storyboards. This is not to dis the many great comics which have used filmic narrative techniques but I wanted to go back and explore some of the possibilities of comics as music.[356]

It is at least possible that the superhero comic book has moved on to the future promised by the presence of Elijah on the superhero landscape into this completely bizarre realm of storytelling. These works do not participate in the tradition of the superhero story as the works studied above do, but find influences in the most unlikely places.

Marvel Boy, for example, is a kind of glossy MTV action flick, in line with Jean Luc-Besson's *The Fifth Element.*[357] The old structures are still there: Midas, whose name invokes gold, gathers cosmic radiation so that he may take on powers like the Fantastic Four (the Royal Family of the silver age); an obsessive and domineering father (and father figure) he hunts after Noh-Varr, icon of the pop comic, who has teamed up with Midas's daughter, Oubliette, a dark young woman dressed in black leather whose name refers to a dungeon, the only entrance to which is the top. But *Marvel Boy*'s surface gloss seems, in the words of John Ashbery, on the outside looking out, and resists interpretive structures like the ones we have invoked here.

Grant Morrison and Frank Quitely's vision of *New X-Men* is of a kind with contemporary Nike advertisements and hip-hop magazines. Quitely's covers invoke the fashion magazine images of *GQ, W,* and *Cosmopolitan* (posed shots of single heroes from the thigh up against a solid-color background). The design of a mutant introduced in their first issue, Ugly Joe (*New X Men* 114), was lifted from an advertisement in the Australian magazine *Free Skier.* In this vein, Quitely simultaneously accepts and rejects the traditional portrayal of the *X-Men*'s women as

---

[356] Ibid., 123.

[357] It might be interesting for a future study to see how these comics might function in the context of *cinéma du look,* and the extension of related film criticism.

impossibly curvaceous superbabes. Jean Grey and the White Queen are still as "beautiful" as models, but the template for their design is now contemporary runway models like Kate Moss rather than the voluptuous pinup girls of the 1950s or their gravity-defying "interpretation" in the bad girl comics of the early 1990s. (In a bad pun, Quitely's X-Women bring new meaning to the phrase "heroin(e) chic.") Morrison and Quitely introduce uniforms that, rather than the traditional spandex and skullcaps, look as if they were designed by Tommy Hilfiger. When Professor X asks what the students think of their new "look," this exchange takes place:

WOLVERINE: Suddenly I don't have to look like an idiot in broad daylight.

THE BEAST: I was never sure why you had us dress up like superheroes anyway, Professor.

CYCLOPS: The Professor thought people would trust the X-Men if we looked like something they understood.

PROFESSOR X: That's correct, Scott.[358]

Morrison doesn't claim that the X-Men are the future of the superhero narrative (as Warren Ellis retroactively configures *Planetary*), but rather claims that they never were superheroes. Something new and strange has emerged from the superhero story, something without a name. In Morrison's first plot arc, "E for Extinction," the X-Men face Cassandra Nova, a villain who is to the mutants what the mutants are to the humans. As the Beast explains:

She's from beyond the biological twilight zone. She looks human on the outside, but nothing like her has ever existed before. And she preys on mutants. Why? Because every few hundred thousand years, evolution, which emphatically does not proceed smoothly, takes huge catastrophic jumps. Old life forms get wiped from the fossil record overnight in periodic mass extinctions, and are replaced. I think Cassandra Nova is the first of a new unforeseen species. I think she'll instinctively use her out-

---

[358] Grant Morrison, Frank Quitely, et al., *New X-Men* (New York: Marvel Comics, 2001–present), #114.

landish natural gifts to wipe us out if she can. . . . The human race is at an end. Within three, maybe four generations, they'll be gone, replaced by us, or something even stranger.[359]

"Something like Cassandra Nova," responds Professor X, ominously. Having reached the end of our study, a detailed examination of Morrison's *New X-Men* is not necessary, but it is clear that Morrison is saying something about the superhero narrative and its progressive ages, about innovation and literary tradition, about the future of the genre.

X-Force is playing further games with the notion of pop comics. A new media-savvy X-Force is recruited, complete with toys, T-shirts, and a teammate whose job it is to videotape the team's exploits. In Peter Milligan and Mike Allred's first issue all but two members of the brand-new team are slaughtered protecting a boy band. The doomed leader of this first incarnation of the new *X-Force* bears the code name Zeitgeist and is gifted with the power to vomit energy on his foes. Morrison has already described the ideal comic as "a holographic condensation out of pure zeitgeist,"[360] and here we have a character whose name means "the spirit of the age," the post–silver age, that regurgitates as surely as *Watchmen* tried not to (see chapter 1). At the end of Milligan and Allred's seventh issue, as the team is gathered in their chic film-screening room, Tike Alicar remarks, as the closing line of the two-part plot arc "Lacuna," "Is it me . . . or is this popcorn, like, stale."[361]

"Pop comics" like *Ultimate X-Men, Marvel Boy, New X-Men,* and *X-Force*—in their glossy, surface-only brilliance—may have achieved something impenetrable to the kind of model offered to explain the arc from *Crisis on Infinite Earths* to *Planetary.* Their status as something different may prove the validity of the approach presented here. Time will tell whether this trend will continue into something lasting, but in any case, there are stirrings here that should be noticed and watched. We began with a Crisis. We end with something New.

As a final word on this subject, I would like to point out a moment within this new phase of the pop comic that properly signifies that the present study has made its argument just in time for the superhero

---

[359] Ibid., #116.
[360] Ellis, *Alone,* 124.
[361] Peter Milligan and Mike Allred, *X-Force* (New York: Marvel Comics, 2002), #122.

narrative to move beyond it: as of *X-Force* 118, Harold Bloom has appeared by name in a superhero comic book. One of X-Force's new recruits was a student at Harvard who not only had Bloom for a professor of English literature—discussing "Hamlet, Freud and the Oedipus fallacy"—but was harassed by fellow superhero teammates for reading his books. To see Bloom and his theory butchered in a mainstream superhero comic book (an *X-Men* spin-off, no less) seems an auspicious moment to declare this study complete. Can there be any greater misprision than to place the Yale-educated Bloom, author of *The Anxiety of Influence,* at Harvard discussing some kind of imaginary crossbreed of the oedipal complex and the affective fallacy?[362] Harold Bloom has left the building; the next book of superhero criticism will have to invent a language all its own.

---

[362] An uncorroborated online report on the Warren Ellis Forum, from someone claiming to have passed the issue on through a friend who worked for Harold Bloom, said he was highly amused.

Unbreakable

U *nbreakable* (2000) is an interesting movie on several levels, not the least of which is that it was marketed solely on the basis of "From the writer and director of *The Sixth Sense*." In none of the advertising is it presented as the superhero movie it actually turns out to be. In a study of the superhero story from the early 1980s to 2001, it seems that one way to illustrate the growth of the superhero narrative would be to ask how the superhero film goes from *Superman: The Movie* to *Unbreakable*. What lies between is *Batman: The Dark Knight Returns, Watchmen, Marvels, Astro City, Kingdom Come,* America's Best Comics, *The Justice League of America, The Authority, Planetary,* and *Wildcats.*

Unbreakable is the story of Elijah Price (Samuel L. Jackson), who is born with a disorder that makes his bones especially brittle. Growing up on superhero comic books, he assumes that his existence implies the existence of someone at the other end of the spectrum, someone as immune to damage is he himself is susceptible to it. When David Dunn (Bruce Willis) is the only survivor of a train wreck, and there is not a scratch on him, Elijah believes he has found his superhero. Claiming that superhero comic books are only exaggerations of superheroics that have always existed, Elijah sets out to convince David of his special status. Dunn slowly "discovers" his modest powers—sensing evil deeds, bench-pressing 350 pounds—and the only thing to which he is not immune (his kryptonite, Elijah says) is drowning. Dunn rescues two hostages from a killer in the suburbs and in the final moments of the film discovers that Elijah Price is the true villain. He is a terrorist who has caused a plane crash, a hotel fire, and David's own train disaster in an effort to discover someone who was unbreakable, a sole survivor miraculously unharmed.

In online message boards, Mark Millar has suggested the possibility that David Dunn is just an ordinary mortal who survived his train crash through luck: his heroics are merely the result of Elijah's placing him in the position of believing he is a superhero. It is an arguable reading, and not wholly convincing (relying, as it does, on the belief that any person properly sensitized would be able to sense evil in others), but it points to an important theme of the film. *Unbreakable* is about interpellation—in the Althusserian sense of the term—of ordinary people into an intentional subtext formed by superhero comic books. DC Comics published a few books under a banner called "Realworlds" (a riff on their "what if" line "Elseworlds") that told the stories of ordinary people who read *Batman, Wonder Woman,* and the *JLA* and how their lives were affected by the comics they read. On some level, *Unbreakable* is this kind of superhero story, with Elijah Price as the tragic lead character.

Elijah's speeches on the eternal existence of the superhero are at odds with what he is actually doing. Initially, it appears that *Unbreakable* is in the Jung–Campbell–Lévi-Strauss lineage, as Elijah claims that superhero comic books are only exaggerations of an eternally true archetype of the hero that has always lived. What he does, however, is bring a superhero into existence through his radical misreading of the world: by looking too much into things through the paradigm of the superhero comic book, he actually causes the sole survivor of a train wreck to interpellate himself into the role of the comic book superhero. Louis Althusser writes:

> I shall then suggest that ideology "acts" or "functions" in such a way that it "recruits" subjects among the individuals (it recruits them all), or "transforms" the individuals into subjects (it transforms them all) by that very precise operation which I have called *interpellation* or hailing, and which can be imagined along the lines of the most commonplace everyday police (or other) hailing: "Hey, you there!"[363]

> The individual *is interpellated as a (free) subject in order that he shall submit freely to the commandments of the Subject, i.e. in order that he shall (freely) accept his subjection, i.e. in order that he shall make the gestures and actions of his subjection "all by himself." There*

---

[363] Louis Althusser, *Lenin and Philosophy* (New York: Monthly Review Press, 1971), 174.

are no subjects except by and for their subjection. That is why they "work all by themselves."[364]

David Dunn does not merely save lives but becomes entangled (interpellated by Elijah's call) in all the tropes of the superhero: the secret identity (his wife abhors violence in any form, and thus Dunn keeps her in the dark about his other life), the cape and cowl (a green poncho that becomes in the course of the film something very much like the Specter's garb), the colorfully costumed villain (a maintenance man in a fluorescent orange jumpsuit), the mentor (Elijah himself), the confidant (his son, Joseph), and finally the mastermind villain behind it all. The tragedy of the film, and the reason that it is really Elijah's story, is that in order to make all this happen, Elijah is forced into the role of the supervillain. Naming is a key strand here: Elijah Price suggests the tax levied against the one who prophesizes the coming of the superhero (his first name clearly resonates with the same signification as Elijah Snow), but his brittle bones earn him another name. As a child in the schoolyard, he was called Mr. Glass. To believe in the existence of superheroes, he must believe that the childhood taunt has a meaning in the matrix of comic books as the name of a supervillain. As discussed above, superheroes only rise to fight threats to the status quo, so to call forth a superhero, Elijah must become a villain. This is the reason for his tears, rather than pride, in the final scene. He says to Dunn at the end of the film, "Do you know what the scariest thing is? To not know your place in this world. To not know why you're here. That's just an awful feeling. I almost gave up hope. There were so many times I questioned myself. But I found you. So many sacrifices just to find you. Now that we know who you are, I know who I am."[365] Elijah's speeches on the eternal archetype of the superhero do not reflect the stance of the film, but rather Elijah's pathological reasoning behind imposing his own vision on the world. This powerful misreading, however, results in a world in which something like superheroes do exist, thus validating the theory of archetypes.

What we discover here is something fundamental about the act of misprision: its Möbius strip quality. One of Žižek's oft-used metaphors,

---

[364] Ibid., 182 (emphasis Althusser's).
[365] *Unbreakable,* dir. M. Night Shyamalan, perf. Bruce Willis and Samuel L. Jackson. Touchstone Pictures (2000).

taken from Lacan, the Möbius strip is a theoretical object, imagined by topology, with only one side (a model of which can be easily made by taking a strip of paper, giving one end a half twist, and connecting the ends together). At any given point, it appears to have two opposing sides, but by traveling on one side long enough, the traveler will discover herself on the opposite side without being able to determine at what point she crossed over. It is an important way of conceiving of binary oppositions (such as inside/outside) and is useful here: Elijah's theories of the superhero archetype causes them to take shape in reality, proving the theory that is believed to be true and misread into the world, and so on and so forth.

This is not, however, an analysis of the film, but only a teasing out of one of its thematic strands. What is important here is that the super-hero comic book's translation into other media, such as film and televi-sion, serve an important function. They represent the superhero comic books (and, by extension, the superhero comic book reader) to the outside world, a point that has been made elsewhere. *Unbreakable* is perhaps the only representative of the revisionary superhero narrative available to the non–comic book reading public.

Bibliography

Works Cited

Ashbery, John. *Self-Portrait in a Convex Mirror.* New York: Penguin, 1975.

Althusser, Louis. *Lenin and Philosophy.* New York: Monthly Review Press, 1971.

Baird, Forrest E., and Walter Kaufmann, eds. *From Plato to Nietzsche,* 2nd ed., Upper Saddle River, NJ: Prentice Hall, 1997.

Bendis, Brian Michael. *Fortune and Glory: A True Hollywood Comic Book Story.* Portland, OR: Oni Press, 2000.

Bloom, Harold. *Agon.* Oxford: Oxford University Press, 1982.

———. *The Anxiety of Influence.* Oxford: Oxford University Press, 1973.

———. *The Book of J.* New York: Vintage, 1990.

———. *A Map of Misreading.* Oxford: Oxford University Press, 1975.

Brennert, Alan et al. "The Brave and the Bold no. 197," in *The Greatest Batman Stories Ever Told.* Edited by Mike Gold. New York: DC Comics, 1988. 321–343.

Brooker, Will. *Batman Unmasked.* New York: Continuum, 2000.

———. "Hero of the Beach: Flex Mentallo at the End of the Worlds." Unpublished.

Brown, Jeffery A. *Black Superheroes, Milestone Comics and Their Fans.* Jackson: University Press of Mississippi, 2001.

Burke, Kenneth. *Permanence and Change,* 3rd ed. Berkeley: University of California Press, 1984.

Busiek, Kurt, Brent E. Anderson, Alex Ross et al. *Astro City.* New York: DC Comics, 1995–present.

———. *Astro City: Confession (Astro City,* vol. 2, no. 4–9, 1/2). New York: DC Comics, 1997.

———. *Astro City: Family Matters (Astro City,* vol. 1–3, no. 10–13). New York: DC Comics, 1998.

———. *Astro City: Life in the Big City (Astro City,* vol. 1, no. 1–6). New York: DC Comics, 1995.

Busiek, Kurt, and Alex Ross. *Marvels.* New York: Marvel Comics, 1994.

Campbell, Joseph. *The Hero with a Thousand Faces.* Princeton, NJ: Princeton University Press, 1949.

Casey, Joe, Sean Phillips, et al. *Wildcats.* La Jolla, CA: Wildstorm, 1998–2001.

Casey, Joe, Travis Charest, et al. *Wildcats: Street Smarts (Wildcats,* vol. 2, no. 1–6). La Jolla, CA: Wildstorm, 2000.

Casey, Joe, Sean Phillips, et al. *Wildcats: Serial Boxes (Wildcats,* vol. 2, no. 14–19). La Jolla, CA: Wildstorm, 2001.

Casey, Joe, Sean Phillips, et al. *Wildcats: Vicious Circles (Wildcats,* vol. 2, no. 8–13). La Jolla, CA: Wildstorm, 2001.

Chandler, Raymond. *Trouble Is My Business.* New York: Random House, 1939.

Daniels, Les. *Batman: The Complete History.* San Francisco: Chronicle Books, 1999.

David, Peter, and Jae Lee. *X-cutioner's Song,* chapter 6 (*X-Factor* 85). New York: Marvel Comics, 1994.

Eco, Umberto. *The Role of the Reader: Explorations in the Semiotics of Texts.* Bloomington: Indiana University Press, 1979.

Ellis, Warren. *Come in Alone.* San Francisco: ATT/Planet Lar, 2001.

————. *From the Desk of Warren Ellis.* Vol. 1. Urbana, IL: Avatar, 2000.

Ellis, Warren, Brian Hitch, Paul Neary, et al. *The Authority.* La Jolla, CA: Wildstorm, 1999–2000.

————. *The Authority: Relentless* (*The Authority,* no. 1–8). La Jolla, CA: Wildstorm, 2000.

————. *The Authority: Under New Management* (*The Authority* no. 9–16). La Jolla, CA: Wildstorm, 2000.

Ellis, Warren, John Cassaday, and Laura Depuy. *Planetary.* La Jolla, CA: Wildstorm, 1999–2000.

Ellis, Warren, Phil Jimenez, et al. *Planetary/The Authority: Ruling the World.* La Jolla, CA: Wildstorm, 2000.

————. *Stormwatch,* vol. 1, no. 37–50. La Jolla, CA: Wildstorm, 1996–1998.

————. *Stormwatch,* vol. 2, preview, no. 1–11. La Jolla, CA: Wildstorm, 1999–2000.

Ellis, Warren, Chris Sprouse, et al. *WildC.A.T.s/Aliens.* La Jolla, CA: WildStorm–Dark Horse, 1998.

————. *Stormwatch: Change or Die* (*Stormwatch,* no. 48–50, Preview no. 1, vol. 2, no. 1–3). La Jolla, CA: Wildstorm, 1999.

————. *Stormwatch: Final Orbit* (*Stormwatch,* vol. 2 no. 10–11). La Jolla, CA: Wildstorm, 2001.

————. *Stormwatch: A Finer World* (*Stormwatch,* vol. 2, no. 4–9). La Jolla, CA: Wildstorm, 1998.

————. *Stormwatch: Force of Nature* (*Stormwatch,* no. 37–42). La Jolla, CA: Wildstorm, 1996.

————. *Stormwatch: Lightning Strikes* (*Stormwatch,* no. 43–47). La Jolla, CA: Wildstorm, 1996.

Emerson, Ralph Waldo. "Circles." In *The Portable Emerson,* edited by Carl Bode. New York: Penguin, 1981.

Evans, Dylan. *An Introductory Dictionary of Lacanian Psychoanalysis.* New York: Routledge, 1996.

Foucault, Michel. *Madness and Civilization.* Translated by Richard Howard. New York: Random House, 1965.

Gruenwald, Mark, Bob Hall, et al. *Squadron Supreme.* New York: Marvel, 1985.

Harvey, Robert C. *The Art of the Comic Book: An Aesthetic History.* Jackson: University Press of Mississippi, 1996.

Hobbes, Thomas. "Leviathan." In *From Plato to Nietzsche,* edited by Forrest E. Baird and Walter Kaufmann, 417–512. New Jersey: Prentice Hall, 1997.

Homer. *The Odyssey.* Translated by Robert Fagles. New York: Penguin, 1996.

Jung, C. G. *Psychological Types*. Translated by H. G. Baynes. Princeton, NJ: Princeton University Press, 1990.

Koike, Kazuo, and Goseki Kojima. *Lone Wolf and Cub*. Vol. 1: *The Assassin's Road*. Milwaukee: Dark Horse, 2000.

Lacan, Jaques. *Seminar 11: The Four Fundamental Concepts of Psychoanalysis*. Edited by Jacques-Alain Miller. Translated by Alan Sheridan. New York: Norton, 1978.

Lévi-Strauss, Claude. *Myth and Meaning*. New York: Schocken Books, 1978.

McCloud, Scott. *Understanding Comics*. New York: A Kitchen Sink Book for Harper Perennial, 1993.

McCue, Greg. *Dark Knights: The New Comics in Context*. London: Pluto Press, 1988.

Meisel, Perry. *The Cowboy and the Dandy*. New York: Oxford University Press, 1999.

Millar, Mark, and Adam Kubert, et al. *Ultimate X-Men*. New York: Marvel Comics, 2001.

Millar, Mark, Frank Quitely, et al. *The Authority*. La Jolla, CA: Wildstorm, 2000–present.

———. *The Authority: Under New Management* (*The Authority*, no. 9–16). La Jolla, CA: Wildstorm, 2000.

Miller, Frank. "Batman and the Twilight of the Idols: An Interview with Frank Miller." In *The Many Lives of the Batman*, edited by Roberta E. Pearson and William Uricchio, 33–46. New York: Routledge Press, 1991.

Miller, Frank, David Mazzuchelli, and Richmond Lewis. *Batman: Year One*. New York: DC Comics, 1986–1987.

Miller, Frank, Klaus Janson, and Lynn Varley. *Batman: The Dark Knight Returns*. New York: DC Comics, 1986.

———. Interview. In *Writers on Comics Scriptwriting*, edited by Mark Salisbury. London: Titan Books, 1999.

Milligan, Peter, and Mike Allred. *X Force*. New York: Marvel Comics, 2001.

Moldoff, Sheldon, George Roussos, et al. "Detective Comics no. 168." In *The Greatest Joker Stories Ever Told*, edited by Mike Gold, 51–63. New York: DC Comics, 1988.

Moore, Alan. *Alan Moore's Awesome Universe Handbook*, vol. 1, no. 1. Los Angeles: Awesome Entertainment, 1999.

———. "Introduction." In *The Dark Knight Returns*. New York: DC Comics, 1986.

———. "Introduction." In *Saga of the Swamp Thing*. New York: DC Comics, 1984.

Moore, Alan, et al. *1963*. Fullerton, CA: Image Comics, 1993.

Moore, Alan, Brian Bolland, and John Higgins. *Batman: The Killing Joke*. New York: DC Comics, 1988.

Moore, Alan, and Dave Gibbons. *Watchmen*. New York: DC Comics, 1986–1987.

———. *Will Eisner's The Spirit: The New Adventures, no. 1*. Northampton, MA: Kitchen Sink Press, 1997.

Moore, Alan, Gene Ha, and Zander Cannon. *Top Ten*. La Jolla, CA: America's Best Comics, 1999–present.

Moore, Alan, and Kevin O'Neal. *The League of Extraordinary Gentlemen*. La Jolla, CA: America's Best Comics, 1999–present.

Moore, Alan, Kevin O'Neal, et al. *Miracleman*. Guerneville, CA: Eclipse Comics, 1985–1989. (See *The Miracleman Companion* [George Khoury, Raleigh: Two Morrows Publishing, 2001] for details on *Miracleman*'s complicated publishing history).

————. *Saga of the Swamp Thing*. New York: DC Comics, 2000.

————. *Supreme*. Los Angeles: Awesome Entertainment, 1999–2000.

————. *Supreme: The Return*. Los Angeles: Awesome Entertainment, 1999–2000.

————. *Swamp Thing;* no. 51–62, 63–64. New York: DC Comics, 1986.

————. *Swamp Thing: A Murder of Crows*. New York: DC Comics, 2001.

————. *Swamp Thing: Love and Death*. New York: DC Comics, 2000.

————. *Swamp Thing: The Curse*. New York: DC Comics, 2001.

————. *Tomorrow Stories*. La Jolla, CA: America's Best Comics, 1999–present.

Moore, Alan, Chris Sprouse, et al. *Tom Strong*. La Jolla, CA: America's Best Comics, 1999–present.

————. *WildC.A.T.s: Gangwar*. La Jolla, CA: Wildstorm, 1998.

————. *WildC.A.T.s: Homecoming*. La Jolla, CA: Wildstorm, 1998.

Moore, Alan, Kurt Swan, et al. *Superman: Whatever Happened to the Man of Tomorrow?* New York: DC Comics, 1997.

Moore, Alan, and J. H. Williams III. *Promethea*. La Jolla, CA: America's Best Comics, 1999–present.

Morrison, Grant. Interview in *Writers on Comics Scriptwriting,* edited by Mark Salisbury. London: Titan Books, 1999.

Morrison, Grant, et al. *Animal Man*. New York: DC Comics, 1988–1990.

————. "Introduction." In *The Authority: Relentless*. La Jolla, CA: Wildstorm, 2000.

Morrison, Grant, Richard Case, et al. *Doom Patrol*. New York: DC Comics, 1989.

Morrison, Grant, and J. G. Jones. *Marvel Boy*. New York: Marvel Comics, 2000.

Morrison, Grant, Howard Porter, John Dell, et al. *The Justice League of America*. New York: DC Comics, 1996–2000.

Morrison, Grant, Frank Quitely, et al. *New X-Men*. New York: Marvel Comics, 2001.

Morrison, Grant, Val Semeiks, and Prentis Rollins. *DC: One Million*. New York: DC Comics, 1998.

Pustz, Matthew J. *Comic Book Culture*. Jackson: University Press of Mississippi, 1999.

Reynolds, Richard. *Superheroes: A Modern Mythology*. Jackson: University Press of Mississippi, 1992.

Rorty, Richard. *Contingency, Irony, Solidarity*. Cambridge: Cambridge University Press, 1989.

Seigel, Jerome, and Joe Shuster. "Superman." In *Action Comics 1*. New York: DC Comics, 1938.

Shelley, Mary. *Frankenstein*. New York: Dover, 1994.

Shoptaw, John. *On the Outside Looking Out: John Ashbery's Poetry*. Cambridge, MA: Harvard University Press, 1994.

Smith, Kevin. "Arrow Heads." In *Green Arrow 1*. New York: DC Comics, 2001.

Teluskin, Joseph. *Jewish Literacy*. New York: William Morrow, 1991.

Waid, Mark, *The Kingdom*. New York: DC Comics, 1998.

Waid, Mark, and Alex Ross. *Kingdom Come*. New York. DC Comics, 1996.

Wertham, Fredric, *Seduction of the Innocent*. New York: Rinehart and Company, 1954.

Wilde, Oscar. *The Artist as Critic*. Edited by Richard Ellmann. Chicago: University of Chicago Press, 1968.

Wolfman, Marv, George Pérez, et al. *Crisis on Infinite Earths*. New York: DC Comics, 1985.

Young, Dossele, et al. *The Monarchy*. La Jolla, CA: Wildstorm, 2001.

Žižek, Slavoj. *The Art of the Ridiculous Sublime: On David Lynch's Lost Highway*. Seattle: The Walter Chapin Center for the Humanities, 2000.

————. *The Fragile Absolute: or, Why Is the Christian Legacy Worth Fighting For?* New York: Verso, 2000.

————. *Looking Awry: An Introduction to Jacques Lacan through Popular Culture*. Cambridge, MA: MIT Press, 1992.

————. *The Metastases of Enjoyment: Six Essays on Causality and Women*. London: Verso, 1994.

————. *The Sublime Object of Ideology*. London: Verso, 1989.

Further Reading

McCloud, Scott. *Understanding Comics*. New York: A Kitchen Sink Book for Harper Perennial, 1993.

For those who have never read a comic book, I will break no new ground in recommending Scott McCloud's *Understanding Comics,* without a doubt the best introduction to the medium.

Further Reading in the Superhero Genre

Bendis, Brian Michael, and Michael Avon Oeming. *Powers: Who Killed Retro Girl*. Orange, CA: Image Comics 2001.

————. *Powers,* no. 7–15. Orange, CA: Image Comics 2001–present. (Uncollected)

Powers tells the story of two ordinary cops assigned to superhero-related crime. Existing on the edges of the superhero genre, it is clearly the work of a crime comic artist entering the mainstream on a superhero-related title. *Powers* is also especially interesting in its perspective, not on the revisionary superhero narrative, but on the fan base that supports it. "Who Killed Retro Girl" (*Powers* 1–6) introduces the world of *Powers* in a case about a superheroine murdered and left in an alley. Her killer, it turns out, was motivated by a desire to have her canonized in the public mind as a saint rather than be brought down by inevitable mortal failings. Here a fan's obsession with purity becomes murder.

Powers 7 guest stars Warren Ellis as himself. Drawn into the comic book, Ellis provides his own dialogue for a story about a graphic novelist tagging along with our protagonists to gather material for his new work. He rants about the state of the comic book industry:

> Fuck superheroes, frankly. The notion that these things dominate an entire culture is absurd. It's like every bookstore on the planet having ninety percent of its shelves filled by nurse novels. Imagine that. You want a new novel, but have to wade through three hundred new books about romances in the wards before you can get at any other genre.

His face is melted by a supervillain when he interferes in a hostage situation.

"Role Play" (*Powers* 8–11) centers on a group of kids who dress up as superheroes as part of a role-playing game. They hire an out-of-work superhero to make their game more realistic, but, completely insane, he kills them all. "Groupies" (*Powers* 12–15) investigates the phenomenon of crazed superhero fans. A plot arc published in issues of *Comic Shop News* involves a man who follows a superhero's public philosophy of stopping what you believe is wrong regardless of conventional morality and legality, and kills her. *Powers* is a reflexive story in a different mode than the superhero narratives discussed above. It looks at the superhero story through the eyes of an outsider and is a vision of obsessed fans gone wrong and heroes' nobility twisted by the perception of others, ideas that find a perfect form in the noir-style detective story.

Luke, Eric, et al. *Ghost Stories*. Milwaukee: Dark Horse Comics, 1995.
———. *Ghost: Black October*. Milwaukee: Dark Horse Comics, 1999.
———. *Ghost: Exhuming Elisa*. Milwaukee: Dark Horse Comics, 1997.
———. *Ghost: Nocturnes*. Milwaukee: Dark Horse Comics, 1996.
———. *Ghost: Painful Music*. Milwaukee: Dark Horse Comics, 1999.

Eric Luke's feminist take on the superhero in Dark Horse Comics' attempt at a superhero line is particularly interesting for its interpretation of the elements of *The Shadow*. Ghost uses the Shadow's trademark .45 automatic pistols but counters the strong strain of chauvinism in the earlier character (and particularly Howard Chaykin's 1980s incarnation). That Ghost's sister, Margo, shares a name with the Shadow's female partner is an allusion easy to spot, but note the sideline presence of a character that might have been Ghost's boyfriend or husband before she was reborn as a specter with few memories of her earlier life. The character sketches in the first trade paperback, *Ghost Stories,* make it clear that it is Orson Welles, voice of the Shadow in the original radio program. This reduction of a predecessor to a subservient status seems concomitant with the analysis in the present book of the superhero comic book's staging of the agon for priority with earlier selves.

McFarlane, Todd, et al. *Spawn*. Orange, CA: Image Comics, 1992–present.

As mentioned earlier, Todd McFarlane's *Spawn* was an incredibly important landmark in the breakaway from the big publishing companies into creator-controlled work, though largely uninteresting as far as this book is concerned. Four issues of *Spawn*—8, 9, 10, and 11—however, are noteworthy because they were written by guest writers supporting the title as an emblem of creator control and ownership. Alan Moore, Neil Gaiman, Dave Sim, and Frank Miller each wrote an issue promoting this monumental industry landmark. Miller, Moore, and Gaiman have already been introduced in the course of this study, but Sim requires special mention. Dave Sim has been writing, drawing, and independently publishing *Cerebus* since the 1970s. *Cerebus,* initially an Aardvark parody of Conan the Barbarian, became a sprawling meditation on a host of subjects (many misogynistic). It is the longest running independent comic book in the history of the medium, with a projected 300 issues. Sim's issue of *Spawn* is a scathing critique of the big publishers and those who would sell their hearts and souls to them, not to be missed by anyone interested in this battle.

Additionally, Grant Morrison wrote "Reflections" (*Spawn* 16–18), and Brian Michel Bendis wrote a spin-off series, *Sam and Twitch (Book One: Udaku.* Orange, CA: Image Comics, 2000), which leaves Spawn behind altogether to pursue a cop drama with two members of Spawn's supporting cast.

Miller, Frank, et al. *Daredevil Visionaries: Frank Miller.* Vols. 1–3. New York: Marvel Comics, 2000–2001.

Miller, Frank, and David Mazzucchelli. *Daredevil: Born Again.* New York: Marvel Comics, 1987.

Miller, Frank, John Romita, Jr., et al. *Daredevil: The Man Without Fear.* New York: Marvel Comics, 1994.

Miller, Frank, and Bill Sienkiewicz. *Daredevil: Love and War.* New York: Marvel Comics, 1986.

————. *Elektra: Assassin.* New York: Marvel Comics, 2000.

Miller, Frank, and Lynn Varley. *Elektra Lives Again.* New York: Epic Comics, 1990.

Frank Miller broke into comic books on this title in the late 1970s, first as a penciler, then taking over as writer and transforming this poorly selling third-string superhero book into a compelling and realistic crime drama. His initial run on the series is a great example of a strong writer's early work, but four later Daredevil projects stand out especially. On *Daredevil: Love and War* and *Elektra: Assassin,* Miller was joined by artist Bill Sienkiewicz, one of the most visually stunning talents in the business. *Daredevil: The Man Without Fear* and *Elektra Lives Again* continued to stretch genre conventions until their connection to superhero storytelling was as minimal as Marvel would allow, and as close to Miller's desired crime genre as he could get.

Moore, Alan, et al. *1963.* Fullerton, CA: Image Comics, 1993.

1963 was an unfinished mini-series by Alan Moore (intended to be six issues and an eighty-page Giant) best described by the quip in *Tom Strong* that "It's not crude, it's classic." *1963*'s authenticity goes further than most satires as the series is printed on grainy low-quality paper and includes no contemporary advertisements (common in most comic books) that would spoil its "retro" style. In place of advertisements Alan Moore incorporates parody "period" advertisements, and a meticulously written "Bullpen" column in each issue that playfully rides the line between crude and classic, between satire and tribute, reproducing Stan Lee's boisterous prose, which uses alliteration like it's going out of style. Moore writes:

> ITEM! Gather round, groveling ones, and get the goods on the gum-grinding galaxy of groovy GUEST-STARS parading through the penultimate pages of the pulse pounding periodical presently pressed in your paw!!! A painstaking perusal of pages 20 and 21 in this potentially perfect publication will provide a plethora of power packed personages, prudently and properly protected by the patents of their perpetrators, proudly presented post-scriptum to prevent possible pecuniarily punitive protests of plagiarism from the pertinent parties. (no. 6, prose)

Besides a lengthy column in each issue, *1963* also features letters pages straight out of the early days of Marvel, discussing such issues as whether a girl can be a valuable member of a superhero team or whether scientific concepts employed in the narrative were "realistic." Readers also attempt to score something like the "no prizes" offered by Marvel to readers who could offer a diegetic rationalization for an artist's error, such as a character suddenly appearing in a different outfit.

Each of the first six issues of *1963* are dedicated to telling a seamless 1960s-style story focusing on a different character—supposedly an issue somewhere in the middle of that character's series. At the end of "The Tomorrow Syndicate" (*1963* 6) the characters must team up and travel into the future, where—in the never published *1963* "80-page Giant"—they would have confronted the "heroes" of the contemporary Image universe, heroes like Youngblood, Spawn, and the WildC.A.T.s. To the heroes of *1963,* these dark, violent antiheroes would have looked like monsters, and had *1963* been completed, the resulting commentary surely would have been given a place in this book. For more information on this, as well as an interview with Alan Moore on the subject, see www.comicon .com/moore/moore.htm.

———. *Miracleman.* Guerneville, CA: Eclipse Comics, 1985–1989 [see *The Miracleman Companion,* edited by George Khoury (Raleigh, NC: TwoMorrows Publishing, 2001) for details on *Miracleman*'s complicated publishing history.]

As influential and important as *Batman: The Dark Knight Returns* and *Watchmen, Miracleman* (originally *Marvelman* in its British incarnation in *Warrior* magazine in the early 1980s) is Alan Moore's legendary pre-*Watchmen* exploration of the superhero. Legal battles over copyright (the original publisher went out of business, and the group copyright changed hands several times) have kept this canonical superhero work from being reprinted.

————. *Supreme*. Los Angeles: Awesome Entertainment, 1996–1998.

————. *Supreme: The Return*. Los Angeles: Awesome Entertainment, 1999–2000.

————. *Judgment Day: Alpha, Omega, Final Judgment* and *Aftermath*. Los Angeles: Awesome Entertainment, 1997.

Alan Moore's run on *Supreme* was the transformation of Rob Liefeld's "dark age" Superman into a playful, metatextual comic: a Supreme who knows he has gone through several incarnations and revisions, whose alter ego is a superhero comic book creator. Giving this previously two-dimensional character life by the inclusion of fake, stylized Supreme "back stories" from the 1950s and 1960s seems important and resonates with this study's emphasis on the influence of comic book history on contemporary narratives. Bloom writes: "Kierkegaard, in *Fear and Trembling*, announces, with magnificent, but absurdly apocalyptic confidence, that he who is willing to work gives birth to his own father. I find truer to mere fact the aphoristic admission of Nietzsche: 'When one hasn't had a good father, it is necessary to invent one'" (*Anxiety* 56). Moore must invent poetic fathers for *Supreme*—previous creators, previous incarnations of Supreme—because he realizes that superhero comic books are invigorated by interaction with their history: Supreme will not be anything more than a grim and gritty Superman clone until powerful anxiety of influence relationships can be built. In *Judgment Day*—the *Crisis on Infinite Earths* for the Awesome universe—Moore attempts to build a history for Supreme's entire continuity with jungle explorers, westerns, and space operas. Moore's innovations on *Supreme* are more fully realized in his America's Best Comics line, especially *Tom Strong* and *Tomorrow Stories*.

————. *Saga of the Swamp Thing*. New York: DC Comics, 2000.

————. *Swamp Thing*, no. 51–62, 63–64. New York: DC Comics, 1986. (Uncollected)

————. *Swamp Thing: Love and Death*. New York: DC Comics, 2000.

————. *Swamp Thing: The Curse*. New York: DC Comics, 2001.

————. *Swamp Thing: A Murder of Crows*. New York: DC Comics, 2001.

Alan Moore's run on *Swamp Thing* was a key point in the rebirth of the horror comic book. In his particularly inspired "Anatomy Lesson" (*Swamp Thing* 21), Moore changed everything readers thought they knew about the character. Alec Holland was a botanist working on an experimental plant formula when his lab, in the Louisiana swamp, blew up. He was transformed by the swamp and his formula into the hulking, monstrous, Swamp Thing. The pre-Moore issues revolved around Holland's hope that he could someday regain his humanity. Moore's "Anatomy Lesson" involves an autopsy on a seemingly dead Swamp Thing, an autopsy that discovers that Swamp Thing has the plant equivalent of human organs—kidneys of yam and a heart that does not pump—none of which could possibly work. Moore introduces the idea that planarian worms can be taught to run a maze; if chopped up and fed to other worms, those other worms will know how to run the maze as well. Alec Holland died in the swamp that ingested his decomposing body. Swamp Thing was not a man transformed into a plant, but a plant that, altered by Holland's formula, thought it was a man. Moore literally takes the center out of the character. In some very intelligent comic book writing, Moore understands the absurdity of Swamp Thing's sharing continuity with Superman, Batman, and Wonder Woman and conceives of Swamp Thing as a hero of the margins. In one instance, a nemesis, Jason Woodrue, achieves the status of a global threat: In the watchtower of the Justice League of America, Green Arrow becomes furious and says: "Man, I don't believe this! We were watching out for New York, Metropolis, for Atlantis, but who was watching out for Lacroix, Louisiana?" (no. 24) The answer, of course, is Swamp Thing.

Morrison, Grant, et al. *Animal Man.* New York: DC Comics, 2000.
————. *Animal Man,* 10–26. New York: DC Comics, 1988–1990. (Uncollected)

Grant Morrison's bizarre run on a title about a third-string superhero who can take on the powers of any animal in close proximity. Includes a high degree of reflexivity (in the final issue, Animal Man meets Grant Morrison and discovers he is a comic book character) and a wonderful conception of Wile E. Coyote as a Prometheus/Christ figure eternally suffering (and eternally being reborn) for the sins of a violent world.

Morrison, Grant, and Dave McKean. *Arkham Asylum: A Serious House on a Serious Earth.* New York: DC Comics, 1989.

Most notable for the unique and stunning visuals provided by artist Dave McKean, *Arkham Asylum: A Serious House on a Serious Earth* is a stand-alone graphic novel in which Batman enters an Arkham taken over by the inmates and fights for his own sanity. *Arkham Asylum* takes the usual stance of stories set in madhouses, questioning who is really crazy, the patients or the outside world. It includes the suggestion, from a doctor, that the Joker is actually superrational rather than crazy, that he achieves "a brilliant new modification of human perception, more suited to urban life at the end of the twentieth century." *Arkham Asylum* also suggests that the doctors have made Two-Face worse: they have shattered his decision-making capability by replacing his coin with a tarot deck, and plan to move toward the I-Ching. Batman is disgusted, but the attentive reader will note that the real world requires decision-making ability across more than a binary spectrum and it is really Batman—with his dual persona and black-and-white morality—who benefits from Two-Face remaining crippled.

Morrison, Grant, et al. *Doom Patrol: Crawling from the Wreckage.* New York: DC Comics, 1992.
————. *Doom Patrol,* 26–63. New York: DC Comics, 1989–1993. (Uncollected)

An important breeding ground for ideas that would be more fully realized in his *Invisibles,* Grant Morrison's powerful and deeply surreal take on DC's response to the *Fantastic Four* includes villains like the Telephone Avatar and the Brotherhood of Dada, as well as a painting that eats Paris.

Morrison, Grant, and Frank Quitely. *Flex Mentallo.* New York: DC Comics, 1996.

Grant Morrison's *Doom Patrol* is also notable for its spin-off mini-series *Flex Mentallo,* one of Morrison's strongest works that presents, in many ways, a variation on the argument of this study.

Smith, Kevin, and Phil Hester. *Green Arrow.* New York: DC Comics, 2001.
Smith, Kevin, and Joe Quesada. *Daredevil Visionaries: Kevin Smith.* New York: Marvel Comics, 1998.

Kevin Smith, who wrote and directed the films *Clerks, Mallrats, Chasing Amy,* and *Dogma,* is also a lifetime comics' fan. Based on the popularity of his films (most of them anyway), Marvel Comics commissioned him to write eight issues of *Daredevil,* then DC asked him to take on *Green Arrow.* Smith is not the greatest writer in the history of comics and never claimed to be, but, despite the wordiness many professionals have teased him about, his tenure on *Daredevil* and *Green Arrow* have been solid and unpretentious. He writes: "I'm not trying to reinvent the wheel here. Like I did on *Daredevil,* I'm only trying to add another spoke. Don't expect any revamps along the lines of 'Everything you thought you knew about Oliver Queen has been a lie!' I'm just trying to tell a good, strong Green Arrow story" (no. 1, prose).

Batman: The Animated Series

Dini, Paul, and Chip Kidd. *Batman: Animated.* New York: Harper, 1998.
———. *Batman: The Animated Series.* Episode 105: "Legends of the Dark Knight." Story: Bruce Timm. Teleplay: Robert Goodman. Directed: Dan Riba. Fox, Fall 1998.
———. Episode 32: "Beware the Grey Ghost." Story: Dennis O'Flaherty and Tom Ruegger. Teleplay: Garin Wolf and Tom Ruegger. Directed by Boyd Kirkland. Fox, Nov. 4, 1992.

A classy, beautifully designed, well-told Batman adaptation, the reader of this study will not find it without interest despite the fact that it is aimed at a much younger audience than the works discussed above. The design of Gotham City draws heavily on *Citizen Kane, Metropolis,* and *The Cabinet of Dr. Caligari,* and the world of *Batman: The Animated Series* does a wonderful job in synthesizing conflicting decades of a character that has been around since 1939. The villains may have laser cannons, and the people of Gotham access to the Internet and fax machines, but all television broadcasts are in black and white, Zeppelins populate the sky, and all the men wear fedoras.

Two episodes stand out: "Legends of the Dark Knight" and "Beware the Grey Ghost." "Legends of the Dark Knight" is a retelling of the most cited comic book moment in academic studies of the superhero. Three kids discuss Batman, and each has a different take on what he or she believes Batman is "really" like. One kid believes Batman is a vampire of some kind (cf. Kurt Busiek's Confessor). Another recalls a story his uncle told him about a time a friendly Batman and Robin foiled a robbery at a museum of giant musical instruments. The third, a girl, believes that Batman is old, grim, gritty, and tough, drives a tank, and has a girl partner. Only the second and third "interpretations" are given accompanying visuals and dialogue, each rendering two very different versions of Batman. The giant musical instrument museum invokes Bill Finger's obsession with having Batman on giant props, and the whole scene is visually rendered to recall the hokey "Good job, old chum" Batman with a silly Joker and bad puns. The second story is a scene adapted from Frank Miller's *Batman: The Dark Knight Returns*.

The children tell these stories while looking through some burned out Gotham storefronts, and in an abandoned theater they discover the Firebug, a costumed arsonist for hire. Just as he sets fire to the theater, Batman enters and saves the kids. The visual trope should be noted: the "real" Batman is on the theater's stage fighting Firebug, and the children watch hidden in the rows of the theater. After being rescued, each child defends his or her story based on the actual encounter with the "real" Batman, staged for their interpretation. Bruce Timm and company present their animated Batman as the synthesis of the previous Batman stories, a space where fans of both classic and revisionary Batman stories may find agreement.

"Beware the Grey Ghost" is about an out-of-work actor who used to star in a television program where he played a character reminiscent of a pulp novel hero, the Grey Ghost. Unable to find work, he is forced to sell his Grey Ghost memorabilia to pay the rent. Meanwhile, a series of bombings are committed in Gotham, and Batman finds them strangely familiar, because (Batman comes to realize) they are modeled after episodes of "The Grey Ghost" that he used to watch with his father when he was a child. Putting on his old television costume, the "Grey Ghost" teams up with Batman to discover a crazed fan committing the crimes. In their interaction, Batman reveals to this washed up actor that "The Grey Ghost" television program inspired him to become a costumed crime fighter, and reveals that the Batcave—modeled after the hideout of the Grey Ghost—contains a hidden shrine to Batman's childhood hero. "The Grey Ghost," to the surprise of the actor that played him for so many years, really mattered after all.

The voice of the Grey Ghost is provided by (who else?) Adam West. More than a tribute to a forgotten actor, *Batman: The Animated Series* manages to admit the influence on a version of the Batman many fans would rather forget, and pays its debt to this part of history without disturbing the continuity of its own vision.

Further Reading in the Comic Book Medium

Bendis, Brian Michael. *Fire.* Orange, CA: Image Comics, 1999.
———. *Goldfish.* Orange, CA: Image Comics, 2001.
———. *Jinx.* Orange, CA: Image Comics, 2001.
Bendis, Brian Michael, and Marc Andreyko. *Torso.* Orange, CA: Image Comics, 2000.

> Brian Michael Bendis's black-and-white crime comics. *Fire* is the story of a Reagan-era spy. *Goldfish* and *Jinx* take place in the same "continuity" and tell the stories of a grifter with a heart of gold (Goldfish) and a female bounty hunter named Jinx. *Torso* is based on the true story of Eliot Ness versus the first serial killer on American soil. Bendis introduces realistic dialogue into comic books in a way that made what most comic book fans had been putting up with look pretty shameful.

Bendis, Brian Michael. *Fortune and Glory: A True Hollywood Comic Book Story.* Portland, OR: Oni Press, 2000.

> Probably Bendis's finest work and one of the funniest things I have ever read, *Fortune and Glory* tells the true story of Bendis's experience in Hollywood, trying to get one of his comic books made into a movie.

Chadwick, Paul. *Concrete: Complete Short Stories, 1986–1989.* Milwaukee: Dark Horse Comics, 1990.
———. *Concrete: Killer Smile.* Milwaukee: Dark Horse Comics, 1995.
———. *Concrete: Think Like a Mountain.* Milwaukee: Dark Horse Comics, 1997.

> Paul Chadwick's *Concrete* is the story of a man kidnapped by aliens and returned to Earth in a body of rock. What is notable about Concrete is that, although this reads like the premise of a superhero story, nothing much interesting happens after that. Or rather, a host of interesting things happen after that, but none of them stretch credibility in the slightest. Concrete goes to a children's birthday party, becomes entangled with a group of Earth First!ers (who want to use him to help fight for ecology), and thinks a lot. A sensitive, introspective book, *Concrete* is the quietest superhero story ever told, though I feel it does Paul Chadwick's creation a disservice by aligning it with a genre that is, if not wholly absent, so far on the margins of his story as to be inconsequential.

Ennis, Garth, and Steve Dillon. *Preacher: Gone to Texas.* New York: DC Comics, 1996.

> Scholars of the western might find something worth discussing in Garth Ennis's contemporary supernatural horror western about a Texas preacher who, given the ability to compel others with the sound of his voice by being possessed by the spawn of an angel and a demon, sets out on a quest to confront God, who has abandoned his position and now walks the earth in human form.

Miller, Frank, and Lynn Varley. *300.* Milwaukee: Dark Horse Comics, 1999.

> 480 B.C. King Leonidas of Sparta and his personal guard of three hun-
> dred men ready themselves for battle. The future of humanity is at stake.
> Out of Persia thunders the mightiest military force ever assembled. The
> earth shudders with the impact of its march. It drinks the rivers dry. It
> devours livestock like some hungry, angry god. It pauses, poised to
> vanquish tiny Greece, to crush her impertinent invention of democracy
> and extinguish the only light of reason in the world. The Spartans are
> outnumbered a hundred thousand to one—but Leonidas has chosen his
> battle site with care: the mountain pass called hot gates. Funneled into
> this narrow corridor, the Persians find their numbers useless. . . . The
> hope of civilization is kept alive by Spartan courage—and a careful
> choice of where to fight. (Frank Miller, *Sin City: The Big Fat Kill,* Milwau-
> kee: Dark Horse Comics, 1995, my ellipsis.)

Frank Miller wrote and drew this true story of ancient Sparta (taken from Herod-
otus' *Histories*), assisted by colorist Lynn Varley. Each two-page spread of the
comic book is conceived of as a single layout, and the trade paperback reprints
each double page as a single: the width of each page of *300* is twice that of an
ordinary comic book, lending the project a rich, windscreen, cinematic feel.

It should also be noted that *300* participates in the superhero story's con-
stant reimagining of origins. The story of a small and noble force holding out and
eventually triumphing against disastrous odds shares obvious affinities with the
standard superhero narrative, but more important is *300*'s emphasis on the story
being retold and entering historical memory as a story. The final image of the
work is that of a single storyteller inspiring those who will defeat the Persian
army, a group of soldiers who fan out in all directions in red garments that look
a lot like capes (and Miller notes that "the sum total of [his] contribution to the
color on *300* was that the capes should be red" [*Writers on Comics Art,* ed. Mark
Salisbury, London: Titan, 2000, p. 180]). While *300* should not be reduced to
an allegorical status alongside the more visible superhero genre, it should be
noted that in a genre that often retells origins Miller seems to have hit upon an
especially early tale of heroism, perhaps a kind of origin story for the whole genre.

Miller, Frank. *Sin City.* Milwaukee: Dark Horse Comics, 1991.
———. *Sin City: The Big Fat Kill.* Milwaukee: Dark Horse Comics, 1995.
———. *Sin City: Booze, Broads and Bullets.* Milwaukee: Dark Horse Comics, 1998.
———. *Sin City: A Dame to Kill For.* Milwaukee: Dark Horse Comics, 1995.
———. *Sin City: That Yellow Bastard.* Milwaukee: Dark Horse Comics, 1997.
———. *Sin City: Family Values.* Milwaukee: Dark Horse Comics, 1997.
———. *Sin City: Hell and Back.* Milwaukee: Dark Horse Comics, 2001.

Frank Miller's hyper-noir, which Harlan Ellison describes as "tougher and meaner
than a drano-Milkshake" (*Family Values,* back cover), *Sin City* is a small body of

interesting and intense work that, as far as I know, has been largely ignored by those undertaking an analysis of noir and neo-noir.

Moore, Alan, and Eddie Campbell. *From Hell*. Marietta, GA: Eddie Campbell Comics, 1999.

Probably one of the only examples of a historical novel in the medium, Alan Moore's *From Hell* is a meticulously researched (and documented) story about Jack the Ripper, culled from a host of sources. This is not the playful, fantastical, anachronistic history of Moore's *League of Extraordinary Gentlemen,* but rather an examination of history that presents, in fictional format, a theory as to the identity of London's most notorious serial killer.

Morrison, Grant, et al. *The Invisibles: Say You Want a Revolution*. New York: DC Comics, 1996.
————. *The Invisibles*. vol. 3, no. 1–12. New York: DC Comics, 2000. (Uncollected)
————. *The Invisibles: Apocalipstick*. New York: DC Comics, 2001.
————. *The Invisibles: Bloody Hell in America*. New York: DC Comics, 1998.
————. *The Invisibles: Counting to None*. New York: DC Comics, 1999.
————. *The Invisibles: Entropy in the U.K.* New York: DC Comics, 2001.
————. *The Invisibles: Kissing Mr. Quimper*. New York: DC Comics, 2000.

Grant Morrison's mind-bending comic book series about a group of rebels (The Invisibles) engaged in an ongoing secret war against the metaphysical forces of fascism. *The Invisibles* contains a raw, uncensored degree of Morrison's particular brand of madness. It is a work that runs the full gamut of Morrison's learning from sci-fi pulps to tantric sex-magic, which (if one believes the hype) Morrison himself endorses. I debated for a long time whether or not to include *The Invisibles* along side *Planetary, The Authority,* and *Wildcats* as a work that stands as a successor to the silver age—as a work that has a heroic theme and truly succeeds as something blisteringly new and strange. Ultimately, however, it seemed to do the series a great disservice to hammer it into the constraints of the superhero genre, constraints that, however interestingly, *Planetary, The Authority,* and *Wildcats* accept.

Ware, Chris. *Jimmy Corrigan: The Smartest Kid on Earth*. New York: Random House, 2000.

Chris Ware's *Jimmy Corrigan* is an intricate and moving tale of loneliness that has much in common with P. T. Anderson's *Magnolia*. Sensitive storytelling that would amaze anyone who thinks the medium is for children, more than any other work this makes the term *comic book* seem vastly inappropriate.

Manga

Manga is a term used to refer to Japanese comic books (as *Anime* refers to the stylized animated cartoons often based on manga texts). Manga reading is indispensable for anyone interested in contemporary comic books. More widely accepted as a storytelling medium in Japan, comic books evolved important storytelling techniques that influenced many western comic book creators, including Frank Miller and Warren Ellis.

Koike, Kazuo, and Goseki Kojima. *Lone Wolf and Cub*. Vols. 1–28. Milwaukee: Dark Horse, 2000–2002.

Kazuo Koike and Goseki Kojima's manga samurai epic is perhaps one of the best examples of mature comic book storytelling. Ogami Itto is the disgraced "second executioner" to the Shogun in eighteenth-century Japan who now travels as an assassin for hire with his three-year-old son. More about characterization and genuine moments of human interaction than sword fighting (though there is quite a bit of the latter), *Lone Wolf and Cub* runs an astounding twenty-eight volumes in reprint, capping out at more than 8,400 pages.

Otomo, Katsuhiro. *Akira*. Vols. 1–6. Milwaukee: Dark Horse Comics, 2000–2002.

The definitive sci-fi manga epic by Katsuhiro Otomo, who went on to write and direct the groundbreaking film of the same name, *Akira* tells the story of government experiments with powerful psychic children in post–World War III Tokyo. The comic book makes the film significantly more lucid.

Index

Endpapers

With impulses, that scarcely were by these
Surpassed in strength, I heard of danger met
Or sought with courage; enterprise forlorn
By one, sole keeper of his own intent,
Or by a resolute few, who for the sake
Of glory fronted multitudes in arms.
Yea, to this hour I cannot read a Tale
Of two brave vessels matched in deadly fight,
And fighting to the death, but I am pleased
More than a wise man ought to be; I wish
Fret, burn, and struggle, and in soul am there.
But me hath Nature tamed, and bade to seek
For other agitations, or be calm;
Hath dealt with me as with a turbulent stream,
Some nursling of the mountains which she leads
Through quiet meadows, after he has learnt
His strength, and had his triumph and his joy,
His desperate course of tumult and of glee.
That which in stealth by nature was performed
Hath Reason sanctioned: her deliberate Voice
Hath said; be mild, and cleave to gentle things,
Thy glory and thy happiness be there.
Nor fear, though thou confide in me, a want
Of aspirations that have been—of foes
To wrestle with, and victory to complete,
Bounds to be leapt, darkness to be explored;
All that inflamed thy infant heart, the love,
the longing, the contempt, the undaunted quest,
All shall survive, though changed their office, all
shall live, it is not in their power to die.

—William Wordsworth, *Home at Grasmere*

"What kind of lectures do you plan on giving?"
"That's exactly what I wanted to talk to you
about," he said. "You've established a wonderful

thing here with Hitler. You created it, you nurtured it, you made it your own. Nobody on the faculty of any college or university in this part of the country can so much as utter the word Hitler without a nod in your direction, literally or metaphorically. This is the center, the unquestioned source. He is now your Hitler, Gladney's Hitler. It must be deeply satisfying for you. The college is internationally known as a result of Hitler studies. It has an identity, a sense of achievement. You've evolved an entire system around this figure, a structure with countless substructures and interrelated fields of study, a history within history. I marvel at the effort. It was masterful, shrewd and stunningly preemptive. It's what I want to do with Elvis."

—Don DeLillo, *White Noise*

I wrote this speech for Helen's encomium and my own amusement.

—Gorgias

Nobody burns the midnight oil for *this,*
Yet I think I shall be a scholar someday, all the same.

—John Ashbery,
"The Burden of the Park," in *Wakefulness*